D0780435

TRAILBLAZER

TRAILBLAZER

The U.S. Navy's First Black Admiral

Vice Admiral Samuel L. Gravely Jr.
with Paul Stillwell

Afterword by Alma B. Gravely

NAVAL INSTITUTE PRESS
Annapolis, Maryland

Naval Institute Press
291 Wood Road
Annapolis, MD 21402

This book has been brought to publication with the generous assistance of Mr. Everett P. Weaver.

Library of Congress Cataloging-in-Publication Data

Gravely, S. L. (Samuel Lee)

Trailblazer : the U.S. Navy's first Black admiral / Samuel L. Gravely Jr. with Paul Stillwell ; afterword by Alma B. Gravely.

p. cm.

Includes index.

ISBN 978-1-59114-338-3 (hardcover : alk. paper) 1. Gravely, S. L. (Samuel Lee), 1922- 2. Admirals—United States—Biography. 3. United States. Navy—Officers—Biography. 4. United States. Navy—African Americans—Biography. 5. United States—History, Naval—20th century. I. Stillwell, Paul, 1944- II. Title.

E840.5.G73A3 2010

359.0092—dc22

[B]

2010031959

Printed in the United States of America on acid-free paper.

14 13 12 11 10 9 8 7 6 5 4 3 2

First printing

Contents

	Coauthor's Note	vii
	Preface	xi
	List of Abbreviations and Acronyms	xvii
1	Richmond	1
2	New to the Navy	7
3	First Sea Duty	20
4	Civilian Interlude	32
5	Recruiting	37
6	USS *Iowa*	42
7	USS *Toledo*	55
8	Com Three—New York City	66
9	USS *Seminole*	76
10	On-the-Job Training	87
11	USS *Theodore E. Chandler*	93
12	USS *Falgout*	107
13	Naval War College	124
14	Housing Still a Problem	128
15	Defense Communications Agency	131
16	USS *Taussig*, 1966	139
17	USS *Taussig*, 1967–68	158
18	Satellite Communications Program	169
19	USS *Jouett*	174

20	Director of Naval Communications	193
21	Cruiser-Destroyer Group Two	202
22	Eleventh Naval District	210
23	Third Fleet	216
24	Defense Communications Agency	226
25	After the Navy	229
	Afterword	239
	Index	263

Coauthor's Note

My first awareness of the name Sam Gravely came in the summer of 1966. I was then a newly commissioned ensign, and en route to my first ship, I attended training courses at the naval amphibious base in Coronado, California. While I was in the base barbershop one day, I picked up a copy of *Ebony* magazine as I waited for a haircut. In it was an article about Commander Gravely, the commanding officer of the destroyer *Taussig*. As I came to discover later, he had cooperated with the magazine only because he had to. His reluctance to blow his own horn or seek public recognition was among his many appealing qualities.

As the years passed, I learned of Gravely's selection for rear admiral in 1971. Then, three years later, while I was on four weeks of active duty with the Naval Reserve, I came in proximity to him, though I had no direct contact. A North Atlantic Treaty Organization (NATO) sea control and transit exercise called Safe Pass involved forty-two ships that steamed in March 1974 from Roosevelt Roads, Puerto Rico, to Norfolk, Virginia. During the exercise I was on board the Second Fleet flagship, the heavy cruiser *Newport News*. Rear Admiral Gravely, as Commander Cruiser-Destroyer Group Two, was on board his own flagship as officer in tactical command of the exercise. Shortly after the exercise concluded, I ran into Lieutenant Commander Mike Pavlik, a former shipmate of mine. He was on Admiral Gravely's staff and told me how much he enjoyed working for him.

My first correspondence with Sam Gravely came in 1986. I was then doing oral history work for the U.S. Naval Institute. Admiral Gravely at that time was retired from the Navy and working with the Armed Forces Communications and Electronics Association (AFCEA) in Burke, Virginia. As I went through the Naval Institute files, I discovered that my predecessor, Dr. John T. Mason Jr., had previously requested that Admiral Gravely do an oral history, but nothing came of it. In May, I concluded it was time to try again, so I wrote to the admiral. In his reply he said: "Frankly, I hate interviews. This I must decline at this time. . . . Also, thank you for asking me. Whereas I do not remember Dr. Mason asking me, I suspect I told him the same thing that I am telling you." But Gravely left the door ajar by adding, "On the other hand, I am willing to listen to further details on this subject." We communicated some more, and finally he agreed. We met face-to-face in his AFCEA office on June 25 and began the series of oral history interviews that are the basis for this book. He was a large, imposing man physically. In personality I found him to be low key and unpretentious.

In 1993, the Naval Institute published my book on the Golden Thirteen, the first black naval officers. I sent Admiral Gravely a copy, along with a note that included something along the lines of his "following in the footsteps" of the Golden Thirteen pioneers. In his gracious way, the admiral responded by letting me know that such a description didn't quite fit him. Even though the thirteen were commissioned six months earlier than he was, that was because their training course was so brief. He had actually been in an officer training program several months before they started.

The Navy honored the surviving members of the Golden Thirteen in 1994 on the fiftieth anniversary of their commissioning at Great Lakes, Illinois. Half a century earlier, the new black ensigns had been admonished not to use the local officers' club. On the golden anniversary, the officer in command of the entire Great Lakes training center was a black man, Rear Admiral Mack C. Gaston. Subsequently I came to know Mack as a friend, and it was he who pushed me to complete Admiral Gravely's oral history transcript.

On Abraham Lincoln's birthday, February 12, in the year 2000, the San Diego chapter of the National Naval Officers Association put on a tribute night for Admiral Gravely at North Island Naval Air Station in Coronado, as part of the African-American History Month celebration. I was fortunate to be able to spend some time the night before the event with the admiral, his wife, Alma, and their good friend Willita "Dede" Reagan, the widow of John Reagan of the Golden Thirteen. The turnout for the tribute was spectacular. It was a public thank-you from many officers whose opportunity to pursue a naval career had been made possible because of what the admiral had accomplished step-by-step so many years earlier. Hundreds of individuals stood in line to greet the Gravelys and shake their hands.

In 2003, as Admiral Gravely's oral history was nearing conclusion, Mack Gaston's wife, Nancy, took an active part. By then Admiral Gravely's eyesight had dimmed, so Nancy read the pages of transcript aloud to him and incorporated the changes he gave her. It was none too soon, because the admiral died the following year. He was honored at two funerals, one in his home church in Haymarket, Virginia, and the other at Fort Myer, adjacent to Arlington National Ceremony. One of those who shared their recollections during the first funeral was Mack Gaston. He told the story of meeting Commander Gravely for the first time many years earlier and the electric feeling he experienced from their handshake. It was, he said, like being touched by the "hand of God." Mack was speaking on behalf of many, many others as he paid tribute to the naval pioneer.

The Navy has further honored Admiral Gravely by naming a new guided missile destroyer for him. On May 16, 2009, at the Northrop Grumman shipyard in Pascagoula, Mississippi, Alma Gravely smashed a bottle of champagne on an extension of the bow and christened the new ship. My longtime coworker and friend Fred Rainbow and I attended the ceremony together. In the process we met Commander Doug Kunzman, the prospective commanding officer of the *Gravely*, and saw many of the young men and women who would comprise the first crew.

At the end of a long and enjoyable day, Fred and I sat in an airport awaiting our flight home. As we talked, Fred said, "You should write a book on Admiral Gravely." This volume, drawn from the oral history interviews with the admiral, is the result of that conversation. Mrs. Gravely has reviewed the text, made her inputs, and given it her blessing on behalf of her late husband. She also recorded her own recollections in an interview that served as the basis for the afterword at the end of the book. I am grateful for her kindness and generosity.

I also appreciate the contributions other individuals made to the project. Everett "Tuck" Weaver, who was a submariner in World War II, made a generous financial donation to support the publication. He was a boyhood friend of Paul Richmond, the naval officer who devised the training curriculum for the Golden Thirteen in 1944.

Retired Commander Jim Jackson, who has made a second career of celebrating the achievements of the Navy's black flag officers, provided suggestions and encouragement. Bob Cressman of the Naval History and Heritage Command has helped me many, many times over the years. This time he came through with annual command histories of the ships Admiral Gravely commanded. The histories were particularly helpful in providing specific dates when events happened.

At the Naval Institute Press, press director Rick Russell and acquisitions editor Adam Kane provided steady support throughout the process of moving from concept to finished book. A Naval Institute Press alumna, Linda O'Doughda, whom I have long known as a friend and able editor, did a superb job in copyediting the manuscript. She provided the extra set of eyes needed to sharpen the prose for the benefit of readers. Susan Corrado, editorial manager of the press, directed the production of the book and Christine Onrubia directed the design. Helpful in facilitating the use of the illustrations were David Gravely, son of the admiral, and Janis Jorgensen of Naval Institute's photo archive.

Lastly, as always, I am truly grateful for the love and encouragement from my wife, Karen, and sons James, Robert, and Joseph.

Paul Stillwell
Arnold, Maryland
Spring 2010

Preface

The long life span of Samuel L. Gravely Jr. encompassed a period of dramatic changes in race relations in the United States. In part, he was a beneficiary of those changes, and in part, he was an active agent in bringing them about. Gravely grew up in Richmond, Virginia, which had been the capital of the Confederacy during the Civil War some sixty years earlier. His boyhood and teenage years were a time when former slaves still had memories of their subjugation, and elderly white military veterans still recalled their days of fighting for the South. Though the Civil War had officially ended southern secession and slavery, in the 1920s both law and custom still decreed that Negroes, as they were then called, were forced to live as second-class citizens.

The era of Gravely's birth was a time when the Ku Klux Klan had considerable power in the United States, and many southern men were lynched for the "crime" of being black. Segregation, based on the notion of white superiority, often condemned blacks to use inferior facilities, do menial jobs, receive low pay, and avoid any behavior that whites could label as "uppity." The jobs in which black professionals could work were largely limited to education, law, medicine, and religion.

By the time of the admiral's passing in 2004, the racial climate in the United States had changed dramatically, albeit often grudgingly. No one has been able to wipe out prejudice and states of mind, which still surely exist, but laws and changing attitudes have provided African-Americans far greater freedom of speech and action than were available in 1922. Through the determined leadership of Chief Justice Earl Warren, the Supreme Court overturned the 1896 decision in *Plessy v. Ferguson* that decreed segregation to be justified, warranting facilities that the court decreed should be "separate but equal." In 1954, Warren's court declared, in *Brown v. Board of Education*, that separate facilities were inherently *unequal* and thus no longer legal. Some schools were integrated easily; others did so only with an accompaniment of violence and death. The civil rights movement of the 1950s and 1960s, led by Dr. Martin Luther King Jr. and others, determined to bring change through peaceful means, had such nation-altering results for black citizens as guaranteeing them voting rights, the barring of discrimination in public accommodations, and a general mind-set that opened a variety of opportunities for black citizens. Within Gravely's lifetime, African-Americans had become military leaders, astronauts, presidential cabinet officers, mayors, senators, and Supreme Court justices. Though surely not perfect, equal opportunity had become a goal realized far more often than in 1922, when the concept was rare indeed. Four years after the admiral's death, the citizens of the United States elected an African-American president, which seemed unimaginable not too many years earlier and impossible throughout much of the twentieth century.

★ ★ ★

One hallmark of a successful leader is the ability to go where no one has gone before, to blaze the trail, and to serve as a role model and mentor so that others may follow. Sam Gravely was just such an individual for the U.S. Navy. Even though the service traced its history back to the eighteenth century, it had no black officers until the 1940s and it had no black admirals until the 1970s. In March 1944, the Navy commissioned the Golden Thirteen, its first black officers. Gravely became an officer nine months later. In the years that followed, he was the first African-American line officer to reach the ranks of commander, captain, rear admiral, and vice admiral.

When Gravely was growing up in segregated Virginia in the 1920s and 1930s, being an admiral in the Navy was not a goal for which he could hope to strive. Indeed, when he enlisted in the Naval Reserve in September 1942, the Navy had only recently allowed black men to serve in occupational specialties other than those of cooks and servants for the white officers. Opportunity opened further in 1943 when the service inaugurated its V-12 program, which consisted of both a college education and officer training. Though the service had a long tradition of separation of the races, President Franklin D. Roosevelt directed that V-12 could include black midshipmen.

Gravely studied at the University of California at Los Angeles and received naval training through Midshipman School at Columbia University in New York City. He was commissioned an ensign in the Naval Reserve in December 1944.

Even as the U.S. Navy was creating its first handful of black officers, the service was still unwilling to have white enlisted personnel serving under those new black officers. The Navy did take the experimental step of commissioning two warships that were manned by black enlisted personnel and white officers. The destroyer escort *Mason* and the submarine chaser *PC-1264* both went into service on March 20, 1944, less than a week after the commissioning of the Golden Thirteen. When Ensign Gravely joined the *PC-1264* in May 1945, he became one of the first few black officers to serve in combatant-type ships. Gravely reveled in the opportunity to serve with an open-minded skipper, Lieutenant Eric Purdon, but duty in the ship was not without its drawbacks. In one instance when Gravely was on liberty in Miami, military policemen arrested him for impersonating an officer. They did not believe that a black man could hold such a rank. After the war ended, Gravely returned to Virginia to complete his college education and worked for a time as a railway postal clerk.

As was the case on a number of occasions throughout his naval service, circumstance and timing played their parts. In 1949, the year after President Harry S. Truman integrated the armed services by executive order, the Navy recalled Gravely for a one-year tour of active duty as a recruiter. That planned year of service turned into a thirty-plus-year career. In 1950, the Korean War intervened, the U.S. Navy rebuilt its strength, and Gravely went to sea, first in the battleship *Iowa* off Korea and later on board the heavy cruiser *Toledo*.

Though Gravely enjoyed sea duty, he found himself pigeonholed in the specialties of communication and operations. Up to that point, he did not have a well-rounded background, nor had he served in destroyers, a type of duty he needed as a stepping-stone for promotion. As a pathfinder, he realized that he would have to make his own opportunities. He initiated a do-it-yourself program of training to become an executive officer. He took courses and spent time on board various destroyers as an extra man. Gravely's method was to familiarize himself with the ships, to watch exercises and training in action, and thus to absorb lessons that can be learned only through experience.

In January 1960, he got orders to become executive officer of the destroyer *Theodore E. Chandler*. It marked a major advance in his career. As Gravely reminisced, "I was just flabbergasted but happy as a lark." He got his first command of an operating ship in January 1962, when he became skipper of the radar picket destroyer escort *Falgout*, homeported in Pearl Harbor. The news media played up the story, but Gravely accepted publicity reluctantly—a trait that was to characterize his entire naval career. He viewed himself as merely doing his job within the Navy establishment, but—like it or not—he was indeed a role model. In 1963, the Navy dispatched him from Hawaii to the Kennedy White House for a celebration of the one hundredth anniversary of the Emancipation Proclamation, which was issued during the Civil War to free slaves. Gravely's professional emergence came as the nation as a whole was changing during African-Americans' struggle for civil rights.

After he left the *Falgout*, Commander Gravely and Lieutenant Commander George Thompson became the first two black officers to attend the august Naval War College in Newport, Rhode Island. As he was nearing the end of the academic year, Gravely and his wife, Alma, began to plan their move to the Washington, D.C., area for his next assignment. A real estate agent called to invite them to visit and see about housing. When the Gravelys showed up, chagrined agents discovered that their potential clients were black and said that there were no available rental places. After a great deal of looking—and with the help of the Northern Virginia Fair Housing Organization—Gravely found a place in which he could house his family.

In the years that followed, Gravely continued to ascend the rungs of the Navy's hierarchy. In the latter part of the 1960s, he commanded the destroyer *Taussig*, which was engaged in combat operations off the coast of Vietnam. It was a dramatic increase in the pace of operations over the role the *Falgout* played, largely on detached radar picket duty.

Gravely then moved to shore duty in the nation's capital to work with the Navy's emerging satellite communication program. His next wartime assignment followed, this time in command of the sophisticated guided missile frigate *Jouett*, which used its radars and electronic tactical data system to monitor air traffic in Vietnam. The chief of naval operations (CNO) at the time was Admiral Elmo Zumwalt Jr., who instituted a wide-ranging program to foster increased opportunities for minorities within the service.

Gravely was in the right place at the right time, with an accomplished record in the essence of the naval service—command at sea. In the spring of 1971, a selection board chose him as the U.S. Navy's first black admiral. He went on to command the Naval Telecommunications Command, Cruiser-Destroyer Group Two, and the Eleventh Naval District. In 1976, he became the U.S. Navy's first African-American three-star admiral and its first fleet commander as Commander Third Fleet, based in Hawaii. He later served as director of the Defense Communications Agency, his last billet prior to retirement from active duty in 1980.

By that time, many other black officers had been inspired by the admiral's achievements. The selection of an African-American or other minority individual for flag rank became part of the regular process, no longer a widely heralded exception. Though he hadn't intended to make history, Admiral Gravely did so by a steady series of achievements. He worked within the system and succeeded by its standards. He took pleasure in serving on the bridges of ships at sea and directing the efforts of his crews. As he describes in this memoir, he succeeded with the help of white officers, for he had no black role models to follow. In the process, Gravely blazed the trail for thousands of other black officers who learned from his example and his success. That is his greatest legacy.

Abbreviations and Acronyms

AFCEA	Armed Forces Communications and Electronics Association
AKA	attack cargo ship
ATF	fleet tug
BOQ	bachelor officers' quarters
BuPers	Bureau of Naval Personnel
Chinfo	Chief of Information
C^2	command and control
C^3I	command, control, communications, and intelligence
CIC	combat information center
CinCPac	Commander in Chief Pacific
CinCPacFlt	Commander in Chief Pacific Fleet
Com Eleven	Eleventh Naval District, San Diego
Com Fourteen	Fourteenth Naval District, Hawaii
Com Three	Third Naval District, New York
CNO	Chief of Naval Operations
CO	commanding officer
CruDesPac	Cruiser-Destroyer Force Pacific Fleet
CVS	antisubmarine aircraft carrier
DCA	Defense Communications Agency
DDG	guided missile destroyer
DER	radar picket destroyer escort
DesRon	destroyer squadron
DEW	Distant Early Warning

DLG	guided missile frigate
FRAM	Fleet Rehabilitation and Modernization
JCS	Joint Chiefs of Staff
MOTU	mobile technical unit
MPA	main propulsion assistant
MPs	military policemen
NAACP	National Association for the Advancement of Colored People
NATO	North Atlantic Treaty Organization
NavElex	Naval Electronic Systems Command
NavShips	Naval Ship Systems Command
NavTelCom	Naval Telecommunications Command
NMCC	National Military Command Center
NNOA	National Naval Officers Association
NROTC	Naval Reserve Officers' Training Corps
OOD	officer of the deck
OpNav	the extended staff of the Chief of Naval Operations
PAO	public affairs officer
PIRAZ	positive identification radar advisory zone
ROTC	Reserve Officers' Training Corps
SCTC	Submarine Chaser Training Center
SecDef	Secretary of Defense
SHF	superhigh frequency
SoLant	South Atlantic Force
SurfLant	Surface Force Atlantic Fleet
SurfPac	Surface Force Pacific Fleet
Task Force 77	Carrier Striking Force, Seventh Fleet
Task Group 70.8	Cruiser-Destroyer Group, Seventh Fleet
TraPac	Training Command Pacific Fleet
UCLA	University of California at Los Angeles
UHF	ultrahigh frequency
USC	University of Southern California
USO	United Services Organization
V-12	World War II officer training program
XO	executive officer
Z-grams	nickname for policy messages issued during Admiral Elmo Zumwalt's tenure as CNO

TRAILBLAZER

CHAPTER ONE

Richmond

My life began in Richmond, Virginia, as a postwar baby—World War I, that is. Both of my parents were native Virginians. My father, for whom I was named, had come from the area near Danville. My mother was from a little place called Clover.[1] My father served in World War I as a draftee, then extended his Army enlistment until about 1921. Soon after his discharge he married my mother, and I came along in June 1922 as the first of five children. I have two brothers and two sisters: Ed, Robert, Christie, and Betsey.[2]

My father worked for many years as a Pullman porter. The porters, known as Negroes in those days, were essentially servants for railroad passengers. They took care of the riders' needs, which included running errands for them and converting the accommodations to serve at night as bunks. He worked for the Southern Railroad, as I recall, and used to run from Richmond to Chase City, Virginia. I got a lot of free rides on trains until it was time to start school.

The Depression began in 1929 and got worse after that. My father was laid off, and so he did a number of other jobs in order to keep the family going. He seemed always to be working toward something in civil service because of the security it would provide. As luck would have it, he went into the post office in 1932 or '33 as a mail handler and worked there until he retired. He was earning an hourly wage. I doubt very seriously if he made as much as six

1 His mother's maiden name was Mary George Simon.

2 As of 2010, only Ed is still living. In May 2009, Ed's daughter Denise Price was one of the matrons of honor when Mrs. Gravely christened the guided missile destroyer that honors her late husband.

hundred dollars a year. But my mother was just a tremendous cook and saver and partner, and as a result they saved money. (I can remember that when I was an ensign in the Navy in the 1940s I told my dad that I was making more money than he'd ever made in his life.)

One of the values I got from my parents was the work ethic. My father was a hard worker, and I'm sure he got where he did in life through hard work, because he didn't have very much education. When he worked in the post office, it was as a mail handler. His job was strictly laboring; he carried sacks of mail from one place to another and dumped them down for others to sort. He taught me that whenever you see a guy's work station without a bag, you put one there so he can keep going.

I remember a specific event that served as an object lesson. I was coming home one day and passed a drugstore. The druggist called out to me and said, "Son, would you like to make a dime?"

I said, "Yes, sir."

He said, "Well, would you mind sweeping my walk?"

I swept his walk, and he gave me the dime. When I got home, I told my dad what had happened. He said: "Son, I just got off the streetcar at that corner, and that place doesn't look like it's been swept to me. You give me that dime. We're going to walk back around there and we'll see if Mr. Harrison will let us do it again so I can show you how."

And, boy, he swept that sidewalk out to the middle of the street, where the streetcar came up the track, right to the gutter, curb, and everything else. I guess it took about an hour—after I'd done it in about fifteen minutes and thought I'd done it right. He knew how to work much harder than I did, and he did it. The next time I saw Mr. Harrison, he said, "How would you like to come back here and work every Friday and Saturday night?"

"Yes, sir." So he gave me a job, cleaning up the drugstore. Obviously, I never forgot that lesson from my father.

★ ★ ★

I have no memory of feeling disadvantaged during that period when I was growing up. We were as well off as, or better than, most of the other people in our neighborhood, particularly after my father went to the post office. When I was born, my father was buying the house in which he and my mother lived. We moved to a larger house when the other children came along, and he bought that one too. We were right along with the norm of the people in that particular area.

Religion was a regular part of our lives. From day one, I was taken to a small church called Rising Mount Zion Baptist. I don't recall my father going very much, because most of the Sundays he was away. He spent his weekends down in Chase City for the longest time. Ultimately, when he got into the post office, he went to Rising Mount Zion. I was expected to be there every Sunday for Sunday school, which I did, and went to church. I went to about two services a Sunday, and sometimes I went in the afternoon to Baptist Young People's Union in another church. I was eventually baptized at age twelve. That experience in church implanted values that have stayed with me for a long time, and we are regular churchgoers today as a result.[3]

My formal education began when I entered elementary school in Richmond at the age of six. It was just a breeze for me, despite the fact that I didn't go to kindergarten or any other preschool programs. I don't think I was that smart, but somehow I mastered most of the things that went on. The other thing I remember is that my mother felt I should go to school year-round. I don't recall what happened with my siblings, but I went every summer, which meant that each fall I started out with a new bunch of kids because I was half a grade ahead of them. The summer school was designed primarily for those kids who had not done well during the regular semesters. But somehow I got forced into summer school, and I went for four years. That put me about two years ahead of my contemporaries.

I was not involved in sports in high school, although I played football and tennis on the local playground all the time. I was very, very sports oriented, and at some point I decided that what I really wanted to do was to become a high school football coach. The problem was that my father was deathly afraid of me getting injured. I can remember that I went out for the high school football team. At that time, the school did not have a gymnasium where you could change your clothes. So when I came home, I hid my uniform behind the refrigerator. When my father found that thing, he made me take it back. That was the end of my football career—at least for a while.

★ ★ ★

In 1937, when I was fifteen years old, my mother died. One week later, my brother Ed lost his right leg because of an accident. It happened right in our front yard as the result of a streetcar jumping the track. So things were traumatic

---

3 The bulk of the interviews on which this memoir is based were conducted in 1986.

about then. The next year I graduated from high school and really had no idea what I wanted to do in the immediate future.

Neither of our parents had a high school education; in fact, they had considerably less. Even so, I can remember knowing by the time I was five years old that my father and mother intended that I would one day go to college. In fact, they had a place in mind, Hampton Institute in Hampton, Virginia. It had been established shortly after the Civil War as a vocational school for black students. I had thought in terms of going to Hampton, but the circumstances weren't right. My father decided he did not want me to leave the family nest at the age of sixteen. So I enrolled at Virginia Union University, which was a religious school in Richmond. I commuted back and forth each day between home and classes. Virginia Union was a very, very good school. All the students were black; the president and some of the instructors were white.

One difference from high school was that I was able to play football without my father knowing it. The college had a gym with lockers, so it was no longer a case of trying to hide my uniform at home. One of the football trips in 1940 had beneficial consequences down the road. At the time, my sister Christie was going to school at Virginia State College in Petersburg. I went over there once with a bunch of football players, and my sister introduced me to one of her roommates, Alma Clark. Several years later, Alma and I were married, which I'll come to.

In the meantime, unfortunately, I didn't quite fit in at Virginia Union. The biggest reason, of course, was my age. When I started, most of the other freshmen were seventeen or eighteen. Those who lived on the campus were not exactly independent, but at the same time, they could make their own decisions about this or that. The other factor was that my father wanted me home every afternoon as soon as school was out. He had a good reason: somebody had to take care of the kids. I learned to cook and do things around the house because I did a lot with helping to raise my younger siblings, including a sister who was only two and a half years old when my mother died.

We tried what you might call maids or cooks, but that didn't work very well. Some of them were much poorer than we were. When my mother was alive, she used leftovers the following day to make soup or something else. But we had the problem that these women felt that my dad was well enough off so they could take food home to feed their families. He was spending more money than he wanted to, and the whole thing was just a big mess.

My classes were a problem as well. Despite the fact that I breezed through high school and the other schools, I found it a little tougher in college. You had to study then, and I didn't do very well. So in 1940, I dropped out of college and thought in terms of possibly joining the Army. I read at that time about a special program in the Army's Transportation Corps. The recruiting pitch was, "Enlist in the Army as a sergeant, and you will be taught to drive all this heavy equipment and trucks." So I went up to the recruiting office one day. I took the examination, and I failed the physical. The doctor said I had a heart murmur. Of course, that frightened me a little, so I immediately went home and talked to my father about it. We went to see a civilian doctor, who declared that I did not have a heart murmur at all. I guess that was the Army's way of getting rid of me in those days of segregation. In any event, I went home and forgot that one.

Since I was no longer in school, I got work in Richmond and still lived at home. My first job was in a tobacco factory, and, my father was just deathly afraid of my being in the tobacco industry. He felt there was no incentive to go anyplace else; he feared that ultimately I'd marry some broad and that would be the end of me. I'd be in the tobacco factory the rest of my life. I stayed there for about a year until a friend of mine, who worked at a clothing manufacturer, got me a job pressing coat linings. I was doing that when World War II started.

★★★

On December 7, 1941, I was at home when I heard the news that the Japanese had attacked Pearl Harbor. That, of course, got the United States into the war. The questions that came to me, as they did to many other people, were, "Where is Pearl Harbor, and what effect is that going to have on me?" Very shortly thereafter, the effect became obvious because the draft was stepped up to provide manpower for the armed forces. I was faced with the choice of sitting around and waiting to be drafted or else volunteering for some branch of service and being able to pick what I wanted to do.

In about May of 1942 I read that the Navy had opened up the various enlisted ratings to Negroes.[4] So, I began to investigate that and talked to my father about it. Even though he had been in the Army, he really didn't try to talk

4 On April 7, 1942, the Navy announced a new policy in which it would accept black sailors into general service ratings as of June 1 of that year.

me into joining that service. He wanted me to make my own decision. Finally it came down to the idea of joining the Navy and learning a trade. We thought it would be a short war, and then, when I got out of the Navy, I'd have something to fall back on, or I could go back to college and finish my education. In addition to discussing my options with my father, I talked to several ministers. There were about three or four churches in the neighborhood, as I recall, and I knew them all. I looked up to the ministers, and they were helpful in my coming to the decision to join the Navy.

I liked the opportunity for training and the challenge of being part of something brand-new—the opening of the general ratings so I could become something other than a servant for officers. I could be a regular sailor just like everybody else. This was completely new to blacks. The change came about because there'd been a lot of hue and cry from the black press and from the NAACP[5] about the Navy's recruiting policies when it obviously needed a lot of men to fight the war.

Though I had no way of knowing what all I would encounter in this next stage of my life, I knew for certain what I was leaving behind. Every school that I'd ever been to before the Navy was all black. Even when I had a part-time job in the drugstore, I couldn't buy a Coke at the fountain and drink it there. I automatically went to the back of the streetcar or the back of the bus. I had to sit in the front of a train, which was the first place the coal hit. It was a completely segregated society, and I knew no other. It was a way of life, it was the law of the land, and it was the way I had learned to live—and had been forced to live—during my years in Richmond.

---

5 The National Association for the Advancement of Colored People was founded on February 12, 1909, the one hundreth anniversary of Abraham Lincoln's birth.

CHAPTER TWO

New to the Navy

After I'd had twenty years of a truly home-centered existence, my life and horizons began to expand dramatically once I decided to join the Navy. That decision led me to the recruiting station in Richmond. Part of the reason I went into the service was for the training, but there was also an element of patriotism. I knew that this is a great country, and I had to do my part to support it, just like anybody else. I probably was not as patriotic as some, but I certainly had a sense of duty.

The recruiting office had several desks. One of them had a white chief petty officer behind it, and he handled the black people who came in. I assume we all took the same aptitude tests as the whites. I don't think they modified the test for blacks. Despite the discrimination that still existed in many areas of life, the recruiter made no overt attempts to discourage me or cause me to want to do anything differently. By this time, of course, World War II was raging. The services now needed manpower much more than in 1940, when the Army played the game on my physical exam. I didn't have any problem this time. I was just another recruit, and, incidentally, I made a good score on the examination. After going through all the necessary preliminary steps, I enlisted on September 15, 1942.

The day after I joined up, I was part of a group of men headed for the Great Lakes Naval Training Station, north of Chicago on the shore of Lake Michigan. Segregation still prevailed. All ten of us were from my hometown, and all were black. An older black guy was in charge of this group. We got on the train in Richmond, and in very short order a Pullman porter came through picking up the tickets. He noticed that one kid in our group was much fairer skinned than all the rest of us, although he had registered with the Navy as a Negro. The porter said, "Hey, you're in the wrong car." Our petty officer in charge objected to him doing anything about it, but this porter moved that guy to the back of the train, and I never saw him again. All I know is that nine of us were admitted to the same recruit company when we got to Great Lakes.

Even though a number of aspects of recruit training—known as boot camp—were different from my civilian upbringing, I was again in a segregated situation. Within the larger training facility at Great Lakes, black sailors were put in a special area called Camp Robert Smalls. It was named for an escaped slave who captured a Confederate ship during the Civil War and turned it over to the Union Navy.[1] From then on throughout the war, he was in ships of the U.S. Navy. Robert Smalls ultimately became a congressman from South Carolina.

This camp at Great Lakes had been in operation for only a few months when I got there in September. Figuring that there were a hundred men in a company, and probably four or five companies there at a time, perhaps eight to ten thousand black men had either passed through Great Lakes or were still there by the time I arrived. My company was number 10-43, which indicated that it was the tenth company to be formed there in fiscal year 1943, which started in July of 1942.

The training itself was almost a breeze for me. The regimentation was no problem; I'd been regimented at home all my life. Reveille at six o'clock in the morning was more than a breeze. One of the things I did as a youngster was carry newspapers. I had to get up every morning at five, so now I could sleep an hour later. We did a lot of drilling and marching, and because I had been a Boy Scout, I had no problem falling into line there.

In the classification tests that led to future assignments, I easily passed the ones that would send me on to service school for specialized training. I chose motor machinist's school, which sounded sort of interesting. I was also thinking ahead in terms of what I could do when I left the Navy. I figured I

---

1 In May 1862, Robert Smalls took over the Confederate steamer *Planter* when the ship's white officers were ashore. With his family and other black sailors on board, he delivered the *Planter* to a Union ship that was part of the blockade of Charleston. Smalls then served as pilot of the *Planter* and later of the gunboat *Keokuk* in service of the Federal Navy.

could run my own gas station and repair cars, so diesel engineering seemed a good fit.

It so happened that the motor machinist's mate school was at Hampton Institute near Norfolk, Virginia. It was the same school my mother had envisioned for me years earlier. The civilian school there was still operating, and now the Navy had taken over a portion of it to provide advanced training for black sailors. It was quite convenient for the Navy to set up a school on the campus. It already had instructors, and the school had shops and various types of machinery available as well. Thus, most of the black sailors destined for artificer ratings went to service school at Hampton.[2] The seaman ratings stayed at Great Lakes for further training.

I should mention that there was an interruption in this process. After I finished boot camp, I went home on the normal nine-day leave. That's the only thing that was ever promised. Richmond, Virginia, was kind of warm that November. Then, even though my next trip defied common sense, the regulations said I had to go back to Great Lakes before reporting to Hampton. It was colder than hell out there next to Lake Michigan, and I caught pneumonia. As a result, I was held over in Great Lakes for a month and lost track of the men I'd been with. Then, on New Year's Day of 1943, I arrived in Hampton with a different group of guys, and I didn't know any of them. We were assigned rooms at Hampton by alphabetical order, and I wound up with three really fantastic roommates—Foster, Green, and Gibbons.

At Hampton Institute I discovered that I was not as technically minded as I thought I was, so I didn't do very well at service school. Some of the men came out of those classes as motor machinist's mate second class, that is, petty officers. I came out as a fireman second class. That meant I was still a nonrated man, not a petty officer. When we graduated from service school, there were six possibilities for our next duty stations: New York, Boston, Philadelphia, San Diego, Seattle, or San Francisco. Since I had grown up on the East Coast, my normal inclination would have been to say New York or Philadelphia. Not only were they close to home, I still had a lot of home in me. My younger brothers and sisters were still in Richmond.

But I was influenced by one of my roommates to look in another direction. Gibbons had been a schoolteacher. He'd been one of the great football

2 The artificer branch of engineering ratings included such specialties as machinist's mate, motor machinist's mate, water tender, and boilermaker.

players of Prairie View A&M, a black college in Texas. He could also hit a baseball a country mile, and he was a man's man. I sort of idolized him because of his various accomplishments. As he and I were sitting around one day discussing the future, he said: "Hey, do you know what Horace Greeley said? Horace Greeley said, 'Go West young man.' We ought to go to San Diego."

So I said: "All right. How do we assure that we go to San Diego?" We talked further and agreed that there was no way to be sure. So we decided to try to outfox the system. We said, "Well, everybody in this class wants to go to New York, so what we're going to do is put down New York as our first choice and San Diego as our second." That's exactly what we did, and we got orders to San Diego.

Even though the new assignment was liberating in a sense, I did have some reluctance to be that far from home. It was not until later that I realized, "Hey, you've got to be your own man." At the age of twenty, I was still quite a father's boy, because he had directed my entire life while I was growing up. For example, I had never been to a dance with a date. I went alone to my own high school ball. Can you imagine a guy going to a high school dance all by himself? During my first years at Virginia Union University, I wanted to go to a couple of fraternity affairs. My father said, "Go, fine, if you're going to be home by ten o'clock." But who in the hell is going to go to something that lasts till midnight and have to be in at ten? My father was a very strict man, but at the same time he was a very fine man.

In any event, Gibbons and I arrived in San Diego, and I thought I had reached the most beautiful place in the world. About fifteen of us mustered in, and the first thing that happened was that the first class petty officer who was the master-at-arms came around and said: "All right, I need one mess cook, and I need one compartment cleaner. Who's going to volunteer for those two?" Since I was one of two or three firemen second class in the group, I knew I was low on the totem pole and I'd get one of those chores. So I said, "I will volunteer for the compartment cleaning job." I simply didn't want to go mess cooking. Mess cooking reminded me of being a steward, the traditional role for black sailors.

The other guys, except for one who was picked for the mess-cooking job, were assigned to various machine shops on the base. At that point, there were very few blacks on board ships, and certainly the naval base commander didn't have any authority to transfer us to a seagoing ship. But they did have some harbor craft that operated in the local area, and some black sailors went there in the engineering ratings.

Despite the fact that I really loved the city of San Diego, I was surprised to discover that the Navy facilities were even more segregated than my own hometown. On this big base, blacks were on one end, whites on the other. In fact, the Navy didn't permit the blacks to live in the barracks. Instead, all of us were assigned to a group of huts on the western end of the base. These huts would hold eight people in four double-decker bunks. As a guy of six-foot-three, I could not stand upright in my hut. The only time I was ever in my hut was when I was asleep, or we could go in there and sit and play cards at a little table.

I did this compartment-cleaning job for about two months. My job was to go around each morning and see that all the bunks were made up, pick up the cigarette butts, and make sure that all of the cigarette receptacles had water in them. I swept the area, went and picked up the mail, and put the letters on each guy's bunk. Also I worked in the office of the chief master-at-arms. One day, while I was doing my job in the office, the chief master-at-arms had to go off someplace, and he said, "Look out for my phone."

The phone rang, and it was the welfare and recreation officer, Lieutenant Stubbs. He was looking for the chief master-at-arms, but since I had answered the phone, he would talk to me. He said: "We have decided that the Negroes aren't really taking advantage of the welfare and recreation things that we have on this base. They are spending most of their time either going to Tijuana or some of the undesirable locations in San Diego. We've decided that we'd like to have two people to work in the welfare and recreation department. Specifically, we're going to run a pool hall, and I want you to put the word out that I'm looking for two people."

I said, "Mr. Stubbs, I'll volunteer for one of these positions, and I'll see if I can find you someone else."

Now, at that point in time—with my sheltered upbringing—I'd never been in a pool hall in my life. But I found another guy, and we went up there that day to work for Mr. Stubbs. Putting us in that pool hall turned things around a little bit because obviously, where you've got two blacks working, others are going to come. It did succeed in bringing people in. Our job was relatively simple: cleaning the tables, charging a nickel fee, making sure the place was clean and orderly. I was quite happy doing that and got to know a lot of people when they came in to play. But I still felt frustrated because the thing that I started out to do in the Navy—becoming a motor machinist's mate—just had not come to fruition.

My big break came about in a quite unexpected way. After I'd been in the pool hall for two or three months, Lieutenant Stubbs came up one morning when I was in there cleaning. He said, "Why aren't you taking the V-12 test?"

I said, "Mr. Stubbs, I'm not sure I know what the V-12 test is."

He said, "Well, you should have read it in the plan of the day." But welfare and recreation, despite the fact it had a division, never mustered people at quarters. They just sort of assumed you were there. You did your work, went on liberty when you were off duty, and that was about the end of it. I had not read the plan of the day, so I said, "What is it about?"

He said, "Well, V-12 is a program where a grown person will get an opportunity to go to college and ultimately become an officer in the Navy.[3] You finished high school, didn't you?"

I said, "Yes, sir." I didn't volunteer that I had a couple of years of college already, but I did say: "Mr. Stubbs, I'm not sure that there's any reason for me to go down there and take this test. To the best of my knowledge, the Navy has no Negro officers, and I don't know of anything about them anticipating any."

He just simply said, "Get your ass down and take the test."

"Yes, sir."

So I went down and took the test. I was one of three people on the base to get into the program. I don't know what the passing score on the test was, but I was selected, along with two white boys.

Shortly after I took the V-12 test, the Navy came out with a new policy that said service school graduates could work only in their ratings. Since I had graduated from Hampton, even though I hadn't been promoted to petty officer I was quickly transferred from the pool hall down to one of the machine shops. But that was even more frustrating than before. By now I'd been away

3 V-12 was a Naval Reserve officer-training program in which individuals worked toward bachelor's degrees and also received naval instruction. The program was held at civilian colleges and universities and took about two years.

from the machinist's mate business for about four or five months. The other guys in the shop were all white and didn't particularly want to help me learn. I was just an odd man in the shop, and their attitude was, "What the hell did they send this guy down here for?"

But I was saved, obviously, by the fact that I had been selected for the V-12 training. The Navy offered me a choice of schools, and there were dozens of units in various parts of the country. I recognized that there was no such thing as trying to come to the University of Richmond, which is where I probably would have liked to come, since that was my hometown. So I just wrote, "No choice." When my orders came, I was sent to the University of Southern California in Los Angeles. I arrived at USC about the thirty-first of October 1943. I began registration and was assigned five roommates, all white, who were there for V-12. I was one of the first five or six blacks to get into this program.

The next morning I was quite surprised when I was called down to the administration office and was told that I had been transferred to the University of California at Los Angeles. Now, I didn't know any more about UCLA than I did about USC. I was a little concerned about this but said I'd go. So they put my gear in a truck and drove me to UCLA, which was across town. I got the impression later, from talking to a few of my friends, that UCLA was the school that most black students went to, although there were a few at USC. Just a couple of years before that, Kenny Washington and Jackie Robinson had been there.[4]

When I got to UCLA, a couple of things really began to hit me. One was that here I had a rare opportunity, and I had to take advantage of it. Number two, there was to be no failure; failure couldn't enter my mind. I had to succeed, not only for myself but also for other people who might come along after that. I watched my decorum, I watched everything. I made sure I was going to do everything right, and I guess I did. I got out successfully.

When I arrived, I was put into a company with a group of premed students from Stanford. One of them was Bobby Brown, who later played baseball for the New York Yankees and still later became a cardiologist. Another

---

4 The Los Angeles Rams became the first National Football League team since the 1930s (when the game was resegregated) to integrate when they hired black veterans Kenny Washington and Woody Strode in 1946. In 1947, Jackie Robinson became the first black major league baseball player.

thing that hit me was that, with rooms all over the building, I was assigned to the basement. I asked the question about why was I consigned to the basement, but I really didn't get a good answer to that one. It was a good room, no complaint about that. There was one other guy in the basement with a good room. But the guy who was my next-door neighbor was fouled up, and they put him down there for that reason. I was a little concerned that I might be perceived the same way.

As it turned out, there were no incidents. I was treated just like any other V-12 student. V-12 was regimented—much more so than the ROTC is now.[5] Today's midshipmen wear civilian clothes, but we wore our uniforms all the time. So I marched with these guys, I played with these guys. We did everything together during the week, but there was no social interchange over weekends. I don't think I expected any real social activity. That just was not the norm in that day and time. As a V-12er during the war, you were kind of restricted to that campus anyway, so there was not much opportunity to go downtown to have a beer. It was basically a policy of separation of the races. Despite the fact that Los Angeles was a little more open on those kinds of things, we didn't do it at all. I did manage to have dates with some black women while I was out there.

Academically I did about as well as the majority of those in the program. I kept my grades up well enough to pass. I didn't work too hard at it. We took college courses, except that every Saturday morning we had about three hours of Navy orientation. The program was designed so that the guy who had finished only high school would be able to pick up about seventy hours of credit in two and a half years, and from there go to a midshipman school and be commissioned. In fact, I had maybe forty or fifty hours from Virginia Union when I entered the program, so I stayed only two semesters, and I left UCLA in June of 1944.

I did not have a major; I just sort of took courses. At Virginia Union I had been a premed student to some degree because I wanted to be an undertaker. I guess I was kind of mixed up in my younger life. I first wanted to be a football coach, then when I went to college I decided that I'd take courses

5 The Reserve Officers' Training Corps, an officer commissioning program, has its origin in the Morrill Act of 1862, which established land-grant colleges that were to include military tactics in their curriculum.

in order to get into embalming and thought about running a garage as still another possibility. When I got to UCLA, I just let it swing. Nobody really asked me about a major. I think I probably put down premed, and so my courses were along that line.

There was some inevitable attrition in the program, because not everybody was cut out for it. I would assume that someone who had previously been a straight civilian and flunked out of V-12 went on to boot camp. The program also took in a lot of enlisted men from the fleet. For example, there was a white signalman first class in the program at UCLA. He couldn't hack the academics, so he went back to the Navy as a signalman first class. I had a black successor at UCLA, from what I hear, although I never met him. He failed the program, and I don't know what happened to him.

Anyway, I got out in good stead and left there en route to pre-midshipman school. The Navy had four midshipman schools: Columbia, Notre Dame, Fort Schuyler, and Northwestern. A new class went into midshipman school every two months, with the duration being four months. There were so many of us to be funneled into these four that the Navy had to send some through the pre-midshipman school in the meantime. So I went through Asbury Park, New Jersey. I was the only black in that unit. I went through all the normal wickets everybody else did. There was no problem. I had five white roommates. Nobody uttered a slur or any of that kind of crap. I did take a turn at mess cooking. I wasn't a very good swimmer so I couldn't be a lifeguard on the beach. But it was just another training camp and nothing untoward happened.

The period I spent in that program was an eye-opener. I was now in a world where I had to compete with the people that I'd be competing with the rest of my life. I knew that this environment was different from what I'd experienced up to then. I realized that if I were to compete successfully, I would have to do it just like everybody else did it. I think I discovered for the first time that all men put their pants on one leg at a time—no matter what their complexion. All men did it the same way.

I think the thing that gratified me the most was the fact that I could do it successfully. That was when I began to think a little bit seriously. "When I get out of the Navy, I'm going back to college and get that degree, and I'm going to do some of these other things that I have been thinking about." I was twenty-two years old, and so I really cut the strings. I knew I was on my own at that point.

By then I had become well acquainted with Navy discipline. I was never unready for an inspection. Some nitpicker might find something wrong, but I took a lot of pride in shining my shoes, and I got a haircut every two weeks, whether I needed one or not. I kept my uniforms up to snuff, so I didn't have any problem. Oh, I was a little nervous at times. Everybody's nervous going through inspection, but I knew that I was in good shape. I learned that the inspection process was a necessary evil as part of the system.

In mid-August of 1944, after roughly two months at Asbury Park, we were transferred up to Columbia University, which is in the Harlem section of New York City. When you started out in midshipman school, you were treated like a boot. That was the first month. Then, finally, you got your midshipman uniform, and you were someplace between an officer and a boot. Treatment got a little better, and the requirements weren't quite as stiff. I developed some really, really good friends there, and we were all struggling to survive.

Midshipman school lasted sixteen weeks, and it was tough. There were some subjects I hadn't taken before. For example, I'd never been through any navigation. I didn't know very much about ordnance. We got into some fairly specific information about the guns and some fairly specific details in engineering courses. We learned about the customs and traditions of the Navy, how to recognize various types of ships and aircraft. Normally, if you didn't pass a subject, you had to stay there some extra time on a Saturday.

As with a lot of Navy training, we did our share of marching. I got caught one Saturday, but it was sort of a minor thing. Our company was the lowest in drilling one week, and I was the guy that caused the low grade. In this particular instance I was on the right side of a column that was marching past the reviewing stand. On the command of "Eyes right," those in the outside ranks immediately turn their heads to the right and look at the reviewing officer. But those of us on the inboard side were supposed to keep our eyes looking straight ahead. And that's what I did. Commodore John K. Richards, who headed the place, marked us down as a result of that. He told my company commander that if I ever passed a reviewing stand again, I was to do eyes right like everybody else.

I tried to object and said, "Sir . . ."

He said: "Don't tell me about that. Do it."

"Yes, sir." From then on, I was eyes right, as the commodore had directed. The next week, we were the outstanding company. Well, it was easy to notice me. We had hundreds of people out there drilling, but I was the one guy the commodore saw out there.

Midshipman school was a very, very, very good course; fairly intensive, highly competitive. Guys were dropping out of there every week. But I'd already told myself I wasn't going to fail, and I didn't. As I recall, my company was originally at about 1,600 men. When we graduated, we were down to about 1,030 or something like that. Roughly a third of the class left, and I was in the top remaining third. So I thought I'd done fairly well.

When I got my commission in December of 1944, there were still very few black naval officers. I was aware that the Navy had commissioned twelve black officers and one warrant officer the previous March. I saw the *Life* magazine story on that. They subsequently became known as the Golden Thirteen. There were also some black staff corps officers. I'm sure there must have been something in the paper at that time about Edward Hope, who was a civil engineer at Howard University in Washington, D.C. He was selected and commissioned as a lieutenant in the Civil Engineer Corps and then finally made lieutenant commander.

But the point is that I didn't really have role models because I didn't have any connection with these other officers from the time they were commissioned until I was. They were out in left field somewhere. I was on my own in that regard, though I had known Johnny Reagan, one of the Golden Thirteen, when he was an enlisted man. He was in the class ahead of me at Hampton, and we played on the same softball team when we were in San Diego together. There were a couple of the other guys whom I had touched base with but didn't know very well. Johnny Reagan was probably the guy I knew best. (In fact, many years later he married a woman named Dede Thompson, whom Alma and I recommended to him.)

Midshipman school kept us so busy that I didn't have time to think about race. For example, as I remember, Johnson Hall had about seventeen floors, and we were timed each time we went up and down the stairs. I ran from the first floor of Johnson Hall all the way to the seventeenth floor for sixteen weeks. And, of course, you ran down to formation and had to be down there at a certain time. I had great leg muscles as a result.

Because the regimen was so demanding, we were happy to get away from school on Saturdays. I spent a lot of time in Harlem, which was nearby. But, as at UCLA, there was very little mixing of social activity. There was no such thing as a club these guys could use. We did some studying together. I always had at least one white roommate. I didn't think very much about it at the time, but I moved around a lot. I'm not sure why, but maybe this was part of somebody's idea of a social experiment. I had about ten roommates during my four months there, moving to a two-man room with one guy, a two-man room with another guy, and a four-man room. But that didn't bother me, because it usually happened when some guy had flunked out and left. So I would move into that open room.

When I went into Harlem, a lot of people weren't aware of what the midshipman uniform signified. At that time, there was a black captain who commanded a merchant ship.[6] And there were a lot of other blacks who got into the merchant marine, so you'd see a lot more merchant marine uniforms out there in Harlem than you would see Navy types. There were no other midshipmen out there. So people just wondered: "What the hell is he? Who is this guy?" But everybody in uniform was treated very, very well in wartime. When you would go into any number of bars, some guy would look at you and say: "Well, I don't know exactly what service you're in, but you must be in some. Come on up and have a drink." I met a couple of girls in the Harlem area. In fact, one girl from my hometown was a nurse there, and she took me around a couple of places, so that was enjoyable.

In any event, after the training period was over, I got my set of orders, and I was very, very disappointed. Now, you think about patriotism, and it hits you. Here were more than a thousand new naval officers—ready to go out and fight the war, fight the Japanese. Most people had orders that either took them to sea or took them to some training course after which they would go to sea. My orders directed me to proceed to Great Lakes, Illinois, to train Negro recruits, and I was let down. I really felt that that was a blow.

In the period between the time we completed all the course requirements and the time we were to be sworn in as ensigns, we got more liberty than before. We had one week during which we were measured for our new

---

6 The black shipmaster was Captain Hugh Mulzac, whose memoir, done in collaboration with Louis Burnham, is *A Star to Steer By* (New York: International Publishers, 1972).

uniforms, and we could go anyplace we wanted. We were permitted to leave in the afternoon and stay out until ten o'clock. The members of my platoon decided that we would go out one night and just have a ball. While we were all out, some guy from the Pennsylvania Dutch country said, "How many of you belong to the fifty-beer club?" I didn't even know what the club was. The requirement was to drink fifty mugs of beer without moving. It seemed like a good idea at the time, and so everybody wanted to join the club, myself in particular. Well, I'm not sure I got past about twenty, so I didn't join, but I got pretty well loaded, and that's what led to my next break.

We all went back to the barracks. I went up to the passageway on the top floor of my building, yelling and screaming: "Goddamn it, if all of my friends are going to sea, I ought to go to sea too. I cannot understand why I've got to go train recruits." The ensign or lieutenant (j.g.) who was officer of the day heard me. He came and put me to bed, but I have always been convinced that something good came out of that. Shortly after I finished midshipman school, I went out to Great Lakes for duty. Six weeks later I was on my way to sea. I think my orders to shipboard duty came as the result of raising a stink after drinking the beer.

CHAPTER THREE

First Sea Duty

The end of midshipman school was marked by a big graduation ceremony on December 14, 1944. More than one thousand of us, wearing the gold stripe of an ensign on each sleeve, took the oath as commissioned officers that day. After celebrating with about two weeks of leave back home in Richmond, I proceeded to Great Lakes as ordered. When I got back to Camp Robert Smalls, where I had started my naval service more than two years earlier, I was shocked to tears. Even though I recognized that we were still living in a segregated world, I had been treated differently during the V-12 training. I'd lived and worked together with white midshipmen, but now I had to drop back down to the same old conditions as before.

As a midshipman, I ate in the mess with everybody else who was on the same level. When I got to Great Lakes, the naval training station had quarters for white officers, but not for me. It had an officers' club for the relaxation of the white officers, but it was not available to me. I was twenty-two years old, and I probably should have had some experience at lining up a place to stay, but I'd never had to find a hotel room in my whole life. So I had to look around to see if I could find a room. And I always ate over in the enlisted mess with the other black men. That caused no major problems because I had never been to an officers' club anyway. But I was still disappointed about the living arrangements.

What made the disappointment even worse was the discrimination when I stood duty watches for the entire station. I was a duty officer not just for Camp Robert Smalls but also for Camp Moffett and the other camps where white sailors were trained. In the "main side" portion of the Great Lakes training station, that is, the headquarters area, there was a bunk in which the duty officers slept—but only the white ones. The routine for a black duty officer at the time required him to go back and forth between camps during the day but at night to sleep in the black camp. That was one of the hardest things for me to take of anything that happened to me during my Navy career.

The chore at Camp Robert Smalls was just exactly what was implied, training black recruits. As an assistant battalion commander, I reviewed the drills and helped the companies. I guess I used to get a little charge out of going over there and taking the kids away from whoever the company commander was, drilling them, and putting them through their paces. I enjoyed giving orders. That duty lasted about six weeks.

It was also during that return stint to Great Lakes that I first saw other black naval officers. At that point in time, we were about five or six black officers at Great Lakes, including some staff corps officers who were jaygees. A fellow line officer there was Ensign Dennis Nelson, who was a member of the Golden Thirteen. He was now running a remedial school for a group of sailors who could not read or write. He was pretty proud of the job that he was doing there, and he was justified in feeling that way. I think he lived in North Chicago, and I found a room someplace else in North Chicago, but we really didn't have that much of an opportunity to get together.

I really didn't have much contact with the other black officers because we had different assignments. So we didn't get much chance to compare notes on how we were being treated. They were older than I was. In fact, there was a lot of discussion about the fact that Dennis Nelson, who was in his late thirties, probably should have been commissioned as a lieutenant, based on an age-rank structure, but here he was an ensign. Most of the Golden Thirteen would have been either jaygees or lieutenants, and probably one or two of them as lieutenant commanders, but the Navy didn't do that. Despite the environment of discrimination, we didn't make any complaints to the chain of command. You sort of wondered whom you would complain to anyway. There just wasn't that kind of an atmosphere. Now you read that every commanding officer has an open-door policy, but I never heard of an open-door policy until much later.

★★★

In the late winter of 1945, I was transferred to the Submarine Chaser Training Center (SCTC) in Miami, Florida, for an eight-week course in antisubmarine warfare. I was quite concerned about going to Miami because it was in the deep South. I was not quite as concerned as I found out later that my father was. He had written a letter to the president of the United States saying, "Hey, you're going to send that boy down there to be killed [or something like that]." I think he got an answer back that said, "Don't worry about your son; he'll be okay."

In Miami, as at Great Lakes, I was again in a segregated situation. All the white students lived in the Biscayne Bay Boulevard Hotel, and I had to go someplace else initially. Later I moved into the same hotel with everybody else. They must have had an officers' club, but I never went there. Social activity was a little bit better because some of the guys from my midshipman company at Columbia University had reported directly to Miami and were still there for another two or three weeks. So I saw a lot of them. We went out to drink on Biscayne Bay Boulevard and see the sights.

The program at subchaser school was sort of a stepped-up midshipman school. You knew that you were going to sea on a ship, and they were trying to teach you to be at least a junior division officer or maybe a division officer, as the case may be. It was a good course. One of the things I'll always remember was that you had to be able to read visual signals. That included semaphore flags and Morse code by blinking light, the dot-and-dash thing. You had to take at least one message, about twenty words, by semaphore. And you had to read the light, fifteen words a minute. You had an opportunity to go over there every morning in one of the three training rooms to take one of these messages. The minute you took one message successfully you were exempted from the course. If you didn't take one message during the first four weeks, then it was mandatory that you went there from then on until you passed. I really don't know what would happen if you never passed it.

We learned the semaphore by practicing with decks of cards that had the flags on them. For the blinking lights, we used flashlights and a little paper device that could open and close like a blinker. I used to play with those cards, and I had done that to some degree in midshipman school. But when I got down there to Miami, it was just a concentrated thing of sitting down there, looking at the signal flags, looking at dots and dashes and those things. A signalman could master the codes in four weeks, so I didn't see why I couldn't.

I was fortunate enough so that I passed the test during my first four weeks down there, and I didn't have to go to mandatory study during the rest of the time.

It was also in Miami that I got my first taste of going to sea. There was a destroyer escort attached to the school. I'm not really sure, but I think we just went out for day cruises. I don't remember spending the night on there. It was quite interesting. I really enjoyed it. We didn't do much ship handling, but we did get the opportunity to be junior officers of the deck, and it all went well. We also had a simulator ashore in which we learned some of the antisubmarine tactics. I think I might have been the object of a few stares, but what the hell, stares didn't bother me at all. No snide remarks.

In terms of off-duty time in Miami, when I went out in town by myself, I lived by the local set of rules. They had a black district outside of town, and that's where I went to socialize more than I did with my Navy classmates. After the departure of the guys whom I had known at Columbia, my relationships with my classmates were only in the professional sense. They were not cold to me by any stretch of the imagination, but I didn't have the openness with them that I'd had with the men I was with as we fought through the battle of Columbia University. That experience had produced a bonding.

Carl Rowan, incidentally, came to Miami four weeks after I did. He was in the V-12 program and in a class right behind me in midshipman school. He went on to have a distinguished career as a newspaper columnist, television commentator, and public official. I got to know Carl fairly well. He and I socialized a couple of times. In fact, we knew two girls who were cousins, so we went on double dates. I see Carl around Washington periodically these days.[1] He and I know a mutual friend, and we sometimes get together at his home. I'm always really pleased to see the extent to which Carl Rowan went from his V-12 experience and on up. He's really a truly outstanding guy. I wish I were that sharp. He's smart, really.

The important thing at school was keeping up with the studies, and that worked out. My next set of orders sent me to the *PC-1264*, which was homeported at Staten Island, part of New York City. It was a 173-foot, 280-ton submarine chaser. At the time, it was one of two Navy ships—the de-

---

1 Rowan died in Washington, D.C., on September 23, 2000, subsequent to the interview in which Admiral Gravely discussed him.

stroyer escort *Mason* was the other—that had a crew of white officers and black enlisted men. The commanding officer was Lieutenant Eric Purdon, who had four white officers in his original wardroom.[2] I reported aboard May 2, 1945, to relieve one of those officers. As I said earlier, black officers had mostly been assigned to harbor craft if they got shipboard duty at all. Even after integration, the *PC-1264* and the *Mason* were the only combatant-type ships with black officers during the war.

There were sixty enlisted men on board when I arrived; all of them were black. Before I got there, I didn't know much about the *PC-1264*, and I'm not sure what I expected. But I did know that these two ships were really experimental. The idea was to find out if blacks could really sail, if they could take orders from one another, and if they could do it successfully at sea. In the case of the *PC-1264*, it started with nine senior white petty officers and five white officers. By the time I got there, Captain Purdon had successfully moved the black senior petty officers up into those positions of leadership, and none of the white petty officers were still there.

My first shipboard job was as engineer. I think it was based on the fact that I did have some enlisted experience, and, secondly, the engineer officer was fleeting up to be executive officer. And, of course, in that case the junior guy would take that empty billet there. Within maybe a week, Ensign Don Morman came on. He was from the University of Michigan, as I recall, had an engineering degree, and he relieved me. In the meantime, we were losing a second officer, and I had fleeted up to be communication officer. That was probably a good change, because I had discovered back at Hampton that I was not as engineering oriented as I had originally thought. And that's always been kind of strange to me because I took a course in automobile mechanics in high school, and I felt that that was something I might be interested in later on.

I was truly welcomed aboard that ship—the first time in my Navy experience that I had the feeling of being at home. That was from the top down; Captain Purdon had made a deliberate effort to get a black officer aboard. The first officer I met on there was an ensign by the name of Ben Shanker, the gunnery officer. Ben greeted me and made me comfortable. If there were any problems, it was simply that the ship was designed for only four officers, and

2 Purdon wrote an excellent memoir of his service in the ship, *Black Company: The Story of Subchaser 1264* (Robert B. Luce, Inc., 1972, and Naval Institute Press, 2000).

the fifth guy had to sleep in the wardroom. When Don Morman came aboard, it meant that two of us slept in the wardroom. They had to set up double bunks right above the wardroom table. So, no matter what time I went to bed at night, I had to be up when breakfast was served in the morning. But then, if I had had the four to eight watch in the morning, either Ben Shanker or one of the other guys would say, "Hey, go on down to my bunk and rest."

The enlisted crew members were delighted to see one of their own as an officer. But ultimately that changed a little bit, and it changed simply because I had certain responsibilities as an officer. When guys were wrong, I'd take note of it. That led them to say, "Hell, this guy's just another member of the establishment." Of course, they were right, because I had to do my job.

Eric Purdon was a top-notch leader. He was easy to get along with. I think he was a great ship handler, and I guess he'd had some sea experience at small boat handling. You couldn't help but admire him because he was just a tremendous guy. He didn't make an obvious push for me to learn and grow, but at the same time it was a sort of compelling thing. He had trained such guys as Ben Shanker and Ernest Hardman, and so I was eager to learn my job and fit in. The skipper was the kind of guy who, no matter what you did, you didn't want to let him down. The crew had tremendous respect for him and liked him. He was kind of easygoing, but at the same time you knew that if you didn't do it right, he could be as hard as nails. He knew when to chew and when not to chew.

In fact, I can remember one time specifically when he wanted a message, and I just happened to be the guy available. He said, "Sam, go get me such-and-such a message."

I was kind of lackadaisical and thought, "What the hell does he need the message for, and blah, blah, blah?"

The next time he saw me, he said, "You didn't bring me that message."

I said, "Well, Captain—"

He said, "Goddamn it, the next time I tell you I want a message, I want that message."

I said, "Yes, sir." I respected him. I knew that he knew what he wanted and how he wanted it done, so I sought to fulfill his expectations as part of the learning process.

I was immediately put on watches at sea as a junior officer of the deck. The guy whom I was to relieve, Ensign Stanley Rhodes, stayed on there for about a month after I arrived, and I learned from him. We escorted convoys. We went down to Norfolk, as I recall, and we did a couple other things. I discovered that I was a fairly quick learner. I just loved being on the bridge of a ship—not only that bridge, but every bridge I've ever been on since then. I love to go up there. I got a sense of "I can do it, and I know I can do it."

Unfortunately, there wasn't much chance to learn the kinds of ship handling you use when going in and out of port or refueling at sea. The PC, of course, was a small ship, went out on a mission, had diesel engines. You could stay out there forever almost, so you didn't do any refueling at sea. We did practice man-overboard drills, in which you could play around picking up Oscar, which was the name of the dummy that was thrown into the water. But you didn't really get a chance to handle it that much in port. The *PC-1264* came into port so infrequently that generally the skipper handled the ship, although Captain Purdon was the kind of guy who would at times let somebody else handle it. He sort of stood over someone's shoulder and watched. But I didn't really get that many chances to handle the ship. I did get a feel for propeller turns, though; for how quickly you could get the speed up.

One thing I discovered, and happily so, was that I wasn't the type who was going to get seasick. In fact, I was seasick only once in my whole Navy career, and it was on that PC, but the reason was my own fault. The ship was down in the South Florida area for training. I went up on the forecastle to lie in the sun and get a little salt spray over my face. A big wave came over. I swallowed some salt water, and I've got to say that it came back out in a hurry. But that experience in the *PC-1264* was where I got my start, my love of the sea, and my desire to be on ships. That came from working with Captain Purdon.

I got aboard the same month that the war in Europe ended. Previously, the ship had developed some sonar contacts on possible German U-boats and worked them over, but we did not have any during my stint. Our emphasis was on training to go to the Pacific for the war against Japan. We constantly had general quarters drills at battle stations and went through lots of other drills, but there were no real opportunities to mix with the enemy during the last days of war.

We had another chore, which I thought was kind of dull, although the Navy discontinued it very shortly after I got aboard. The ship was operated off New York City on what was called the buzz bomb patrol against attacks by German rockets. I guess the Navy used four escort ships to patrol around the area. If the buzz bombs came toward New York, we were going to shoot them down. We did that patrol only once, as I recall. The rest of the time we escorted convoys.

In the summer of 1945, the *PC-1264* went down to Norfolk for a shipyard period to prepare for the planned deployment to the Pacific. We stayed there for about two or three months. I was walking through the shipyard one day, and one of the workers there, a stevedore named Clyde Hassell, spoke to me. We struck up a conversation, and Clyde said, "Well, hey, why don't you come around my house with me?" He had a car, which I didn't, so that was welcome in terms of getting around. Clyde was a very, very energetic young man who was constantly striving to go places and to do things. He had not completed high school, but he had a lot of drive, a lot of energy. Soon after I got acquainted with him, he said, "Come on, go with me. I play with a little football team down here, and we're going out to practice." The team was called the Brown Bombers.

That sounded appealing, so I joined the team during the time the ship was there. Clyde played one end, and I played the other. And that's the way we'd always refer to each other, as "the other end." Clyde and I became great friends, and I saw him many times after that when I was in Norfolk. When I go to Clyde's house today, his kids call me Uncle Sam, just like my kids call him Uncle Clyde. So that was a fortunate meeting for both of us.

After the yard period we had some training for the crew. Then we were due to go down to SCTC in Miami for some more refresher training prior to proceeding to the Pacific. We arrived there on August 5, 1945, and that visit was memorable because it was where I got in trouble. I guess I had the deck watch when we were proceeding into Miami, and one of the young enlisted men said, "Mr. Gravely, are you going ashore?"

I said: "I'll tell you what. I've been to Miami. I know the town; I know the people. In fact, I know a bunch of girls, and I know some clubs there." I gave some of the men an address, and I said, "Why don't you guys meet me over there about noon, and I will be there, and I will have three or four girls that I know."

That's when we started designing a party. The ship got in, and, of course, I went on in, made the arrangements, and I met a number of the enlisted men at a restaurant ashore. It was, oh, three or four o'clock in the afternoon, and I must admit I'd had a couple more than I was used to drinking, but I wasn't drunk. Then a military policeman, an Army guy, came over. He said to me, "You're out of uniform."

I said, "Well, I don't know what you mean."

He said, "Well, you're not an officer. I've never seen a Negro Navy officer."

I said, "I am." I was getting ready to pull out my ID card, and he said something else, but, in any event, I was pulled off my stool, and they decided to lock me up for impersonating an officer. Well, whenever you find a military policeman or shore patrolman, you're going to find a patrol wagon very close behind that, so I was put in the patrol car. The fellows off the ship just weren't going to let that happen, so they began to riot. I quelled the riot, but I was still taken down to the shore patrol headquarters in Miami. I went through the routine of getting a physical examination and being checked to see if I was drunk. But nothing untoward happened to me, because my commanding officer came down very shortly after that, when he discovered it, and took me back to the ship.

Unfortunately, the charges were brought up to the naval district commandant down there, and the charges were much more than impersonating an officer. Drunk and disorderly in public, and I really hadn't done any of that. Using foul language, and I hadn't done that either. Associating with enlisted men, yes, I was doing that. I suspect all of these charges were to cover themselves for the mistake the MP made initially.

In any event, two or three days later I heard from my commanding officer. He had met with a lieutenant commander on the staff of the admiral in command of the Seventh Naval District. He told Captain Purdon that the admiral expected the skipper to court-martial me. One of the points the skipper had raised in the discussions was that there were no other black officers for me to associate with on liberty. In reality, I guess I shouldn't have been fraternizing with the crew, but there had been no point made that I wasn't supposed to. I guess nobody really thought of warning me about that. Certainly there's a fine line between an officer and an enlisted man, but I'd been to social affairs with enlisted men even before that. This was just another one of those stacking of charges, I think, more than anything else.

In the meantime, as the skipper was negotiating with the staff, I was sweating tears as to when my general court-martial would be. He said that they finally had agreed that he would write me a bad fitness report.[3] He said what he had to say in order to get me off, but Captain Purdon understood the situation, and I hadn't done that much anyway. In fact, it had all started because some guy just had never seen a black naval officer. But, anyway, I got out of that one.

The war against Japan ended in mid-August of 1945, while the *PC-1264* was still in the States. The victorious fleet came home and was honored in a Navy Day celebration in the Hudson River off New York City in late October. There was a lot of publicity with the review of ships by President Harry Truman. Despite the fact we were the smallest ship up there, we led the line. In fact, we were the first ship that he was to see on his southbound leg down the Hudson. During that celebration we got all kinds of ship's visitors, but the publicity went to the bigger ships, especially the battleship *Missouri*. The news coverage didn't talk about any specific person from our subchaser—me or anybody else.

We later went to New London, Connecticut, where we operated as a target vessel for submariners who were practicing how to make approaches on surface ships. Very shortly after that, in February of 1946, the *PC-1264* was decommissioned. By that time I had moved up from being the communicator to serve as executive officer of the ship.

★★★

Shortly before that, I'd gone home on New Year's leave, and I revisited Alma Clark, whom I'd met earlier through my sister at Virginia State College. By this time Alma was talking about marrying some guy in June. She and her intended were going to the University of Wisconsin. He was working on his PhD, and she was going to work on her master's. But in about five weeks I convinced her that that wasn't really the right thing to do. I told Alma that she should marry me, and I was coming home on thirty days' leave. I'm pretty convincing when I want to be, so we got married on the twelfth of February 1946, five days after the ship was decommissioned.

---

3 Purdon's account, contained in his book, *Black Company*, differs slightly in the details. He did not mention a promise to write a bad fitness report. He was able to tell the admiral's staff officer that he, Purdon, couldn't be ordered to conduct a court-martial of Ensign Gravely. To defuse the situation Purdon did agree to restrict the officers and enlisted men of the *PC-1264* to stay on board ship during the remaining few days it would be in Miami.

Following the marriage and my transfer off the *PC-1264*, we came down to Virginia, where I spent roughly thirty days on leave between duty stations. Then I reported to the fleet training group, which was at Little Creek, near Virginia Beach. My job there was not particularly challenging. I was a communications watch officer, so I had to look through all the messages that came in to make sure the pertinent ones got to the right people, routing the traffic. Even though the mission of the command was to provide training for ships' crews, I didn't do any shipboard stuff because blacks were not allowed on warships at that time as officers. The *PC-1264* had clearly been an exceptional case.

What was challenging about being at the training group was that I once again had to go out and find a place to live. As at Great Lakes, I did not go to the officers' club or officers' quarters. Finally, one day my commanding officer, who was a captain, said, "Sam, why don't you live in the BOQ?"[4]

I said, "Sir, I'm not permitted to. I'm married."

He said, "Where *do* you live?" I had rented a room that, frankly, was pretty bad. When Alma came down to see me once, I wasn't there, so she called one of my friends to find me. He took her by there, and he said, "He's not here, and I'm not going to let you stay over here." So that's the kind of place it was.

The captain had sufficient concern that he went to see my place, and he said, "What a dump." He went back and wrote a message to the Bureau of Naval Personnel, and the next day I was told I could move to the BOQ. By that time I think there must have been some rules set up that you could go to the BOQ, and probably the officers' club. But obviously the word hadn't filtered down to me, and it hadn't filtered down to the yeoman in the office who stamped my orders "No quarters available." So I moved into the BOQ. I lived there for about two months, and then I was discharged.

There were a couple of reasons why I left the Navy at that point. The uppermost one in my mind was that I'd heard about the government paying for postwar schooling under the GI Bill of Rights. I determined to go back to college and finish. My father had tried awfully hard to support my education before I went into the Navy. I didn't know what school cost, but he paid it,

4 Bachelor officers' quarters.

and I knew he couldn't spare it, particularly while he was trying to raise my four siblings. So now I was going to be able to do it on my own.

That was the first reason that I was leaving the Navy. The second reason I left at that point in time was that nobody really asked me to stay. I knew of an awful lot of people who had not really made up their minds, and I was in that category. When many men got down to a discharge station, someone would ask, "Have you ever thought about staying?" And they'd remain on active duty. But nobody asked me, so I just took my discharge and went home.

CHAPTER FOUR

Civilian Interlude

Even though I had decided to take advantage of the GI Bill and go back to college, I still had some time before classes started. I got out of the Navy in May 1946, and school didn't start until mid-June. I decided I might as well work for six weeks or so. One of the things most of the commercial businesses had said when employees went off to war was, "We will rehire you in your old job." I went back to the clothing company where I had worked before as a clothes presser. After that temporary job, I went back to Virginia Union with a determination to finish it as quickly as I could. I now had a wife and hoped we were going to have more family. Obviously, by then I was a lot more mature than I'd been when I started college at the age of sixteen.

Alma had been living in a little place called Blackstone, Virginia, where she taught home economics. When I enrolled in Virginia Union for the summer, I decided I was going to live on the campus rather than commute between Richmond and Blackstone. We planned that she would continue to work there until I finished school, and then we would move someplace together, and either work together or at least work in the same city. Until then, we would live apart, but Blackstone is only about sixty miles away. I got down there quite frequently, and she came to Richmond often.

My career goal at that point was to be a football coach. I was not a basketball player. I wasn't very good at baseball either. Football was going to be my future. Most of the black high schools, which was where I expected to work, required a degree in a subject an individual could teach, because they didn't have people who were only football coaches. I would major in history and play football for Virginia Union. I hadn't really been away from it long. I had played on a semipro team in Norfolk while the *PC-1264* was down there. One of our games was against Virginia Union, and we won it, fourteen to nothing. In the process, I talked to the coach, Sam Taylor, a guy I liked. He had also been coach for Roger Gibbons, whom I mentioned earlier. Gibbons was the man from Prairie View who was my roommate in V-12. I looked forward to playing football for Sam Taylor.

During my previous time in college I had still lived with my father and my siblings. Living on a campus was different from living in town, but it was easy to get adjusted to it. I'd lived on the campus of UCLA. I'd lived on the campus at Columbia, no big problem. At Virginia Union I was not a big man on campus by any stretch of the imagination. Even though I was probably the only naval officer they'd ever had there. I enjoyed the experience. I'd made up my mind I was going to concentrate on my studies, and I did. I probably had close to a B average when I graduated because I made some good grades in my second go-around. I played football down there for two years, 1946 and '47.

My father was still working in the post office, and each year he would remind me that the post office hired extra people during the Christmas holidays. As a matter of fact, I did it before I went into the service, and I started again after the service. I went down there and worked as a mail handler. I worked twelve hours a day as long as the Christmas holiday ran. I made a chunk of money.

In the following year, 1947, Alma decided our commuting was just out of this world. She felt we should do something about settling in Richmond. The main reason was that the campus had a group of trailers available for married veterans and their wives, and we took one of those. Rent was ninety dollars a month, which was quite a bit in those days. But that wasn't hard to manage. During our time in Richmond, she worked but not steadily. Because she had been a home economics major she was hired as a helper for the guy who prepared the food for the students on campus. She'd get winter jobs at Christmastime helping with one of the big stores when most of the kids weren't on campus. She did quite a bit. At Virginia Union I had an athletic scholarship as well as the GI Bill, so we were fairly comfortable.

When Christmas of 1947 rolled around, my father got me my same old job at the post office. During the holiday period someone said the examinations for postal clerk and for railway mail clerk were open, and they were giving the tests such and such a day. I took those tests, and at the beginning of 1948, I just continued to work twelve hours a day; nobody told me Christmas was over. Then I looked very carefully at what I was doing, as far as school was concerned, and I realized I had to give up one or the other. I had enough credits to graduate in February, so I just kept on working as a "Christmas helper" rather than going back to school in the spring. That routine continued until March. Then the post office sent me a letter saying, "We've had you on as a Christmas helper for too long; in short, Christmas is over. And there's nothing else we can find." Alma and I moved to her folks' place down in Roanoke, Virginia, where I did some odd jobs.

Then one day I got a letter from the post office saying they wanted me in Richmond for some interviews. I had been selected as a potential railway postal clerk. They were short of people after the war, so they took on a few temporary guys. In those days, when airmail was far less common than today, much of the mail moved by train. Each passenger train included a special car with postal clerks in it to sort the mail. That sounded appealing, so I went up, faced the interviews, and started to work there less than a month after I left the post office. In about five months' time I was notified I was a regular railway postal clerk. Here again, to some degree, I was breaking barriers, but the people on the railway car just made me as comfortable as anything. They tried to teach me the various things about it. There was no problem whatsoever, and I became a member of a regular crew. I just enjoyed the hell out of it.

Since I was based in Richmond, Alma went back there, and we were able to have time together when I wasn't on duty. The way they worked it, I had about eighty hours of work in two weeks. I would go to work in Richmond at four o'clock in the afternoon on, say, a Monday. The train left about 6:30 PM, got to Washington about nine o'clock, and I worked about an hour. Then I went out in town, got a meal, came back, and slept on the car until about one, when I started again. I worked enough time in three days that I had the next three days off. Despite the fact that Alma didn't see much of me, say, Monday to Wednesday, I was home the rest of the week. We had plenty of time together.

When one of the runs started, we picked up loose mail from the post office. For the most part, mail was sorted and shipped on, and we put it off the train at the next stop, which is where it came to a post office. While we were coming up, we worked the mail, which meant sorting it by hand in those days before ZIP codes and bar codes. We had three guys who broke the mail down by the states to which it was headed. Then we had the mail headed for the city of Washington, and a couple of guys would break it down right to the individual post office as a head start. I learned a lot of geography in that railroad car. I found out there were about nineteen hundred post offices in Virginia, and I knew where every one of them was and how to route mail to it. It was quite an interesting job.

As the train made its journey, it didn't stop in every little town, but it was still able to pick up the mail. Someone in the station would hang out a pouch of mail for further delivery. Then, as you came along the track near the station, the postal car had an arm that would reach out and grab the pouch. It was quite interesting to watch the process while the train was speeding along. Our rail car was essentially a small post office. We did everything the other post offices did except deliver the mail to individuals and sell stamps.

I don't know how many college graduates had that kind of job, but the range of opportunities was not large. In those days, things were limited so far as employment of blacks was concerned, particularly in businesses. If you taught school, you taught school in a strictly black school, and there were few of those. If you were a lawyer, if you were fortunate enough to go into business with somebody, you probably had a job, but you didn't expect to go into some white firm as a lawyer or even as a law clerk. So getting into the post office was appealing. As I said before, my father thought in terms of security and government service and this was a fairly good job for me. There were debates, believe it or not, between my father and my father-in-law. My father-in-law said: "Hey, here's a young man who has prepared himself to teach and coach, and he ought to do that. He owes it not only to himself but also to a lot of people who have helped him."

My father would always say, "Yes, but whether he wears dungarees or a blue suit, the guy is making a lot more money and has got more security, and can take care of your daughter better as a regular postal clerk." I think my father won the argument.

I had the postal job for about a year, and then one day I got a letter from the Navy Department. It said: "We plan to select twenty-five young Negro officers to bring them on active duty for one year, and place each of them in a recruiting station. Would you like to come back on active duty? If so, write a letter requesting it."

I thought about the offer for a while, and I said to myself: "It'll be almost like a year's vacation. Why not do that?"

I still had a certain amount of love for the Navy. I missed the Navy atmosphere. Despite the fact that I hadn't gotten a real flavor of Navy life, I did miss what little I'd seen. When I was discharged in 1946, it was basically a case of being released to inactive duty, and I still had a reserve commission. I had applied for a reserve two weeks' active duty program on two occasions. On one I was accepted and was at the point where I was awaiting orders. But there were no funds available, so I had missed out on it. In the meantime, I'd kept up enough to get my reserve promotion to lieutenant (j.g.).

I did not do any Naval Reserve drilling during that period with Virginia Union and the post office. I guess there were paid drillers, but I was not one of them. I'm not sure a black officer would have been very well accepted as a driller in Richmond, unless a set of orders said, "You will do this." But, in any event, after I got that letter in 1949, I applied to return to active duty. In 1946 I had left active duty in part because no one asked me to stay. In 1948 President Truman had directed the desegregation of the armed services.[1] Things were changing, and now the Navy had specifically asked me to come back.

---

1 On July 26, 1948, President Harry S. Truman issued Executive Order 9981, which said, "It is hereby declared that there shall be equality of treatment and opportunity for all persons in the armed services without regard to race, color, religion, or national origin."

CHAPTER FIVE

Recruiting

In 1949, Secretary of Defense Louis Johnson was really cutting back on the budgets for the armed services. This was at the same time the Navy was deliberately trying to bring in more black recruits and officer candidates because of the Truman directive. I think Johnson's approach on funds probably shortchanged the program. As I remember, the original target was to recall twenty-five black officers. The actual number wasn't that high, but I think there were at least five young black officers who came back on active duty. I believe all of us in this program were jaygees. One of them was my friend Johnny Reagan, whom I'd known since we were enlisted men.

Since I was living in Richmond, I guess that's the reason the Navy sent me to Washington, D.C. I reported to the recruiting station as assistant to the officer in charge for recruiting. My job description didn't specifically say I was to bring in minorities or Negroes, but I knew that was my forte and the area in which I was expected to work.

Even though I had been gone from the Navy for only three years, I was really surprised and pleased by what I found. The commanding officer said to me, "Have you found a place to stay yet?"

I said, "No, sir, I have not. I expect to try to find a room tonight, sir."

"Well, what do you mean? Are you going to have your wife here?"

"No. My wife is working in Richmond, and she's going to stay down there, and I'm going to sort of bach it until we decide whether or not she wants to come here, and whether or not I'm going to stay more than a year." (The letter that offered to bring me back on active duty indicated it was for a one-year tour of duty.)

"Well, wait a minute. Chief, take Lieutenant (j.g.) Gravely over to the officers' BOQ and get him squared away." I was really flabbergasted to learn I was going to live in the BOQ. I'd never been able to do that except, as I said, when I got into one in Norfolk as an alternative to living in a dumpy place. But I didn't expect the Navy had really advanced to the point where that had become routine. I was introduced around the office and welcomed aboard in a big way.

Everything went fine except for one minor thing, and I'm glad it came up. We had weekly staff meetings. After I'd been around for about two weeks, the senior enlisted recruiter, who was a white guy, said at the meeting one day, "Captain, you know, Lieutenant (j.g.) Gravely is here, and I assume he is supposed to enlist Negro recruits, but can he swear in white recruits as well?"

The commanding officer stuttered briefly, and then he said, "Lieutenant (j.g.) Gravely is assistant officer in charge of this recruiting station, and he can enlist anybody you guys get." His statement really made my day, and it certainly paved the way for me to have a successful tour versus an unsuccessful one.

There began to be a little bit more of a move toward social activity, but not from the officers because there were only about three of us there, and we had some social affairs in maybe a hotel. But there were a couple of chief petty officers around also, and I was wary about officers associating with enlisted men, especially after the incident in Florida when I was hauled in by the MPs. But these chiefs invited me into their homes, and I've kept in touch with them ever since.

In terms of the recruiting itself, I'm not sure I got any more people than anybody else did, but I got my share. The quota then was very small. It actually was eight men a month, and six of them had to be high school graduates. It didn't say anything about the other two, but certainly if they could pass the test, the other two were accepted.

In trying to sell the Navy to potential black recruits, I was able to make the point that it was more appealing than it had been a few years earlier. I did that indirectly by giving a little history of the Navy. I talked in terms of what the Navy was like in 1941, at the beginning of the war. Then I could bring them through my experience at Great Lakes and at Hampton, and how, ultimately, I got commissioned. What I really tried to tell them was: "Hey, there's an opportunity out here, and there's more opportunities opening up all the time. This is not necessarily the thing you've got to do, but you ought to look at it as a viable alternative when you get out of high school." That was the approach I took most of the time.

We were selling the benefits of learning a trade, travel, and security because those were what we were advertising in those days. I could tell them about my experience and some of my travels. In those days particularly, when you talked to the young black high school student, he'd never left his hometown. I didn't leave my hometown, really, except for a little rural place where my mother had been born, until I traveled with the college football team. Even though I hadn't been on any ships except the *PC-1264*, I mentioned San Diego, Key West, and some of the great things that had happened to me.

What we didn't do was try to sell the Navy as an alternative to being drafted into the Army. We sold it as an alternative to something else in life, and as an opportunity, really. Early responsibility was also one of the things we emphasized. You've got to remember that most of these people weren't looking forward to a responsibility beyond teaching another bunch of kids. I challenged them to do more than that.

★★★

The most significant event during my tour of recruiting duty was the outbreak of the Korean War in June of 1950. That essentially changed the rest of my life. Instead of just serving one year on active duty as planned, I was extended another year when the war came and wound up staying for another twenty-nine years.

The Korean War also changed our job requirements dramatically. The purse strings were no longer tight, and the quota of recruits to be brought in just ballooned. We were now told to get as many men as we could. We were kicking that one around one day when the commanding officer asked this question: "How do you sell the Navy?"

I'm not sure who said it, but someone said, "Well, we've got to put more guys on the street." He was right. We had to get more recruiters out and ask more people if they wanted to join the Navy. The way to ask them was to see them, to walk around all day.

The commanding officer made the decision and said: "Okay, I want everybody out on the street who's not assigned to a regular sub recruiting station. Sam, that means you too."

I said: "Sir, I don't think you really want me to do that because, as you well know, there are no officers out doing this thing. You mean the chiefs?"

He said, "No, no, no, I mean you too."

"Okay. Yes, sir." And then, after I thought about it for just a short while, I said: "You know what? Now, it seems to me that with conditions being what they are, probably I would be more successful if I went into a predominantly Negro area and set up a small recruiting station where they would all be coming by, and I wouldn't really have to walk the streets."

"Okay, do what you can."

"Thank you, sir."

I went up to the area around 14th and U streets, which is in the northwest sector of Washington, and I found a government building. I talked to the guy in charge there. By then I had been promoted to lieutenant, so I had a big two bars on. He said: "You know, that might be a good idea. You can set up down the corridor."

I said, "Fine." I went back and I told the commanding officer, and he agreed with it. There was a black chief petty officer, a reservist who had been recalled to duty from civilian life because of the Korean War. He and I went up there and set up our station. We'd been in there for only about two or three days, I guess, when in walked a black man. I sensed he didn't really want to enlist in the Navy, but he said he did, so we began to process him. We went through all the papers and everything else to the point when he was supposed to come up for his physical in the next couple of days. He didn't show. We didn't pay any attention to that, but one day I got a frantic call from the commanding officer: "Come back to the recruiting station right away."

"Yes, sir." So I went back there.

"I'm taking you out of there."

"Oh?"

"Well, look at this." The *Chicago Defender* is a predominantly black paper with wide national circulation. It carried an article that said, "Navy sets up segregated recruiting station." Obviously this guy who pretended he wanted to enlist was a reporter. Well, the station remained open for a while, but the solution obviously was that two blacks couldn't be in there running a recruiting station. We sent a young white yeoman up there, and I came back to the main station.

Another aspect of this job was that very shortly after the Korean War started the naval officer recruiting stations and the naval officer procurement stations, which had been separate activities, became combined. That added about three officers to our staff. About six or seven of us were there, and we handled the Naval Reserve Officers' Training Corps (NROTC) and various other procurement programs. I got familiar with those as well as did a lot of work in processing people for them. I was no longer concentrating on blacks but was part of the overall effort. I helped with the interviewing of the NROTC candidates, and I helped with all the other programs.

We had one officer who was much older than I was. He was a temporary officer who was recalled to active duty. He and I had a ball; we really did. I socialized with the guy a lot because we both lived at the BOQ, and we could ride back and forth together. We could have our dinner together and then sit around a bar together and talk.

That time in Washington was really a great experience for me. Near the end of my second year there, I decided I wasn't really being truthful with myself. Here I was, a Navy recruiter who hadn't really seen very much of the Navy. Rather than just sit around the recruiting station and constantly go to these high schools and other places, talking to these kids, I concluded I ought to go out and experience some of these things myself. I wanted to see if I really thought conditions were as good as I was telling these kids they were. I volunteered for sea duty, and very soon afterward, I received a set of orders sending me to the battleship *Iowa* via communication school in Monterey, California.

CHAPTER SIX

USS *Iowa*

By the time I got my orders to the *Iowa*, more than five years had passed since I'd last had sea duty. So, en route to the ship, I went to a sixteen-week communications course in Monterey, California. I'd been communication officer in the *PC-1264*, so this was part refresher and part updating on the changes since then. The course itself was not hard for me.

Monterey was a very interesting place, in a beautiful area, and I enjoyed the tour out there. One of my classmates was Lieutenant Spence Matthews, who ultimately was selected for rear admiral a year before I was. In the meantime, Alma stayed back on the East Coast.

Unlike my early experiences after being commissioned, there was no longer any question about my being welcomed in an officers' club. I can remember one time being at the club in Monterey with a group of guys. We had a little party going. We were shooting the breeze, and some of the other officers had their wives there. At one point I decided to call Alma. I searched around and found enough change to call her. I was just outside of the bar, making this phone call, and suddenly the telephone booth was upside down. Spence and some of the others guys were just playing a prank on me. I was talking to Alma, and she said, "I can't hear you."

I said, "You'd probably hear me better if this telephone booth was right side up." By then, they'd all disappeared, because they expected me to come charging out of there like a bull, which I probably did after I recovered my wits. But it was all in good fun. We had a great group of guys—about fifteen of us—in the course. We were almost like college students again, except we did wear uniforms all day. I went to San Francisco a couple of times with some of my classmates. During weekends we chased around bars and other places.

I guess the main drawback to the school experience was my perception that black officers were relegated to communication as a less desirable specialty than some of the others. I had the feeling the Navy didn't really pick its best people for it. This was particularly true after I got aboard a couple of ships, and I watched what happened to people who were sent down as assistant comm officers, or who were sent as cryptographers. This pigeon-holing probably explains why I was sent to communications rather than going, say, to one of the operational-type schools or a short course in engineering on my way to the *Iowa*. But if that's the way it was in that era, so be it. I completed the school and left there in January 1952 to report aboard the *Iowa*. Most of the transportation was by train, and I discovered I would never make Long Beach in time with my luggage. I dragged my feet a little bit, so when I arrived, there was the *Iowa* sailing out of the harbor.

Instead, I reported in to the naval base and wound up with a very interesting week as an assistant to one of the harbor pilots. He and I would go out to various ships and give the officers the port directories and all the other information they needed. Then I could watch this pilot handle each ship. It was the greatest thing in the world. I really enjoyed it. There was a Navy small boat—I guess it was about an 80-footer—that made the trip from Long Beach to San Clemente Island. I was put in charge of it one day, and, boy, I really felt great about it. Here I was, I thought, already commanding officer of this small vessel. Of course, a petty officer was really in charge of the boat. But before it was over, he knew I was also in charge. We did have a couple of discussions when I thought at one point he wasn't handling it as safely as I thought he should. I had to bring him up short a couple of times, but we made it.

★★★

When I got in that weekend, the *Iowa* had just come back in, so I was transferred and went aboard. What a contrast to my first ship, which was 173 feet long and displaced 280 tons. The battleship's comparable figures were 887 feet and 45,000 tons. The *Iowa* had been put in mothballs after World War II and then was reactivated and recommissioned in September 1951 as part of the fleet buildup during the Korean War. The crew had had a chance to go through its shakedown cruise down in San Diego, and the ship was just doing some routine operations when I arrived. In fact, we were about two months away from deployment to the war zone.

The first thing you do on ships that size is to go in to see the exec, who was Commander Edward Stephan. He was great. He took me up and introduced me to the commanding officer, who was Captain William R. Smedberg. Then I began to meet the officers in the wardroom, and there were no problems. They all appeared to welcome me. I found out subsequently that this reception was not spontaneous. I learned that the chief of naval personnel had sent a letter advising the ship I was coming. There had been a meeting in the wardroom to prepare the *Iowa*'s officers for this young Negro officer. I think that worked well, except for the one thing I learned later. I saw the letter and discussed it with my roommate, Lieutenant Herb Yarbrough. He said he was the only officer who would agree to room with me. He was not a Naval Academy guy. Maybe a Naval Academy guy would not have done that. Herb was an ex-enlisted man who had gotten a regular Navy commission.

When I arrived, the ship didn't have a radio officer. In fact, I was assigned as the assistant radio officer. A ship of that size had a communication officer, who was a lieutenant commander; it usually had a radio officer who was a lieutenant; and it normally had a signal officer who was a lieutenant. There was at least one warrant radio electrician attached to the group, and they had an electronics department with two or three radio electronics types. We normally got two or three other junior officers who served as communication watch officers. The ship had a radio division with about forty people and about four or five officers, but the *Iowa* had never before had a guy with the title of assistant radio officer. In fact, the radio officer was acting as communication officer, and I became his assistant.

Within about a week of my arrival, in came a lieutenant commander named Gene Horrall, who was to be the communication officer. I happened to be talking to Gene one day, and I guess I was making a little complaint. Having just gotten out of comm school, I didn't think the guy who was the radio officer knew how to write a comm plan. He had not been to this great school at Monterey like I had been, but he did write something that passed as a comm plan. When I told Gene how I felt, he said, "Well, you do it then, obviously." I did from then on.

It wasn't too much longer before I became the radio officer myself, but it was a bit awkward until then. Very shortly after I got there, and I think it might have happened before Gene and I had this discussion, the guy who was radio officer got orders to another ship. When his orders came, for some reason he did not want to leave. Somehow a message was sent off saying the ship could not afford to lose this officer because it was just getting ready to go on deployment, and the *Iowa* needed an experienced radio officer to work with the Seventh Fleet people while the ship was out in the western Pacific.

The ship requested non-detachment of this guy, and a message reply from the Bureau of Naval Personnel said, "Negative, recommend Lieutenant Gravely as a relief." A message then went back from the *Iowa* and said that even though I was a recent graduate of comm school, the command didn't feel I had enough experience.

Another message came back from BuPers. This one said: "In view of the fact you have three radio electricians aboard, Lieutenant Gravely having finished comm school at Monterey, your signal officer has also finished comm school at Monterey, your [message dated so-and-so] declined. Lieutenant Gravely will be his relief." Fine. So I got to be his relief.

I think that was about the time Gene Horrall and I got to talking about race. I never will forget it, because Gene said: "Sam, I might as well tell you now. I don't give a goddamn whether you're red, green, black, or what color you are. All I want is a radio officer, and you are it." Once I got into the new job, I worked as closely with Lieutenant Commander Horrall as I've ever worked with anyone in my life. I think he respected me, and I certainly respected him. That was the beginning of a wonderful relationship. In fact, he and his wife later became the godfather and godmother to our son David. We got to be great friends and remained so afterward.

★★★

In March of 1952 the *Iowa* deployed to the Far East. As the radio officer, I didn't get a chance to spend much time on the bridge as a routine deck watch officer. But the general quarters spot, that is, the battle station, for the communicator was on the bridge. Gene may have felt that with his experience he could run the radio shack better than I could, so he decided to go to the radio shack. I swapped with him, and I went to the bridge during general quarters, which was where I really wanted to be.

This was a great learning experience for me because I could watch the conning officers handling that big 45,000-ton battleship, and I really got a kick out of doing so. I also got fairly familiar with the signal book, which helped me in my next ship because my next job was as communication officer of a cruiser. Once again, as in the patrol craft during World War II, I got a real feel for the sea. I knew I loved it, and I knew if there was ever an opportunity for me to apply for the regular Navy, I would. I bided my time while waiting for a chance.

During the deployment we operated a good deal off the east coast of Korea. Sometimes we were with the aircraft carriers of Task Force 77, and at other times the ship was doing shore bombardment with its 16-inch guns. We did an awful lot of shore bombardment. I remember one incident specifically. It involved a destroyer that had been fired on at Wonsan Harbor in North Korea. We went alongside this destroyer to take off the wounded, and I was really flabbergasted, because this was the first time I really saw men bleeding. I was looking over the port side, and I saw the legs of a man hanging on a life raft, and I didn't see the rest of him. It almost made me sick.

I don't think the *Iowa* itself was fired on during the whole time we were out there. If the enemy doesn't have much of a navy, there's not much of a naval battle. When you've got nine 16-inch barrels to fire at the enemy, he's got to be fairly close or way back to shoot something, and the North Koreans didn't have that much capability, as I recall.

★★★

Another role for the *Iowa* in 1952 was as the flagship for Commander Seventh Fleet. First it was Vice Admiral Robert Briscoe, and then he was relieved by Vice Admiral Jocko Clark, who was a colorful character. I got a little chance to work with him. I remember once there was a discussion between his combat information center people and his radio officer. I got invited up because I was radio officer for the ship. We were talking about air controlling by the various destroyers we were assigned. For some reason, I felt one of those destroyers should have been able to handle the air control assignments for the group. There weren't many. When we were talking about them, Admiral Clark said something, and I said, "Well, why can't destroyer so-and-so handle it?"

I was told: "Hey, I'll make the decision on who handles it. All I want to know from you is, does the guy have equipment enough to do it?"

"Yes, sir. Fine." But I respected the man, certainly, because he was a great admiral.

When the *Iowa* was the flagship for the fleet, the communications requirements were trebled compared with operating alone. While operating alone the basic responsibility is to copy the messages on the fleet broadcast. You don't have anybody in company, so you don't have to worry about ultrahigh frequency transmissions, which are short range. But as a flagship, you copy broadcasts for yourself and for the fleet commander. He had half a dozen different titles, so you'd have to be alert for three or four times the normal amount of message traffic to make sure you got everything intended for the admiral.

In addition, usually the flagship was dragging a couple other ships around with it, and you had to have instantaneous communication to them. You normally had enough radio equipment. Part of your problem, though, was keeping it up and operating. We had a couple of good radio electronics technicians, as well as some good radiomen who could shift those frequencies at the snap of a finger; they worked together to do a good job. Except for at times not having enough of the proper equipment on board, we didn't have any major problems with broadcasts.

The high frequency radio broadcast was quite unreliable, so we missed a message every once in a while, but somehow, using hook or crook, we could get it in a fairly short time. We would hate to miss a message that said move, for instance, because the ship was supposed to move instantaneously. Sometimes we might miss one of those, so we had to ask somebody to send it again.

Another area where the admiral's presence made a difference was in cryptology, that is, coding and decoding classified messages. When the ship was operating by itself, we normally had one crypto watch officer, whose job was to decode a few messages. When Commander Seventh Fleet and his staff came aboard, the decoding went on twenty-four hours a day. A couple of the admirals I worked for—and I think Jocko Clark was one—not only wanted to look at all of their own message traffic, but they wanted to see everything on the fleet broadcast. That meant the ship had to supply six crypto watch officers a day with at least two people on watch all the time.

I have been wearing glasses for years now, and I contend that I really lost my eyesight as a result of being in the little dark hole of a crypto room, sitting down there breaking messages. It was a tedious system. You broke them all by hand. You didn't have anything that would automatically do it as we do today. The easy messages to break, I guess to some degree, were those that came in on a fleet broadcast, because you got a considerable number of those by teletype. And you could really read the teletype, which was fairly smooth. But then when you got them by Morse code, in which a radioman might mistake one letter for another, it got to be a mess. But we had some good people who did the job, and that's all you could ask for.

One significant thing that I can remember happening in communications was a foul-up on my part. I was responsible for making up all of the movement reports for the ship. If you missed one, you immediately got a growl. There was also a problem if the report was in any way screwed up, such as somebody saying the ship's track was plotting over land, or it couldn't possibly make its estimated time of arrival based on its speed and position. Those reactions were kind of embarrassing, so ships didn't like to receive them. I watched the movement reports very carefully.

On one particular day, however, the flag radio officer cornered me, and we were discussing the assignment of one of my men. Then, with the movement report in my pocket, as I was getting ready to go to the bridge, somehow I got turned around, and I didn't go to the bridge. It wasn't until the next day, when I was showering and changing uniforms, I discovered the message in my pocket. I quickly went down to the radio room, upped the precedence to operational immediate, and sent it out. Then I decided I'd better tell somebody about it. I told my boss, Gene Horrall, who then said go tell Commander Herman Rock, who was ops officer. Then we went to see Captain Smedberg. He gave me a little lecture on the importance of getting these out, and never missing one again. Fine.

Unfortunately, the movement report I sent didn't arrive in time, and so we were reported, along with our destroyer escort, as two Russian cruisers going through the Tsugaru Strait between the Japanese islands of Honshu and Hokkaido. The Air Force came out en masse, and, we went to general quarters, the whole bit. Finally, it was all sorted out, and Admiral Clark wanted to know what had happened. The explanation, of course, was my delay in sending out the movement report.

Another problem was that we missed getting mail at the next port, and I guess that's what really brought it to Admiral Clark's attention even more. I survived it. I always felt a couple of people either wanted me reprimanded or certainly chewed out, but Captain Smedberg felt, I believe, he had already done so. There was no sense in doing anything else.

The captain was a very enthusiastic individual. Someone told me that during his recommissioning speech he made a statement something like: "All of you guys now have at least one chance. Everybody starts out equal here." As a result, he had to punish a lot of men at captain's mast, because everybody took his one chance. When I came aboard, he certainly was not a hard man by any stretch of the imagination, but sailors knew he was serious. He was just a tremendous ship handler, had all kinds of leadership abilities, and I liked him. He was just a great skipper, really. A really good man.

We had a fairly good team of people on board there. Most people tried to help me. I got into one little minor scrape in the wardroom with a Marine who said something I didn't think he should have said, and we got into it. He wanted to meet me down on some corner, but I knew I should stay out of that kind of trouble. One of my best friends was the medical service officer on board. In fact, one thing I remember him doing for me was advising me to drink my coffee black, with no sugar, because he was concerned I was putting on weight and increasing my blood pressure. The wardroom officers were a great group. I don't have any feeling other than goodness at having met and been associated with them.

When the ship wasn't operating off the coast of Korea, we went over to Japan. Yokosuka and Sasebo were the principal liberty ports. I certainly went to the local clubs. Most of the time I went alone, although I seldom came back alone because I generally had to carry somebody. I wasn't a big drinker and really didn't get out into the towns other than to do some shopping. I didn't have any bad experiences.

While we were deployed, there was an unusual case that involved one of my fellow officers, and it set me to thinking for a long time. I'm not sure exactly what this man's problem was, but he was an oddball. He did something—and I really don't know what it was—but the ship decided to get rid of him. One day I was called to Commander Rock's stateroom. He was the ops officer, and he said: "Sam, here's a message. It's classified confidential, and it has to be sent out, and I want you personally to handle it."

I said, "Sir, as you well know, any messages that go off classified have to have a check decrypter."[1]

---

1 The normal procedure was that another officer would decrypt the coded version before it was sent out to ensure that the coding was done correctly.

He said: "I don't want anybody else to see the message. Do you hear what I say?"

I said, "Yes, sir." I took the message down, and I wasn't even supposed to read it. But how do you encrypt one without reading it? Of course, I did read it, and I encrypted it. I did not have a check decrypter. I sent it out.

It obviously went out on the right system because we got an answer shortly thereafter. The oddball officer was detached immediately, and I've never seen anybody leave a ship so fast. He didn't even have time to pack. He was told to get off the ship right away. A boat came alongside and took him over to Yokosuka. The ship sent his gear about four hours later after an inventory. He was a sick sister, and I'm not sure what the problem was. But I remember that, and it set me to thinking, "Please don't make these people angry, because they know how to take care of those situations."

★★★

In the summer of 1952 the *Iowa* got a new skipper when it was time for Captain Smedberg to leave. The new man, Captain Joshua Cooper, was even friendlier—if that could be possible—and greater to me than Captain Smedberg had been. He was particularly pleased in that I handled the movement reports well. He also knew he could count on me if something came up. Joshua Cooper ultimately did me a couple of favors, and I'll describe them later. He was just a tremendous leader. He had the proper carriage, straight like a ramrod, the whole bit, and I really did like him. When we got back to Long Beach, we had the ship's party, and Captain Cooper made sure I was well taken care of. Maybe he thought he had to mother me, but it was a fine relationship, and I had a great tour.

As I mentioned earlier, my purpose in going to the ship was to learn some specifics about the Navy for any future jobs. Therefore, I took correspondence courses and also ship's courses. I was exempted from most of the ship's courses because I was a mid-grade lieutenant, and usually junior officers took them. But I felt I just had to do some of those courses to learn about the ship. I almost got us in trouble once because I took a classified course run by Commander Seventh Fleet. It described the communications equipment on board the ship. I sent the thing off to be graded, and I forgot to classify it. We got a nasty little letter, but there weren't very many people taking courses, so they were happy I was doing so. But, at the same time, I was reminded that you obviously have to classify things correctly, and I did from then on.

There wasn't really a specific training program laid out for me. Nobody took me under his wing as a mentor, so I learned mostly by observation. I had a very fine communicator, who was my boss, but I think he was more interested in making sure the communications job was done well. One of the things done for me was that I was put on different inspection parties, and so I was constantly getting around to all the spaces on the ship. I made my own damage control inspections, which meant I had to go through the fourteen radio spaces every week. But I also got around through the engineering department, through the gunnery department, etc. But communicators generally stood watches down in the radio shack, and not so much on the bridge or in the combat information center. CIC was almost a mystery to me for the longest time.

One other thing that happened during my *Iowa* duty was that I received a letter from the chief of naval personnel, talking about my augmenting into the regular Navy. BuPers wanted a certain number of reservists to apply. I guess the notice said that the bureau was going to select about twenty-five. I applied for the regular Navy at that point in time, but I have never, to this day, found out what happened to my application. I am positive it left the ship. I don't know what happened to it when it got to BuPers, but I was not selected. With a limitation of about twenty-five, I imagine they got thousands of applications, and I just was not picked.

During this time Alma and I wrote to each other regularly, and it was certainly a source of enjoyment to hear everything was fine back home. It was a real blessing to have her back there and know she was well and she was going to take care of herself. Fortunately, she is quite independent. She's not a dependent, nagging, crying wife. Her feeling was that no matter what I did, so long as I liked it and it was honorable, I would do my thing and she would do her thing. If something interfered with what we were doing, then we'd make some more decisions about it.

The separations weren't easy, but we had gotten used to them by then. Back when I returned to active duty in 1949 to do recruiting, she had gone down to southeast Virginia to take a job in the town of Franklin as an Agricultural Extension Agent for Southampton County. When I got the orders two years later to go to the *Iowa*, we sat and discussed it. She wasn't quite ready to leave the job, and because I faced a rather uncertain future as far as going to the *Iowa* was concerned we decided to leave things at the status quo.

I knew the ship would return to the West Coast in October of '52, and also very shortly afterward we would change homeport. The four battleships that were in commission belonged to Battleship Division Two. Shortly after returning to the States, we were scheduled for Norfolk, which was only about forty miles from where my wife was living, so that was a most welcome change.

Socially, so far as going to ship's parties and things like that, I went with no problem. I didn't really have a problem with either the young officers or the enlisted men taking orders from me. Years later, I was invited to a party given by a black group who call themselves "Young Navy Retireds" or something similar. Interestingly enough, the president of that group was a young man who had come on the *Iowa* as a seaman apprentice. I really had forgotten the story, but he told me that when he came aboard I invited him to come up to my stateroom. I talked to him a little bit about where he'd been, the rate, and everything else. He said he'd been through radio school, and he was striking for radioman. And he said I told him I wanted him to be a radioman seaman within three months, or I was going to kick his tail out of my division. Eventually, he retired as a warrant officer, which I thought was pretty good. At least I led him along the right path.

During the Korean War, there was a shortage of radiomen throughout the fleet. As I said, Captain Cooper was very helpful to me. He established a policy that I would receive two new men in my radio division every month. But if I had anybody who wasn't learning, or whom I didn't think was cutting the mustard in the radio gang, then I could boot him out, and I got two more. I had a real flourishing gang. Of course, a lot of people elsewhere in the ship were a little angry that I was getting such a good group of men. I handpicked them, which was a considerable advantage.

★★★

After we had left Korea and made our stop in Long Beach, the *Iowa* came through the Panama Canal, which was quite an interesting trip for me because I'd never been there before. We arrived in Norfolk sometime in November and I had a grand reunion with Alma. There's an interesting story about that. I seemed to be doing quite well, and the wives were really interested in seeing that my wife did well, and that she was comfortable and enjoyed the wardroom. The first wives' luncheon she was invited to, they practically babied her. They took care of her, made sure she was invited to everything I was invited to, and she became a really dedicated Navy wife.

After the *Iowa* reported to Norfolk, we went into the Norfolk Naval Shipyard for repair. The battleship was there for about four months; we had just a routine yard overhaul. Of course, the ship had been back in commission for less than a year and a half by then, so it was in pretty good shape. We did get some updates in terms of equipment.

Though the radio gang was made up of fine young men, there was one interesting exception concerning a seaman I picked up out of the gunnery department. When we got to Norfolk, he went on his normal leave and didn't return. Then one day I got a call to report to the quarterdeck. I went up there and met the mother and father of this young man, and they had him with them. The mother said: "Our son has been home for about thirty days, and I know darn well that he doesn't have that much leave. So we felt that we would bring him back."

I said: "Yes, Ma'am. He really had fifteen days' leave, and he's been over the hill for fifteen days. I'll take care of it." He came aboard, went on down to the radio gang with me, and I told the chief to put him on report, muster him, take him to his bunk, and get him squared away. At the next morning's muster he wasn't there again. Then one day about a week later I got a call from his mama, who apologized and said that, believe it or not, when they got to New Jersey, he was in the trunk of their car. They wondered what had happened to him. But this kid just wasn't about to stay in the Navy. Thanks to Captain Cooper, I was able to send him back to the gunnery department and could get another man to replace him. Naturally, the gunnery people were a little unhappy with me about that.

★ ★ ★

In early 1953, after we got out of the shipyard, we went on a training exercise in the Caribbean. The Battleship Division Two staff rode with us during Exercise Springboard. The most interesting part about it was that this staff, contrary to the practice with the Seventh Fleet staff, made all the movement reports. I never will forget that very shortly after we got under way, maybe about the first day or something like that, I got a call to go to Captain Cooper's cabin. I went up there, and he was practically in hysterics laughing. I wondered what this was all about. Finally he said; "Sam, you're a real jewel. I've been on here now for about six months, and you've never missed a movement report, and the first time we turn it over to the staff, they miss it."

The staff had failed to send the movement report, and we got a big blast back: "Your movement report not received." Captain Cooper was, in my mind, a great man. I liked him, worked well with him, no problems. A lieutenant doesn't normally have that much direct contact with the captain. But he and I got along really great, and he wrote me some good fitness reports.

Thanks to the experiences I had on board the *Iowa* and the people I came in contact with, it was really a useful tour of duty and prepared me for what came next.

CHAPTER SEVEN

USS *Toledo*

During the period before the *Iowa* resumed operations again, I received a set of orders to become communication officer of the heavy cruiser *Toledo*, which was on the West Coast. I had no problem with the assignment, but I really wanted to stay in Norfolk, so I called the Bureau of Naval Personnel. I talked to the detailer there and said that our signal officer, for example, had gone to the *Wisconsin*, and someone else had gone to another one of the battleships and cruisers around there. So I talked to him in terms of maybe swapping me with somebody else and letting me stay in Norfolk. But he said, "No, you've been specifically picked to go to the *Toledo*, so here you go."

The *Toledo* was homeported in Long Beach, but at that point in time it was in a shipyard in San Francisco, so that's where I was to meet it. I got off the *Iowa* down in Guantánamo Bay, Cuba, and went over to the local transportation office. I'm not sure what our problem with the Cubans was at that time, but we were not taking anything out of Cuba but dependents. So there I was, "tail-end Charlie," and I had promised Alma I would be home to see her the next day. The young lady in transportation said, "You might as well go over to the BOQ, because we don't think we're going to get you out of here for another five or six days." I was signing into the BOQ when a young lieutenant, a naval aviator, just happened to be there, and he said, "You look like you're going someplace."

I said: "Well, I thought I was. I wanted to go to Norfolk. I promised my wife that I'd be there tomorrow, but it looks like I'm going to be around here for five or six days."

He said: "Well, I'm going to Patuxent River [Maryland] tomorrow. If you'd like to ride with me, I'd be happy to take you. But I'll tell you what, we are going to operate with the *Iowa* this afternoon." So I joined him for that before our flight the next day. It was a specifically radar-configured aircraft that was to operate with the *Iowa* for the Fleet Training Group. Afterward we went to San Juan, Puerto Rico. It was the first time I'd been there, and I enjoyed it.

The next morning we got up for the flight to Patuxent River. He told me he would be passing over Norfolk on the way. I said, "You really could do me a favor if there was some way to let me off in Norfolk." And damn if he didn't drop the plane down and let me off in the middle of the runway—my bags and everything else. I called Alma, and she came and picked me up. I never will forget that guy. I don't think he violated any rules. I'm sure he did it all right, but he could have very easily said no and just kept on to Patuxent River. But he dropped me off, which was kind.

Alma had never been to the West Coast before. I had a new car, so we decided we would drive to San Francisco. The plan was that she would probably come on back to Virginia, because we weren't going to set up a home on the West Coast. We took off with probably about twenty-five to thirty days to drive across country. We enjoyed the trip, but in those days it was always a problem as to where to spend the night. We drove the southern way, Route 66, which went from Chicago to Los Angeles. There just weren't places to find good motels that would take blacks. Whenever we reached a town, we saw where the railroad tracks were, and we went across to the other side of the tracks. We either got a room, which was hotter than hell, or we slept in the car at night. That's the way we got across country.

Things really didn't change a hell of a lot even in California. Alma had cousins in Los Angeles, so we stopped there for a while. Then we went to San Francisco, where there was a Navy–Marine Corps hotel. We also visited some friends for a while, and then she caught a train coming back East.

★★★

I reported to the *Toledo*—I never will forget this—the Fourth of July 1953. I was amazed at the difference in the size of ships. I'd spent eighteen months on board the *Iowa*, which had a huge beam, 108 feet across. The *Toledo* was only 70 feet in the beam. I walked on the quarterdeck, and I started through a little passageway, and I was getting ready to jump over to the other side, it was so small in comparison to the *Iowa*. That was kind of amazing to me, but they took care of me in good shape, the normal routine. No one was surprised about my coming aboard because I relieved Lieutenant Herb Yarbrough, whom I had known on the *Iowa*, and he was able to tell his shipmates about me.

The next day I went up to see the commanding officer. This was Captain F. B. C. Martin, who was a fine gent. He welcomed me warmly, shook my hand, and said: "You know, I'm really happy to meet you. You took care of a friend of mine once."

I said, "Oh?"

He said: "Yes, a friend of mine from North Carolina came up to see me about getting his son into the ROTC program. I really didn't have all of the specifics at hand, but I called the Washington office, and you were the guy that met this gentleman when he came in there and gave him all the information. The guy called me back and thanked me profusely because he thought you had done a good job in explaining the program, etc." So F. B. C. Martin had heard of me, and in some way he knew me.

I got introduced to the wardroom at breakfast the next morning. My good friend Herb Yarbrough didn't particularly want to leave, because he'd taken the ship through the early part of the yard period, and he wanted to see it operate with all the new equipment on board.[1]

I soon got a roommate by the name of Norman Algiers. He was the damage control officer, a former enlisted man. Both of us were lieutenants, and Norman was just a tremendous guy. Norman was a very good conversationalist. We got along famously. One of the really interesting things about Algiers was that he wore his hat cocked to one side. It was about thirty degrees off center. And he drank his coffee from his cup without ever touching the cup: he always poured it in a saucer first and drank it from there. Besides being a character, he was also an artist. He drew a lot of cartoons that wound up in the cruise book that covered the *Toledo*'s deployment to the western Pacific.

The yard period went along fairly routinely, and we were preparing to go overseas. As we were getting ready to go, we got a brand-new chief radio-

1 Prior to Gravely's reporting aboard, the *Toledo* had made three separate combat deployments to Korean waters. When he arrived, the ship was partway through a five-month overhaul and modernization period that lasted from April to September of 1953.

man. He had been on shore duty at a communication station for something like six years, and he hadn't really been working in his rating. He had been the chief master-at-arms. What he needed to know about shipboard radio procedures, and what he had known six years earlier, just were not the same. He had lost his proficiency as a result. He tried to lead the guys, but the man I really relied on was a radioman second class. The main way I found out this chief didn't have it was that he was unable to give the Morse code part of the test to a second class radioman. And he'd lost proficiency on an awful lot of other things too. One of my hardest jobs was trying to figure out how to get rid of this guy and get a new chief radioman. This chief was a problem because of the awkwardness it created in the chain of command. I had to work around him all the time. He had another unfortunate trait, and I'm not speaking about his character at all, but he had an effeminate-type voice. When he'd get on a squawk box, God, everybody on the bridge was laughing.

The *Toledo* finished that yard period. When we got there, I discovered that Captain Joshua Cooper, who had been my skipper in the *Iowa*, was by now the chief of staff to our type commander, Commander Cruiser-Destroyer Force Pacific Fleet. One day Captain Martin said he was going over to the flagship, so I asked, "Captain, do you mind me riding over with you, because I'd like to see Captain Cooper?"

He said: "Oh, jump in, jump in. Yeah, we'll take you."

We went over, and the next thing I knew, there were gongs rung on the quarterdeck to indicate Captain Martin was leaving. I rushed up to the quarterdeck and said, "Well, I haven't seen Captain Cooper yet, and I'll stay over here. I'll get back somehow."

He said, "Fine."

Captain Cooper took the time to see me, and he said, "Sam, how are you getting along?"

I said, "Fine."

"Is there anything I can do for you?"

"Captain, yes there is. I need a chief radioman." Immediately he got on the squawk box and called a personnel officer.

The personnel officer said: "Well, they have a chief radioman. They're only allowed one. Chief radiomen are hard to find."

Captain Cooper said, "Get him a chief radioman."

The personnel officer and I went and sat down. He said: "Well, let me tell you. I've got just one guy that's possibly available. He has just finished the teletype repair school [I believe it was]. And he's sitting around here now and getting ready to go to crypto repair school. When are you guys sailing?"

I said, "We're sailing Monday." This was a Saturday.

He said, "Well, I can't get a message to him for certainty to get him aboard."

"Give me the orders. I'll find him." He gave me the chief's address, and I went to his house. Like most chief radiomen about noon on a Saturday, he wasn't home.

His wife said, "He's at [such-and-such] a beer garden."

I went down to this beer garden, and I said, "I'm looking for Chief Gause."

Some guy said, "He's over there." Sure enough, there he was with a crowd of sailors. They were sitting around swapping lies and everything else. I went over and introduced myself to him. I said, "Chief, I'm the communication officer on the *Toledo*. I've got a set of orders in my hand for you, and I need you aboard tomorrow morning." He almost upchucked. In any event, Monday morning when we set sail Chief Radioman D. C. Gause was there. He made my life much easier.

With Chief Gause in radio, refresher training just became a dream. I had a really strong guy in the radio shack. During maneuvers, I was on the bridge doing the tactical communicating. Had a good signal gang, and we went through with a fairly good set of colors. I had the general signal book memorized; I really did. When somebody said tactical signal—well, the turns and corpens and those things were sort of understood, but most of the two-letter signals would come in, and I had them broken.[2]

The reason I had the signal book was just to double-check. I usually told the captain right away what the meaning of the signal was, and then I'd double-check the signal book. I'd learned fairly well on board the *Iowa*, and we'd gone through it frequently at comm school, so I was pretty well up on it. I think a couple of times people were impressed because official procedure called for checking the signal book.

---

2 A turn signal generally means following the ship ahead, while a corpen calls for a group of ships to turn simultaneously. Two-letter signals dealt with other topics; while some individuals might have had to look up their meanings, Gravely had them largely committed to memory.

As we got going, I made the movement reports, as I had on board the *Iowa*, and I also wrote up the logistics requirements messages. Professionally, I wasn't content with being on the bridge just as tactical communicator during such events as general quarters and special sea detail. I wanted to be up there during normal steaming as well. Finally, I talked with the senior watch officer, and he agreed. I began to stand regular deck watches in the *Toledo* and qualified as officer of the deck during independent steaming. There were about ten officers who stood deck watches during normal steaming and four who had it during task force ops. In task force ops you usually got into a much stricter watch condition than at any other time. I just loved the bridge on ships, and I think they all knew it. I made a couple of tactical errors, but who doesn't? I didn't collide with anybody, although one night I thought I would. Things went fairly well up there, and I continued to progress.

★★★

We left Long Beach in October 1953 and went on out to the Seventh Fleet. We were deployed for about seven months. Nothing untoward happened there, except I remember once we were under way and I was told I had to get the radio shack painted. I told the exec, Commander William Groner: "Sir, I would like to do that, but frankly, that's unheard of during an operating period. The radio gang needs to sit down to do their job while the painting is going on at the same time. You just can't shut down your gear."

He said, "I really don't give a damn whether it's unheard of or not, but it is filthy down there, and I want that place cleaned up."

"Well, yes, sir."

We got it painted, and when we were all through, he came again, and he said, "Sam, it looks good down there."

I said, "Well, sir, normally, as I told you, people don't paint radio shacks while they're under way."

"Hell, I know that. I just wanted to see if you could do it." We became great friends.

Commander Groner was quite a guy. He had a love of birds, as I did. He had spent a lot of time in Japan, and when the ship got there, someone gave him a pair of lovebirds. The impression I got was that they specifically gave him two male birds, because if he'd gotten a female and a male they'd probably breed, and obviously the ship was no place for birds to breed. He kept them in his stateroom in a little cage. Periodically you could go there, and the exec would be in his stateroom with his door locked. He was playing with his damn birds. Birds were fluttering about the room and everything else, and then he'd put them back in the cage. Well, one day one of the birds died, and we had a wardroom meeting to determine who had killed the exec's bird. This was sort of like, "Who killed Cock Robin?"

Obviously nobody volunteered that he had killed the bird, so the ship's doctor was ordered to do an autopsy to find out what happened. The doctor was really upset, protesting to the commander that he was there to treat the humans, not any bird. The exec told him to go do it anyway. The doctor performed an autopsy, and lo and behold he discovered that the bird was egg bound. Commander Groner had been given a female after all. And so all the officers got off scot-free.

★★★

By the time we got to the Seventh Fleet, the Korean War had been over a few months. The armistice had been settled in July of 1953. We showed the flag, operated with carrier task groups, and took part in various exercises. In December of that year, when the ship was in Hong Kong, Captain William Cockell came aboard and relieved F. B. C. Martin as skipper. Captain Cockell was another real fine gent. He had been a dirigible pilot. Since he was a different kind of aviator, he got a cruiser command rather than a carrier. Captain Cockell was a fairly good ship handler, kind of meticulous, an easy man to work for. Treated me no differently from anybody else, and I had a lot of respect for him.

He was fairly well satisfied, I think, with his communications. I can remember specifically one time, and this was after we got back to the States. The *Toledo* went to the Seattle Seafair. Rear Admiral Maurice Curts was on board as Commander Cruiser-Destroyer Force Pacific Fleet, and he was to make a radio broadcast to the city of Seattle. We had to pipe him into a radio station and pipe him out. We were all set for it, with a handset on the bridge. There was a red light on each of these handsets to indicate the transmitter was working. I looked and saw no light as Admiral Curts was coming to the bridge. I started calling radio frantically, and as he stepped up to pick up that handset, the light came on. I'm not sure what happened, but boy, I was sweating blood in the meantime. He made the broadcast successfully, so there was no problem after that.

We got back from our deployment in the spring of 1954, and Alma was still in Virginia. I remember specifically that after the *Toledo* moved from San Francisco down to Long Beach the year before, a couple of the young officers asked me why I didn't have my wife with me. I told them she was on the East Coast, and I said, "There's probably a little bit of a problem trying to find housing out here."

They pooh-poohed that. One guy told me he lived in a group of apartments in Long Beach, and he said, "I know you can get a place where we live." I investigated that, and they would not let me in because we were black. They just weren't quite ready. In fact, we'd already made up our minds that we would wait until the tour was completed to rejoin. By the end of the first deployment, my time in San Francisco plus this deployment equaled about eleven months. When the ship returned from deployment, I took some leave, came back home, and saw Alma. We expected that my tour of duty would be up within the next year, and at the end of the *Toledo* tour, no matter where I went, we'd set up a home.

Well, much to the chagrin of most of us, the *Toledo* stayed in Long Beach for only about three months. Then we were turned around and went back out again in September of 1954, and I stayed on board for the next deployment. What I remember more than anything else from the second cruise was the ship's involvement in the evacuation of the Tachens, two little islands off the mainland of China.[3] The biggest thing about the operation was that we went to general quarters at dawn every morning, for some ten or twelve days, and then we stayed at general quarters until about ten o'clock at night. What we were doing was lying off the Tachen Islands with an anchor down, really, and watching the evacuation. Then at dusk we'd steam out and operate with the task force all night. At dawn the next day we were right back in there near the islands to start the same procedure. It was tiring, because I stayed on the bridge as tactical communicator from dawn every morning till about ten o'clock every night. It was a long haul up on that bridge, eating sandwiches to keep going.

We had several liberty ports while we were in the western Pacific. I went most places alone rather than going ashore with a shipmate. In Japan I got to

3 The small Tachen Islands, north of Formosa (as Taiwan was then called), were subject to attack from mainland China in the early 1950s. In February 1955, on the advice of the U.S. Government and with the assistance of the U.S. Seventh Fleet, the Nationalist Chinese evacuated the Tachens.

like Yokosuka and Sasebo quite a bit. We also went to Hong Kong and to Subic Bay in the Philippines. Rear Admiral Ralph Wilson was on board then as cruiser division commander. I remember he insisted that all officers had to wear hats ashore, and I normally didn't. So when I was in Hong Kong, I purchased a thing I could fold and put in my pocket as soon as I got to the end of the gangway.

I can remember one port when I went on liberty with my roommate. We were sitting around in a bar talking to some girls. I heard snickering going on, and I couldn't figure out why. My roommate said they were trying to find out if Negroes really had tails, because that was one of the stories.

★★★

One of the significant things that happened during the cruise was that I began to really love the Navy. Even though I was still a reserve officer, I knew I wanted to make it a career. As far as black officers in the Navy were concerned, there were Dennis Nelson, who was a regular Navy officer; John Lee, whom I'd met, and who was also a regular Navy officer; and I didn't know too many other regular Navy officers.[4] I think Thomas "Dave" Parham, who was a chaplain, might have gone USN by that time.[5] Wes Brown had graduated from the Naval Academy, and there were a few others.[6]

It was a pretty exclusive group, roughly twenty-five or thirty people. I hadn't been picked earlier in my quest for a regular commission, but some new opportunities arose. While I was in the *Toledo*, a couple of programs opened up that would at least extend my active duty time, whether I became regular Navy or not. One was the TAR program—training and administration of reservists. I looked into that. Generally, you spent some time at a reserve training center, and then, whatever your subspecialty was, you would do a tour in that subspecialty. It seemed like a good program, so I applied for it.

Shortly before I got an answer, I learned of a contract program wherein a reservist could get a contract that assured him a maximum of five years on

---

4 On March 15, 1947, Lieutenant (junior grade) John W. Lee Jr., USNR, became the first black officer with a commission in the regular Navy. He served on active duty until his retirement as a lieutenant commander on July 1, 1966. His oral history is in the Naval Institute collection.

5 Lieutenant Thomas D. Parham Jr., CHC, USN. Years later, in 1966, Parham became the first black officer in the U.S. Navy to be promoted to captain. He retired in that rank in 1982.

6 Ensign Wesley A. Brown, USN, became the first black graduate of the Naval Academy in 1949 and then entered the Civil Engineer Corps. He retired as a lieutenant commander in 1969. His oral history is in the Naval Institute collection.

active duty. I said, "That looks pretty good, and so I'll try that." Then the next thing that came out was a regular Navy program. The problem was that I wasn't eligible, simply because of seniority. The program stated that you had to be a lieutenant with a date of rank of something like '52, as I recall, as a lieutenant. My date of rank was '51, so I was about a year too senior for the program. But I kept reading everything about it, and lo and behold, one day there was a change to the program.

They had not received enough applications, so anybody could apply to the program if he met the eligibility requirements—including date of rank, no matter what it was. You just had to agree that if you were selected your date of rank could not be senior to a lieutenant of 6-1-52 or something like that. I applied for that too. And shortly thereafter I got a change in designator to 1107. I was a TAR. The next thing that happened was that I got a four-year contract. And then the last thing that happened was I got selected for regular Navy.

That was my good year. No matter what I touched, it turned out gold. I sacrificed the seniority of about a year's drop in date of rank. I was being transferred at this time from the *Toledo* and was to go to the Commandant of the Third Naval District headquarters in New York City for duty. I was going as an 1107, but my appointment to regular Navy was transferred up there, so when I got to New York I received the new designator of 1100, an unrestricted line officer.

What else the future held, who could say? I was essentially taking it one tour of duty at a time. I really didn't think at that time that I would go past lieutenant commander. There'd been no black in the Navy who'd ever done that, so I felt that would probably be as high as I could go. I didn't ever think in terms of being passed over for promotion, but I felt I would put in my twenty years, which was what you had to do to be eligible to retire. I would retire as a lieutenant commander, and then go do something else. I didn't have any idea what that would be, although I guess if I had really sat down to think about it, it would probably have been getting in the public school system—coaching and teaching, as I had previously wanted to do.

★★★

The *Toledo* came back into Long Beach and stayed there for about a month. The ship then went to the Puget Sound Naval Shipyard in Bremerton, Washington, for another overhaul. On July the fourth of 1955, two years to the day after I reported aboard, I left the *Toledo*. I rode a train down to Long Beach. I had my car there, so I picked it up and drove across country to meet Alma. She and I had decided that no matter where I went next time, we would go together. She was on a year-to-year contract in her teaching job, so about December of the previous year she informed her employer she was going to leave. Then she went to live with her folks in Christianburg, Virginia. I met her there, and we then traveled up to New York together.

CHAPTER EIGHT

Com Three—New York City

Officially, my new assignment was to the staff of the Commandant of the Third Naval District; unofficially, the command was known as Com Three. The headquarters office was at 90 Church Street in Manhattan. The building housed both Com Three and Commander Eastern Sea Frontier. Those two, plus the shipyard over in Brooklyn, gave the Navy a large presence in New York City. All three commands have since been disestablished, but at the time it was a thriving Navy town. The naval district dealt with a variety of issues in the states of New York and Connecticut. Com One, in Boston, was our counterpart to the north and Com Four, in Philadelphia, to the south. It was my first time as a member of a large naval staff, and it was also the first time Alma and I had really made a home together. Both proved to be interesting challenges.

I did run into one unexpected hassle right away. When I reported, I needed to pass a physical to qualify for my appointment as a regular officer. I went down for my exam, and I could not pass the eye test. I had one hell of a time with my eyes. I really credit my becoming a full-fledged naval officer to a young warrant officer who was there. He insisted, "Okay, so the poor guy can't read 20/20 on the chart, but that's really not what we're interested in. Is there anything really wrong with his eyeballs?" I took the test about six times, and I don't give a damn what it is, if you keep reading it over and over again, you get so you can learn it. That was what I did with those eye charts. I did manage to get through the exam and accepted my regular Navy appointment. But if it hadn't been for a good warrant down there, this young lieutenant doctor would have just sent me on my way, saying, "Not physically qualified," and I probably would have killed him before the day was over.

★★★

As far as my billet assignment on that staff, I had thought in terms of only two ways I could go. My first was that they would probably send me to the reserve section since my TAR designator qualified me for reserve work. The second possible direction was in the communications gang because of my course at Monterey and my two shipboard tours. But, much to my surprise, I was sent in to meet a little guy who was the district security officer. He was Lieutenant Commander Ski Kucharski, a former enlisted man. I became his assistant for ABC—atomic, biological, and chemical—warfare defense matters. I was really taken aback by this assignment but fine with it. Ski was a really gentle man who had been a POW during World War II in Japan, and we frequently talked about his experiences there.[1]

I happened to talk to him one day and said I was curious as to how I got to his office. He told me he needed an assistant for the job, and he was very happy I came there, because it didn't make any difference to him if I was black, blue, green, red or anything else. I'd heard that once before—when I reported to the *Iowa*. Kucharski was very happy to see me, explained the job, and we hit it off like two peas in a pod. In fact, it was he who helped Alma and me find a better place to live.

When we first went to New York, Alma had a sister there. We lived with her for a short while until we moved into an apartment over in Brooklyn. Brooklyn, not too far from the naval shipyard, was not my idea of the nicest community in the world. At the same time, however, it provided us our first real home, though we'd had rooms and those kinds of things before. We really enjoyed the opportunity to live together.

When we'd been there for about three months, I came home one day and noticed there was half of a red brick in the living room. I discovered it had come in through the window, which was broken. Then I looked further, and somebody had been in the house, had been through the refrigerator, and had drunk a Coke. The most shocking part about it was that I had a piggy bank that contained the coins I was saving to buy a fish aquarium. The guy had not

---

1 Boatswain's Mate First Class Leo F. Kucharski was serving at the Navy yard in Piti, Guam, when the Japanese captured that island in 1941. He was imprisoned in the Osaka area of Japan during the war.

only taken my piggy bank, he'd also lain down on my bed and counted my money as he stole it. Then he left the broken bank under the pillow.

I decided we had to get out of that area. When we had tried previously to move to some Navy housing over in Bayonne, which was on the New Jersey side of New York Harbor, I was unable to do so. But Kucharski somehow made the necessary arrangements, and the next thing I knew I was offered an apartment over there. Kucharski's wife worked over in the Navy annex at Bayonne. All four of us socialized after we made our move there.

★★★

In my new role I got to know and work with the Eastern Sea Frontier staff as well as with the Com Three staff. Lieutenant Dennis Nelson was stationed there also, so we saw each other periodically. Though we had known each other a long time and certainly were friendly, Dennis was fifteen years older than I, so we weren't buddies. In addition, my wife was there and his was not.

It's worth going into detail about Nelson. He was one of the original thirteen black officers commissioned by the Navy in the spring of 1944. I first met Dennis at Great Lakes shortly after I became an officer the same year. Dennis was definitely one of the smartest of all of us. He remained on active duty until retirement, which was different from all the other members of the Golden Thirteen. Of the few dozen black line officers who were commissioned as reservists during World War II, John Lee was the only other one besides Dennis who stayed for a full career. John Lee left active service after the war ended but then was called back and in 1947 became the first black officer in the regular Navy, as differentiated from the Naval Reserve. Dennis transferred to the regular Navy very shortly after John did.

Overall, in terms of the integration of blacks into the Navy, I think Dennis did as much or more than any of the rest of us. He fought some really impossible odds to become a naval officer. The opportunity really didn't come soon enough for him. He was born in November 1907, so he was thirty-six years old when he became an ensign. The typical white ensign was probably in his twenties. As an officer, he became a specialist in the public information area, through which he was certainly able to do a lot of positive things. He worked with all of the major black groups of that time: the NAACP, the Urban League, and so forth. I think he knew at least a couple of secretaries of the Navy because he worked in the Washington area.

He also wrote the book on the integration of the Navy, which became sort of a bible for all of us.[2] So Dennis, despite the fact he got only to the grade of lieutenant commander, was one of the stalwarts among the black officers we had during that time frame. We can speculate on why he didn't reach a higher rank. Age very likely was one factor, but I also think it was a result of the course of action he set for himself.

He felt very strongly that he should be at the scene of activity relating to integrating the Navy. I can remember at one time Dennis probably should have gone to sea, and he insisted on staying at that scene in Washington. I think if he'd gone to sea then, he might have gone higher. The Navy wants seagoing officers and not people who stay ashore. Another factor may have been his personality. He was very, very aggressive, and straightforward, and maybe that turned some people off. He was a no-nonsense guy.

In that era, the average black person couldn't live or stay in certain places. In my case, I guess I took the easier route. When we drove across country, we'd stay only in places we knew would accept us. If we knew we were going to be turned down in a given area, there was no sense in going there. Nelson, on the other hand, wore his uniform; in fact, he drove across country once in his white uniform. He stopped anyplace he wanted to, and it looked as if in some of those places they thought he was sort of an African prince or something, when he was just another black naval officer. So at times he got accommodations when I just went across the tracks. I'm sure that if some people in the Navy knew about that kind of activity, they resented it, and they would have stopped him right there.

He was a very proud, very determined man. I firmly believe he sacrificed himself so that others might succeed. He was just a tremendous naval officer. He was the kind of a guy a lot of us went to for advice. In my own case, he was almost like a father figure. And he knew how to get things done. By what I was later able to accomplish in my own career, I may have been one of the primary beneficiaries of the work he did.

★★★

Rear Admiral Milton E. Miles was Commandant Third Naval District and just a fantastic guy. He and his wife had a beautiful set of quarters in the

---

2 Dennis D. Nelson II, *The Integration of the Negro into the U.S. Navy* (New York: Farrar, Strauss and Young, 1951).

Brooklyn Navy Yard. It was a highlight when Alma and I were invited to a Sunday afternoon affair at their place, the first set of flag officer quarters I'd ever been to. We just thoroughly enjoyed ourselves. In fact, I took a young nephew with us. Admiral Miles seemed to like kids, and he sort of took to our nephew. We were quite pleased by the hospitality, and I was quite pleased to be a member of his staff.

That visit, incidentally, was a contrast to the norm for us. In that day and time our social activity was mostly in the black community. Alma came from a rather large family. Her father had fifteen brothers and sisters, and only two of them stayed down in Christiansburg, Virginia. As a result, she had cousins galore, and they populated a good part of the United States. I couldn't drive across country without running across them.

★★★

Things really proceeded fairly normally for me in that job, and I found it to be quite interesting. As I said, we ran the district security office, which meant we conducted security inspections as well as introducing passive defense, a new term then in fashion. We visited every naval activity in the Third Naval District: we inspected the large activities once a year and the minor activities once every two years. Bayonne, for example, was a major activity, and it got inspected every year. I can't remember all of the large activities, but I do know we were on the road quite a bit. We'd plan each trip to visit eight or nine of these places. For example, when we went to the airfield at Niagara Falls we also hit Scotia, New York. Scotia was the processing center for Navy correspondence courses, and it was also the alternate command center for Com Three if something happened to the headquarters in Manhattan. We went out Long Island Sound and also to the bigger ones elsewhere. Ski took me along with him on the first couple, and then we sort of alternated. He let me go on my own, and I would do a few.

A big emphasis was on the physical security aspects, as one would imagine. We checked the size of the guard force, whether they had too many, too few. Looking at gates, seeing what should be locked and what shouldn't be locked. In terms of passive defense, we went into the operational control center to see if it had the proper radio communications down there, as well as supplies of food and water. We wanted to make sure they would be fairly well set up in the event of a nuclear attack. We looked to see that they had the required supply of gas masks and the suits for fighting chemical warfare, certain things for biological warfare, and so forth. We were concerned about possible Soviet nuclear attacks, so we were building our fortress America. We were talking in terms of deep underground shelters and those things, and we looked at their plans to see if they could properly take care of the people in case of an evacuation. In fact, there was normally an exercise at least once a year. The Com Three staff would go up to the command center in Scotia and fight the imaginary battle from there.

It was because of this emphasis on Cold War concerns that I had been assigned as Kucharski's assistant. One day, not long after I had arrived, he said to me, "I'm going to send you down to Fort McClellan, Alabama, to go through a five-week course in ABC warfare." The training would be great, but I'd never been to Fort McClellan and really didn't have much of a desire to go. He also said to me, "There'll probably be about twenty students in the class, and you're to be number one."

As I recall, it was in January of 1956 when I went to Fort McClellan, and it was a very good school. We started with one week atomic, one week biological, and one week chemical, and then the last two weeks were passive defense against those things. I didn't have any problems down there at all. I enjoyed Fort McClellan. I met a guy who was in the Army, and he became a friend of mine.

I met another really interesting character down there, a commander who was in the training section at the Bureau of Naval Personnel in Arlington, Virginia. He and I were sitting around talking one day about the black officers in the Navy and what the future might be. I gave him a rundown on my experience, and he told me, "You know, you probably are on the five-term list." It was for a training program at Monterey, California, for ex-reserve officers who had augmented into the regular Navy. Basically, this was to bring us up to snuff with the regulars. Then we talked more, and he said: "You know, if you don't go to that program then you're ripe for a destroyer. What you need to be is ops officer on a destroyer."

I said, "Well, both of those sound intriguing, but could I come by your office on my way back to New York to see about it?"

He said: "Please do. Stop by my office and we'll talk about it."

Well, I graduated out of the course number four, not number one. That probably disappointed Ski, but in any event, I stopped in BuPers on my way up. When I got to this commander's office in BuPers, he was not there that day. I got to talking to his deputy, and we were looking through the school lists. He said, "Let's talk about your experience a little bit."

I went and gave him the same pitch. "The *PC-1264*, went out of the Navy, came back into recruiting, spent a year and a half on the *Iowa*, spent two years on the *Toledo*, now I'm at Com Three. Yes, I'm now qualified OOD independent steaming, blah, blah, blah, went to Monterey, etc."[3]

"Well, your name's on this list here, but you don't need that." He struck my name right off the list, and he said, "We've got more people on there than we can possibly send to school, and we certainly don't want to send a guy there who doesn't need it." Well, I could understand that. Then he repeated essentially what the other officer had said. "I got to tell you, with your experience and background, you really need to go as an ops officer on a destroyer. Now, you go down and see So-and-so," and he gave me the name.

I went down to see the man he recommended, but that's where I got derailed. This guy said: "Hey, what makes you think you're qualified to go on a destroyer? Hell, you don't have the background for destroyers. We like to send our ensigns out of the Naval Academy to the destroyer Navy. Grow them up in destroyers. You've never done that. Christ, you couldn't hack it as ops officer on a destroyer."

I said, "Yes, sir," and I walked out of his office. Essentially, I was told I was too fat for thin work and too thin for fat work. I was very disappointed in that and apparently the victim of bad timing. I drove straight from Fort McClellan to BuPers. I'd planned to take Monday off and see the officer I'd met in the course. Maybe he took the day off to work in his backyard, forgetting he'd promised to see me. I think it would have gone better for me if he'd been there. At least I don't think he would have deleted my name off of the school list right in front of me, which his deputy did. After that fruitless stop at BuPers, I went back to Com Three and just determined to do the best possible job.

One other thing that happened there was prior to Ski's departure. We were responsible for the reserve destroyers and destroyer escorts in the Com Three area. The naval district commandant was in the administrative chain of command. Each of those ships had to be inspected once every six months. When Kucharski was there by himself, he did it. My predecessor in the job

---

3 OOD—officer of the deck

had been detached without relief. He was a reserve officer who'd never been on board ship, and Ski wouldn't let him do the inspections. Ski did them all, but he wanted help. He said to me: "Sam, you've been aboard ship, and it's nothing but a damage control inspection. You do it." Then he added: "I've got to warn you about Kowalzyk. Kowalzyk is a demanding guy, and I got to tell you, you will never pull any wool over his eyes, so don't try. But at the same time, just go down there and do your normal good job, and everything will come out okay."[4]

We inspected the ship, and then we were scheduled for a critique in the wardroom. I was still inspecting the ship when most people went to lunch. I had done lots of inspections on board the *Toledo* and lots of inspections on board the *Iowa* as part of inspection parties, but I'd never really been on one on my own. I was just walking around the ship, and I passed the ship's office. There was a yeoman in there banging away, and I said, "Hey, what are you typing?"

He said, "Oh, I've got Captain Kowalzyk's inspection notes."

This may not have been quite appropriate, but I said, "Let me see those notes." I had jotted down practically all of the damage control discrepancies myself, but there were a couple that Captain Kowalzyk highlighted in his report. So at the critique, I highlighted the ones on the captain's list, and I gave the ship a satisfactory for the inspection or something like that. The exec, who became a great friend of mine, was a little upset I didn't give him a good or something like that. Captain Kowalzyk said to me: "Boy, oh boy. That's what I call a good inspection."

I was welcome on all the inspection parties from then on. I learned a lot from Captain Kowalzyk. There are times when you've got to be demanding, and you've got to call some spades a spade. You cannot sit around and say, "Hey, this guy is my friend, and he really ought to get a good grade." If it's wrong, it's wrong. People's lives could depend on it, plus there are an awful lot of other things at stake. Unfortunately, my friend, the exec, got passed over for lieutenant commander.

As it turned out, Com Three proved to be a very, very interesting assignment, as well as a good job for me, because I got to know some people

4 Captain Alexander M. Kowalzyk Jr., USN, was the Third Naval District chief of staff.

who began to have a lot of faith in my ability. I can remember when Ski left, a new officer came in to take over his job. Very, very competent officer, also ex-enlisted. He didn't quite understand the program and unfortunately made the decision to go to Scotia to run the operations for the ops officer, who was a gruff, demanding old Navy captain. The captain got on the phone, in the midst of the exercise, when he didn't believe what my new boss was telling him. He called me to give him answers. Then finally he said, "Get your ass up here."

Of course, I went up there, and my immediate boss was flabbergasted. He didn't know the ops officer had been calling on the phone asking for the answers that he'd been giving them. I thought he'd been giving them fairly correctly, but the captain had more faith in me than he did in my new boss.

During the time I was at Com Three, I was continuing to do things to build my professional development; that included correspondence courses. I know I completed more correspondence courses there than in any other tour of duty. There was time to sit down and do these things, not only in the office but also in the afternoon. I probably completed about fifty correspondence courses administered by the center in Scotia. You name it and I took it.

In addition to those, I finally decided I would tackle the Naval War College correspondence courses. They had one on operational tactics, as I recall. It was an eight-assignment course, but it was divided up into part one and part two. I did the first four lessons. I never could have done it alone. I had two or three friends on the staff who were also taking it, because you had three options: to take the exam, to get the correspondence course completed on a subject, or to go to a short course. If you didn't do the short course or somehow get exempted, you had to take this exam. And we were all painfully aware that we didn't particularly want to take the exam. So the four of us used to get together on a Saturday morning and sit down and discuss it. We discussed the problems, and then we'd all go home and write out our individual answers to it, and there was no problem to that, I'm sure. Anyway, I did complete an awful lot of correspondence courses there.

★★★

On the personal side, Alma had a back ailment, and we went through a series of doctors on that. Finally, they decided they would take her into the hospital. We could have gone to the naval hospital out on Long Island, but as I recall, it was much closer to use a merchant marine hospital on Staten Island. It was a short hop over there on the ferry. In addition was the fact that they were supposed to have a good gynecologist over there. The doctors did an exploratory operation, and ultimately, she ended up with a complete hysterectomy.

At that same time, since I'd just about completed my two years there, I began to think in terms of my next assignment. About September of '57 I wrote my letter to the bureau asking for sea duty. I was really surprised when I got a letter back saying, "Yes, we've been looking at your jacket [service record], and we have decided you're going to an AKA out of San Diego as operations officer."[5] I really felt great, because now I was moving up in the world a little bit.

Unfortunately, Alma was still in the hospital at that time, and when she got out she was not able to travel long distances for a while. I took her down to her mother's home in Christiansburg, where she stayed and convalesced until December of that year. In the meantime, I went on out to San Diego.

---

5 AKA was the designation used at that time for an attack cargo ship, one that was specialized for use in delivering cargo during an amphibious assault.

CHAPTER NINE

USS *Seminole*

After my trip across country in the autumn of 1957, I reported in for training at the naval amphibious base in Coronado, California, across the harbor from San Diego. Now a bridge connects the two, but in those days you got from one side to the other either by taking the ferry or driving a long way around. After I arrived, I settled in at the BOQ and was prepared to take some courses designed to acquaint students with amphibious warfare.

My predecessor in the *Seminole* was also the training officer, and he felt I should go through a different set of courses than the Bureau of Personnel directed. So he wrote a letter over to the amphib base and described the courses I should take. One consisted of three days in cold-weather communications. Another one was communicating with the amphibious ships of the task force and several other things. When I got there, it was all confused because they'd have to keep me there for not just eight weeks but sixteen. I expressed my concern about that amount of time because I was eager to report to my ship.

In the meantime, I knew the *Seminole* was in San Diego. The commanding officer was an interesting guy, Captain James W. "Bobo" Thomson. The first lieutenant, who was in charge of the boats and the deck equipment, was Lieutenant George Mau. George called over to the amphibious base, located me in the BOQ, and invited me to his house for dinner on my first Sunday there. I went over, met George and his family, and we had a great relationship, starting right then. We really became fast friends, talking about the ship and everything else.

I said: "George, you know, I think somebody should tell the skipper they're not going to keep me over here for sixteen weeks. My curriculum is only for eight, and with this second letter from the ship there, I've got eight weeks to do nothing." They were concerned about it.

After I had been in the school for a few weeks, I got a call from Captain Thomson. He said: "Sam, you don't need all that crap. Get your tail over here. We're getting ready to go on an operation."

So instead of going for the full time planned, I went through part of the course and then reported to the *Seminole*. It was a World War II-vintage attack cargo ship used for transporting men and supplies during an amphibious landing. It carried a collection of landing craft to get the equipment from the ship to the shore. The *Seminole* was different from the ships I had been on a few years earlier, a battleship and a cruiser. Instead of being able to make thirty-three knots, AKAs in those days were not really fast movers. They could go seventeen or eighteen knots max.

You're also talking about ships that had a lot of reservists on them; they didn't get the personnel talent I'd seen in the big ships. The exec was a fine guy, but he shocked me one day when he told me he felt amphibious ships did dirty work, so they could be dirty. He said, "Not like that cruiser you came off of, spit and polish." But I was determined to clean up my spaces. I didn't give a damn what the rest of it looked like, but I was going to clean mine up.

It was also quite interesting to learn that instead of having one senior watch officer, they had two. One was senior watch officer at sea and the other one in port. The guy I relieved was the senior watch officer at sea: a lieutenant commander senior to every other watch stander on board. And they had another guy who took it in port. I could never really figure that one out. But very shortly after I got there, I quickly told them they had one senior watch officer, and I was the one.

Fairly soon, I was beginning to speak a little out of turn because of what I saw. My predecessor as operations officer had made up his mind he was not going to leave the ship until Christmas, and I got there about the first week in November. I had to live with him for about six to eight weeks, trying not to step in even though I thought I saw a lot of things I could improve upon. Now, I do not mean to discredit the guy I relieved, but he was an aviator, and this was his first shipboard duty. He got sent down because of ulcers, and he probably should have gone to something to learn first. But anyway, he got this job and did the best he could. I didn't think he really knew the job, particularly the communications part of it. I didn't think he was well qualified as a watch stander. At some point in time, everybody thinks a lieutenant commander can handle a ship, but that isn't necessarily so.

There are a lot of special requirements for amphibious warfare, and this ops officer seemed to have done fairly well with some of the special requirements, but there were little things that bothered me. We were with this operation during the first two or three days, and the ship had a message to move in to unload, and the *Seminole* didn't receive the message. Everybody was moving in and beginning, and we got a message from the squadron commander saying, "Why haven't you carried out my so-and-so [order]?"

The captain said, "I haven't seen anything."

My predecessor said, "Well, we haven't gotten anything."

I said: "Hey, it's quite obvious to me you've missed a message. Now go down there."

This officer said, "Well, how am I going to get it?"

I said, "Have the radioman get on the task group commander's net, and ask him for it." We did, and we learned that the ship had been told to move about two hours before.

★★★

In the course of taking over the operations department, I discovered that the responsibility of running the department on the AKA was less trying, really, than being communications officer on one of the other ships. Certainly when we had an amphibious operation going on, it was kind of demanding, but the duties were just a little bit expanded on what I'd been doing all the time. The CIC officer worked for me, the communicator worked for me, the signal officer worked for me. I also had an intelligence responsibility, and there was some awkwardness involved in that. When I relieved on the *Seminole*, my predecessor told me I was the intelligence officer, so I simply asked him, "Well, what do I do as intelligence officer?"

He said, "Well, there's nothing to do." (I sort of wondered why I would have the job if there really were nothing to do.)

I said, "Well, are there any publications around here or anything?"

"Oh, there's something; it's someplace around here."

"Do I sign for anything?"

"No, you don't sign for anything."

Well, my predecessor got off just about the Christmas holidays, and shortly thereafter Amphibious Group Three inspected the *Seminole.* The staff came aboard with a team of people, and I had a communications inspection type, I had a CIC inspection type, I had a signal type, and I was running around. Suddenly a lieutenant came up and said, "I'm the intelligence officer, and I want to inspect your intelligence department."

I said, "Oh, come on, sit down. I'll answer your questions for you."

He said: "Well, as you know, there isn't much of an intelligence nature for an AKA to do. What I really want to do is to go through and see if you've got this list of intelligence publications you're supposed to have on board, and that's about it."

"Well, do you see that safe over there? If you tell me what you want to see, I'll go over there and find it for you." I unlocked the safe, and the guy started reading from his list of publications. Though it's hard to believe, an AKA was supposed to have about thirty intelligence pubs, and there wasn't a one there. There was nothing in the damn safe. We sat there and discussed it for a minute, and I said: "Let me tell you something. My relief left here about three or four days ago, and he told me the pubs were here, so if the pubs are on this ship, I'll find them. Now, when are you giving your critique?"

"Well, I'm going to give my critique at ten o'clock tomorrow morning, and I got to tell you, you get an unsat unless I can see those pubs."

"Okay. I will have the pubs tomorrow morning."

"Well, I'll be here about nine."

"Great." So I looked through that ship. The ship's office didn't have any. They weren't on board. I realized then I should have questioned my predecessor more thoroughly. I guess I was kind of thoughtless in this regard. I thought if it was of an intelligence nature it probably would have been classified, but no, they were all unclassified pubs, and he just didn't have them. I started to think about it. Now, where could I go to do something about that?

The ship was moored down at the foot of Broadway in San Diego, and the only place I could think about was the Eleventh Naval District headquarters. I knew Com Eleven had an intelligence officer, so I went over to see him. I told him what my predicament was, and I said, "Do you have these pubs?"

He said, "Yeah, I have them."

So we went down the list and I said, "Now, the first thing I want to do is to order me a set." And we made arrangements for a set to come. Then I said, "But I've got to have these tomorrow." Sure enough, I signed out a copy of each of these pubs, and I took them over there, and I showed these to the staff inspector the next day. I don't know how carefully he looked them over, but at least he said, "I'm happy to see you found your pubs."

I said, "Yes, sir."

Then I had to take them back to Com Eleven, but I had a set coming, so I was in pretty good shape. From then on I kept an inventory of those damn things so I could turn them over to my relief when the time came. Maybe I had been too trusting, and maybe my solution wasn't quite on the up and up, but I was in an emergency situation, and the inspector seemed to be happy when I showed him the pubs. In fact, his statement on the critique was, "When I came over here yesterday and inspected this officer, I would have given him an unsat, but today he's much better. I will give him a good." I was very happy about that.

At other times I wound up as an inspecting officer myself. We were in a transport squadron that was divided into two transport divisions, or transdivs. Captain Thomson was the senior skipper in the second division, so he hauled me over every Saturday morning to inspect somebody else's ship after having inspected ours on Friday. I spent a hell of a lot of time in whites and sword, going from ship to ship.

Within our organization we took part in various competitive exercises. I remember the ones in communications more than anything else. So far as the competitive year was concerned, we used our refresher training grade for part of it, and then there were just some individual exercises bringing the boat groups over there. We did okay. I don't think we ever won the squadron E award for excellence, but we got by them fairly satisfactorily.

The biggest one I remember was a security exercise, which people held on the various ships and other commands. The *Seminole* happened to be in the shipyard up in San Francisco at the time, and a group of three of us was directed to go over to break in and test the security of a tactical air control squadron in Alameda. I must say that their security was good, because they caught us. When I tried to explain to them that this was just an exercise, and that my skipper had sent me over, they decided to call him. Captain Thomson said, "No, I don't know the guy." I thought I'd been had, but it was just a little joke on his part. Shortly thereafter he admitted I was part of the ship's company.

In a way, that kind of trick was an indication of the relationship we had. Captain Thomson was just an outstanding guy, and he and I hit it off like two peas in a pod. When I first got aboard, we were down in San Diego, and we were about ready to go through the regular underway training. That was about five weeks, and then we went through another couple of weeks of amphibious training to make sure we could get the boats to the line of departure for making their runs in to the beach. In that case, you had to be especially concerned about communicating with the landing craft. The ops officer's task was to write up a little op order that specified what the ship and boats would be doing. Well, I dearly loved tactics. Captain Thomson knew where I had come from, and he had a hell of a lot more faith in me than I had in myself. But we would be on underway training, and the *Seminole* would be the senior ship. So usually for an exercise of "tictacs," as we called tactical maneuvers, we were the number-one ship.

A couple of times I went up there to Captain Thomson and told him what I'd like to do that day. I had it all plotted out with the signals I was going to give: the turns, the corpens, and all the rest of the stuff. Make one ship move from point A to point B, etc. And he liked that. He'd just leave me up there, and he'd go off someplace else.

I enjoyed it, and I guess that's where I really got the feel I could hack it. I guess the thing that really built up my confidence came at the completion of refresher training, during which we made a decent grade on our operations portion. We were under way, coming out of San Diego, and then had to go over and anchor off the Strand, which is the beach near the amphibious base at Coronado. Captain Thomson said: "Sam, I'm going down to talk to the boat group. Now, take the ship over and drop the hook." Nobody had ever told me to anchor a ship before, but I anchored this one. The navigator told me when to drop, and I let her go. We might have been a little off, but not far, so we didn't move.

Captain Thomson had let me handle the ship one other time too. We were anchored in San Diego, getting ready to go out for the battle problem. The first exercise started when we were moored in San Diego: it was an emergency sortie, and you had to get the ship out without tugs or harbor pilot. And it just so happened that this, being a single-screw ship, was hard to turn. It didn't make any difference if you were going this way or that way, backing, or going in the same direction. And I had to get the ship under way without it. But I did it. The only discrepancy was that I forgot to use the Papa boats, which were the 36-foot-long landing craft we carried. But I got it out without those things, and we did fairly well on the battle problem.

★ ★ ★

There was another bright spot that year, 1957: I was selected for lieutenant commander. The letter that appointed me came in, and it said, "We've got to make sure he's gotten all his correspondence courses, or he takes the exam, etc."

I went up to Captain Thomson with the letter from the administrative officer, and I said: "Captain Thomson, here in my hand is this little notebook which shows the list of correspondence courses I've completed. So I'm exempted from the exam."

He said, "Oh, Sam, give me that damn thing." He signed his name on the letter, and I was approved.

One day very shortly after that a new squadron commander came aboard. He was crossing the *Seminole*, and the quarterdeck sounded the appropriate bells to honor him. I had duty that day, so I went out to the quarterdeck and escorted the commodore across the ship. About that time Captain Thomson came down and met him. I was a little ahead of the two, and I could overhear them talking. This commodore said, "Hey, Captain, I notice you have a colored lieutenant commander on board."

Bobo Thomson said: "I do? What color is he?" He acted all sincere and everything. The commodore stuttered a little bit, but that was the end of that conversation. I've sometimes wondered if the commodore didn't get some revenge for that remark on the skipper's next fitness report, but Captain Thomson was a strong supporter of mine, and so was his successor.

We had a change of command, and Captain Vern Allen came aboard. I had first met him when I was on board the *Toledo* when he was the staff operations officer for Cruiser Division Three. So I knew him, he knew me, and we just hit it off from day one. I mentioned earlier how I had consolidated the position of senior watch officer business, under way and in port. I took it all over and did. It was my responsibility. In fact, Captain Thomson was just delighted to see that one guy was in charge. He now knew which guy to call on. Captain Allen insisted that I not only make out the watch bill and put the people on it he wanted, but when we were operating with task groups, he would say, "Sam, I'm going to bed at midnight, and I want you on this bridge." And I'd stay there till dawn. I could even sit in his chair. I got an excellent feel for operations with him on board.

There was really a problem in this setup, however, because the executive officer was a reservist who could not handle the ship. And it was too bad. He resented my closeness with both skippers, and even though I think he might have tried on occasion to give me a hard time, I really didn't care about that. We were rather friendly from all outward appearances, but he made racial slurs at me a couple of times on the bridge. He even accused me of not letting him see classified messages. Generally, we didn't get much classified traffic on the AKA, but sometimes I'd route the board around, particularly on messages that were of immediate concern to the captain. I took it to the captain, or I'd let somebody else take it to him, and the exec resented that a little bit.

★★★

As for our family life, Alma joined me in California in December of 1957, and we got a set of quarters without much of a problem. A guy who had been in recruiting with me in Washington as a chief petty officer had since become a limited duty officer. He was now an ensign and was out in San Diego. I told him I was having a little problem getting on the housing list. Suddenly I was on the list, and there were quarters available in a development called Bayview Hills. If you go out of the Eighth Avenue gate of the naval base, the road comes right straight through National City, and you just keep going till you get to Bayview Hills. They had some really fine quarters up there. They were four to a unit, and we had a good-sized one around the top of the hill. Also, our social life had certainly improved. I knew a lieutenant named Gene McGuire, and he and his wife, Iris, lived up in that area. There were several other Navy families nearby. We visited each other, enjoyed each other, and had great times.

In the years before this, Alma and I had discussed having children. She hadn't gotten pregnant during the first years of our marriage, but we didn't give it a lot of thought. Now, of course, we knew there was no opportunity after the hysterectomy. We thought we'd turn to adoption, so we began working with an adoption agency in San Diego. In June of '58, the *Seminole* departed San Diego to begin a deployment to the western Pacific. When the ship arrived in Hawaii, I got a message that Alma and I had been approved for adoption. However, they would wait until I got back from the deployment. There wasn't anything we could do about it then. But it was approved, and I just sort of sat back and said, "Well, when I get back we'll contact them and see what the score is."

During that deployment, the ship was involved in two or three amphibious exercises. None was of any major import because they were just for training. We spent some of the time down at White Beach in Okinawa. Probably, I felt more black at that time then at any other primarily because Okinawa was not an integrated place. I can remember sitting in a club there with my good friend George Mau, and somebody told him either take me out of there or they were going to put me out. We saw that kind of stuff. The Marines were not our friends at that point in time.

Overall, nothing really untoward happened, but I do recall one incident. One night during that deployment we were in port, and I think it was probably Yokosuka, Japan. George was the command duty officer, and he said, "Sam, would you stand by and take my duty tonight?"

I said, "Well, I'm not going anyplace, so sure, I'll take your duty."

When I got up the next morning, the engineer officer, who was a department head and a friend of mine, said: "What are you going to do about it? What are you going to do about it?"

I said, "What the hell am I going to do about what?"

"Well, didn't you know about the officers having a party on board last night?"

"No, I didn't know about it. Let me investigate it."

Well, I went on down to breakfast. I felt I had plenty of time to find out about it. There were two or three of the young officers talking about this terrible thing that went on during the night. I still didn't know enough about it, but I began to get bits and pieces of it.

One of the officers on the ship was a young ensign who was ex-enlisted. He and two other guys congregated in the engineer officer's stateroom, which was right across the passageway from where George Mau lived. And they proceeded to have a party that included liquor and loud music. Finally, about five o'clock, they were knocked out.

Drinking on board ship was obviously a violation of regulations, but nobody had told me anything about it. The officer of the deck was normally on the starboard side, since the quarterdeck was there. The people having the party all moved over to the port side, so the quarterdeck watch couldn't hear anything.

So here it was, Sunday morning. The captain was away, the exec was away, nobody was around. I called a wardroom meeting on Sunday morning. I told them that I had been informed as to what went on, and I was very sorry I didn't hear about it the night before because I would have taken some action. I wanted to tell all of them, right there, that so far as I was concerned, the *Seminole* bar was closed, and it would be as long as I had the duty.

Then I said, "I've got to do a little bit more than that." So I wrote a letter to Captain Allen, reporting all the facts. I wanted to deliver the letter directly to the captain, but the exec came aboard so I gave it to him, and I kept a copy. I'm not sure the exec planned to give it Captain Allen, so I made sure the skipper got the copy. The captain read it, and a couple of days later he decided to have mast on the three officers, and I had to be the witness against these three.

I went up there and described what had happened. I think the captain said he was going to write it in the fitness report, or something like that, but anyway, it was a matter that was taken care of. I think in the end I gained an awful lot of respect from all those officers on board who knew that the party was wrong, including the three guys who were involved. We all remained friends despite the fact I had an unpleasant chore to perform against them. But that came off okay.

That deployment was pretty routine, and I got along well with Captain Allen, who was a very, very sharp guy. He had a good rapport with the entire wardroom, and our wives all loved his wife. In fact, he had even better rapport with the wardroom than Captain Thomson had had.

The ship returned from WestPac in early December of '58. At that time, Alma and I checked with the adoption agency. We picked up our first son, and I named him Robert Michael. Robbie was about eight months old, so he had been born just about two or three months before we were approved. We probably would have gotten him even then if the ship hadn't deployed. He was just a tremendous young lad.

Things were obviously beginning to change for us, too, because now we began to think in terms of what you do as parents. We wanted to become a part of a neighborhood. We bought a house in San Diego and had the backyard for Robbie. We joined the neighborhood church. In fact, each time we lived in San Diego we always came back to the same church. We met a lot of good people there and just had great times in that city.

The wardroom officers really adopted Robbie. He was quite a good baby. He wasn't crying all the time. Whenever I had the duty, which was one night in four, Alma and Robbie would come down. The ship's officers bought him a folding high chair. So he had his own little place to sit in the wardroom. He was just, just tremendous.

The ship went up to the shipyard in San Francisco after returning from the deployment. One evening Alma and I were having dinner down at Fisherman's Wharf when two guys came over and complimented us on how good our baby was. They were interested in talking about how good the Navy seemed and everything else. We started talking about my background, and a guy said, "Hey, how'd you like to have a job in civilian life?" I had never really thought of that. It looked like here were two guys who wanted to hire me just because I had a good baby. But I had talked about my background a little bit, and they knew I'd been a communication officer who had had a little bit of electronics, things like that.

But I turned them down; I decided I wasn't quite ready to do that yet. Besides, the Navy had other things in store for me.

CHAPTER TEN

On-the-Job Training

As I continued to add to my portfolio of experience, sometime in the spring of 1959 I began to think in terms of, "Where do I go next, and how do I get there?" I'd had some time on ships' bridges, in which I had been left up there all by myself and taken charge. So I decided it was now time to strike out for an exec's job. I was a lieutenant commander, and I really wanted to go to destroyers. I wrote a letter to the Bureau of Naval Personnel and described my desire.

I got back a very nice letter that said, basically, "Our plans are that when you finish your tour on *Seminole*, and we plan to keep you there for twenty-eight months, you will then go to the Fleet Training Group of San Diego for shore duty." I didn't like that answer, having been through several tours of amphibious training. You hear things about various commands, but I frankly didn't think they had the best officer talent there, and I felt I was pretty good. I wasn't ready to retire, and I felt I shouldn't accept the BuPers plan.

I sat down and I wrote another letter. I incorporated in it all of the reasons why it was time for me to go to a destroyer. For the first time, ever, I wrote on a piece of paper, "I have an urgent desire for command." Then I let that letter sit for a while. In the meantime, I continued to be a little disturbed by the answer I'd received out of BuPers. I told my skipper, Captain Allen, I'd like to write an official letter and asked if he would endorse it. He said, "Sure, write it."

So I wrote an official letter to BuPers, which the captain endorsed favorably and then sent on. At the same time, I sent my second personal letter to the bureau. I got back in short order two different answers from the same person. To the personal letter he said: "I told you once, and now I'm telling you again. You're going to stay aboard the *Seminole* for twenty-eight months, and then you're going to Fleet Training Group San Diego."

To my official letter he said, "When we have found a relief for you, you will be transferred to a destroyer squadron, in training for executive officer of a destroyer."

Here were two completely different responses, both from the same guy, so I gave that some thought. There were a couple of possible explanations. Number one is that a detailer has a job of putting a round peg in a round hole. Sometimes he'll put square pegs in those round holes, but he needs to fill the hole. When you write a letter to the chief of naval personnel, maybe he doesn't see them all personally, but some folks do see them. Then that detail comes up, and he briefs the chief as to what he plans to do. They may have thought, "Well, this guy's got more on the ball than that." I think that's what happened to me. In addition, I had some rather good friends along the way, influential people.

What I didn't see at all in that period was any deliberate impulse on the part of the Navy to groom black officers for higher rank. The impulse that did exist was that there were a lot of ex-reserve officers who had been in miscellaneous type jobs and were now lieutenant commanders. BuPers realized, "They're all going to get passed over for commander unless we can do something with them." So there was a program called "Training for Exec of a Destroyer," and it wasn't very widely known. It wasn't designed for black officers, but neither were blacks excluded. I spent six months doing this, and I met several guys who had either been in the program or were there at that time. I think somebody looked and said, "Hey, we ought to at least give this guy a chance," and I got it.

As it turned out, I was in the *Seminole* almost two years. I got off in the summer of 1959. My orders sent me to the Destroyer Squadron Seven staff for duty in training for executive officer. We had the normal good-bye parties, and I really had a lot of good friends in the *Seminole*. In fact, I think my wife and I were probably closer to that *Seminole* group than we'd ever been with any other group of people, other than just one or two individuals. But we certainly were a close-knit group on board that ship.

When I reported to DesRon 7, the commodore and his staff were on board the destroyer *Lofberg*.[1] I've forgotten the other ships in the division, but I ran into an old nemesis, a temporary officer. He was the chief staff officer and engineer of the squadron. My personal feelings are that some temporary officers are very, very smart guys in their specialties, but unfortunately when you take them out of those specialties, they don't know what to do. It's quite unfortunate that a guy can't just be an engineer and that's it, because he was a good engineer. But when he saw my orders he said, "My God, what are you to do?"

Referring to the program of training individuals to become destroyer executive officers, I said, "Well, obviously there's such a program set up here, and I thought you would know what to do."

"No, no, I never heard of this before. What would you like to do?"

"Well, I would imagine that someone should know something about what some of the short courses are that I could take over at TraPac [Training Command Pacific Fleet], number one. And number two, I probably ought to ride some destroyers and watch some execs in action."

He agreed that that would be a good thing to do. "Now, take the TraPac book and go up there and see what courses you want to go through, and then maybe you want to ride a destroyer. Just pick any one of the destroyers in the squadron and go out there and get a ride."

I thought about that for a while, and I said: "Well, you know, I can find the courses in the TraPac book that I think I need to get some training in. But I'm going to feel kind of like a bum going up and asking some exec if I could ride his destroyer that week."

He said: "Oh, don't worry about it; they all belong to me. They'll take care of you."

Well, that's what I did for three months. I took several of the three-, four-, five-day courses out at TraPac. Then I came back on a Friday, and if I saw somebody was getting ready to get under way, I'd go over there and say, "Sir, I'm staff DesRon 7, and I'd like to ride your ship next week if you don't mind."

This guy might say, "Well, I really don't have any room." That was true in many, many instances—they simply didn't have room. But there were

1 The commander of a destroyer squadron is normally an officer in the rank of captain. As a unit commander below flag rank, he rates the honorific title "commodore."

other guys who said: "Sure, be happy to. Go and find yourself a bunk and you've got it made."

The skipper of the *Lofberg* at that time was Commander Russell Prout, an officer who had been the first lieutenant in the *Iowa*, so I knew him. I don't think he ever knew this, but I was never assigned a bunk on board the *Lofberg* during the three months while that ship was in the yard at San Diego. If you're attached to a ship, you need to have a little space where you can put some things. And certainly you don't want to sit in the wardroom all of the time. But I never was assigned a bunk for three months, and so I was a little disturbed about that. Now I must admit, though, it was in the yard, which meant I could go home every night. So that arrangement was fine. I got invited to the social affairs, etc.

Generally, when you have command of a ship and you get so-called guests or a training officer, if he's a lieutenant commander, you give him quarters appropriate to a lieutenant. During my time on board various destroyers I slept in the bunkroom there in the top bunk, in the first compartment down in the bowels of the ship sometimes. I slept in anybody's room; it didn't matter. I watched an awful lot of execs in action and tried to learn from them, see what they were doing.

Most of the people were willing to help, but the thing that bothered me more than anything else was that there wasn't any glad hand when I came aboard. I'd hear, "Yeah, there's a spare bunk back there in the junior officers' bunk room," and certainly, "Pay your mess bill before you leave." But I liked most of them, and I got along fairly well with the skippers. I think they knew what I was trying to do. The best way I can describe what happened when I went up to a ship's bridge was that I was not in the way.

Then one day I was called up to the commodore's room, and he said, "How are you getting along?"

"I'm fine. I'm going to the short courses, I'm riding what destroyers I can."

"Well, you know, we're getting ready to deploy, and I don't have room to take an additional officer. What I plan to do is to send in a letter to BuPers saying you are qualified for exec of a destroyer, and I think you are. And probably they'll find a destroyer for you."

"Yes, sir."

He sent off his letter, and he transferred me to the tender to await orders from BuPers. But before I could report to the tender, I got orders from BuPers that said, "Go to DesRon 5," which I did. The commodore of that squadron happened to be a guy that I had met in the amphibious forces, Captain Terrell Nisewaner. We had briefly known each other, and I guess I'd seen him a second time in one of the short courses in electronic warfare, or something like that. So we had touched base and talked with each other a little bit previously. When I got to his flagship, the *Somers*, he was a little surprised to see me. He said, "What have you been doing?" I gave him a rundown and told him that BuPers obviously didn't have a job for me yet, so this was what I was to do in the meantime.

He said: "Well, the *Somers* will be going to sea soon, so you can learn a little bit here. I'm going to give you the CruDesPac [Cruiser-Destroyer Force Pacific Fleet] inspection lists, pre-deployment inspections. I want you to take this book, and I want you to go down and inspect every department in this ship. In the meantime, I'm going to transfer you to the ship to work with the executive officer, and you can catch on from there."

The skipper of the *Somers*, Commander Ed Cummings, was a really great guy so far as I was concerned. He did not make admiral, but he was a tremendous individual. Had a good wardroom. He gave me a room and bunk, and my new roommate was Larry Layman, who later became an admiral. The experience in that ship was a good one. It was not the easiest thing in the world to be a one-man inspection team, particularly since the department heads didn't really have a lot of time. So usually I'd get assigned some guy who was fairly junior in the department, but at the same time I got it done. I stayed there with him for about a month and a half, when one day Commodore Nisewaner called me up and said: "Sam, I really don't understand this, because I thought you'd have orders by now. I'm leaving, and I'm going back to Washington, but I'd like to finish up all my unfinished business. What I'm going to do is write a letter to BuPers, tell them you're qualified for exec of a destroyer, and I imagine they'll find you a destroyer."

So he left, and I was still sitting there. The next commodore was a captain by the name of David Nash, and I knew Nash very well. He was a tremendous sailor. He was happy with what I was doing, and he said: "That's the best way to learn destroyers. You know, seeing them in action, etc." I stood regular officer of the deck watches on the *Somers*. There weren't very many lieutenant commanders in that day and age standing OOD watches. But that was all right; that's how you learn things. This was beyond independent steaming. I was getting some fleet experience and loving it all the way. The biggest thing was that I had a bunk, and I had a seat in the wardroom. I had good people to work with, and I enjoyed it.

The *Somers* was a brand-new ship. Commander Cummings was the first skipper, and he was a tremendous help to me. His exec let me do some navigating coming into port. Larry Layman was the operations officer, and I worked with him. I'd had a background in operations in my previous ships, so there were no big things I had to learn there. Weapons and engineering were the areas in which I needed much more training, but I really didn't have sense enough to ask very intelligent questions when I got there. I could follow the inspection form, and I got a lot of good answers. I watched the guys in action and everything else. Well, as the end of the year approached, Commodore Nash said, "Sam, I am going back to BuPers over the Christmas holidays on a little leave, and I will have you a job when I come back."

I said: "Yes, sir. Thank you. I'll be happy, because I've done this for four and a half months now." Well, Commodore Nash came back just before New Year's, and I think he avoided me a little bit, but in any event when I did get to see him he said: "Sam, I just have not been able to do anything for you. As you know, we're going to deploy about the first of February. What I want you to do is to take the TraPac catalog, and go through there and find yourself enough five-day, two-week courses to stay here in San Diego for seven months, because we don't have a room for you."

That was a letdown, but I just said, "Yes, sir."

Starting about New Year's Day, I began to look through the TraPac schedule, and I had to have it all done by February the first. Sometime in January, when I had my list partially done, dispatch orders came in for me to go as exec of the *Theodore E. Chandler*. I was just flabbergasted, but happy as a lark.

CHAPTER ELEVEN

USS *Theodore E. Chandler*

My life changed in January of 1960 when I received orders to destroyer duty. They were "proceed immediately" orders, which meant I had to get to the *Theodore E. Chandler* within twenty-four hours. Fortunately, my new ship was right down the pier in San Diego. Alma drove me to work that first day, and she and I said a little prayer on the pier. Unlike the previous destroyers in which I had served, I would not be on board this one as a visiting trainee. Now I was to be the full-fledged executive officer. On the morning when I reported, it appeared to me the watch standing was a little loose. The people on duty were expecting something, but I don't think I was it. I couldn't find the officer of the deck, but the quarterdeck messenger took me up to the exec's stateroom. I said, "Sir, I have a set of orders, and I guess I'm your relief."

He said, "You know, I expected a relief, but I didn't know you were going to get here this quick."

I said, "Well, here are my orders."

He said, "Come on, I'll take you up and introduce you to the captain." We went up, and the skipper was Commander Galen C. Brown. He was one of the nicest people I have ever met in this man's Navy. He was not surprised to see me. The exec said, "Captain, let me introduce you to my relief." We shook hands.

Then, honest to God, the exec said, "By the way, Captain, you remember I wanted to go on thirty days' leave? Do you have any objection if I leave today?"

The captain said, "No," and the exec took off. So there was no turnover period in which to learn the ropes from my predecessor.

I have really tried for the life of me to figure out what had taken place in that ship, and I think I've come to some conclusions. The biggest thing was that the ship had gone through a yard overhaul during the fall and part of the winter. They had a FRAM inspection—that was the fleet rehabilitation and modernization program—and they busted it miserably. They'd had their overhaul, and then they came down to San Diego to go through refresher training. They also had material and administrative inspections, and they busted those. The next thing that was hell on them was that they busted a pre-deployment inspection by CruDesPac.

Captain Brown had arrived about mid-December 1959, so there wasn't anything you could blame him for. Each of the department heads had shifted, so you really couldn't blame the department heads. The exec had been the guy who had been through it all. I do know that Brown's predecessor, as a result of CruDesPac's inspection, got a letter in his service record, and it took him, as I recall, several selections to make captain. He finally made it, but he bore the brunt of this. Essentially, I had finally gotten orders to be a destroyer executive officer because the *Theodore E. Chandler* really needed a change. When I went aboard, I thought there was no way to go but up, and Captain Brown admitted it.

I don't think my predecessor was relieved for cause—not officially—but I think he got blamed for some of the conditions of the *Chandler*, and someone had decided, "Hey, that's the guy." That's why there was a job available, and that's why I had no advance notice. As I began my new role, the first thing I did on my second morning aboard was to have quarters for muster. I'd been used to executive officers who gathered the department heads together and said, "Report." So that's what I did. I was somewhat shocked, because a couple of them said, "What the hell's he talking about?"

I said: "Normally, you report 'all present and accounted for,' or so many men absent. And you tell me anything you think I need to know at this point in time."

The guy said, "Well, we don't normally do that."

I said: "Okay, you guys go back down there, and let's muster these people at quarters, and let's read them the plan of the day. Then you'll come back in, and we'll do this again."

We did, and we started our routine there. My predecessor might have lost the bubble during the yard period. I don't know what had happened, but they weren't quite the destroyer Navy I was used to from my on-the-job training. The other thing about the ship, so far as I was concerned, was that it was filthy, and Captain Brown wouldn't admit that. It took some detailed cleaning and scrubbing—what I called the "toothbrush brigade," because that's how we cleaned up that ship, getting into corners and crevices and everything else.

★ ★ ★

Captain Brown was a competent naval officer, but he wasn't the greatest ship handler in the world. Fortunately, he had three or four good junior officers who were fairly competent ship handlers, and they did a lot of it. I got to conn the ship, which was the first time since the *Seminole* and certainly the first time I handled a destroyer. I got a lot of experience from it. In fact, it profited all of us. Fortunately, Captain Brown and I hit it off famously. He was just a tremendous guy. He knew how to handle people. He had a lot of respect for me; I had a lot of respect for him.

Operating with the fleet at sea was a real learning experience for me because destroyers, I discovered, were a bit different from other ships. They went faster, and things happened much more quickly. You had to be able to see a situation forming and take action in time. With an AKA such as the *Seminole*, you generally had plenty of time to think it through, but here you had to have the ability to anticipate situations and decide quickly how to react. But it was a most interesting facet, and I discovered I really enjoyed running at top speed.

One task for the *Theodore E. Chandler* was plane guarding with carriers. That is, we would steam astern of a carrier so we could be ready to make a rescue if a pilot ejected and wound up in the water. I didn't really enjoy steaming close to a flattop, but I certainly got used to it. There was one incident that frightened me, and this was a time when we were with a carrier I remember as being the *Ranger*. We were sitting at a range of about a thousand yards, about twenty degrees off of its port quarter. The carrier may have sent out a signal by infrared light for a left turn, but we didn't get it. Infrared was known as "Nancy," and the procedure was that you got an announcement by voice radio on the bridge that said, "Nancy Hanks." When you got that word, then you had your signalman alerted to look at the other ship's signal bridge and expect a message to come to you.

Unfortunately, the carrier executed the turn without sending the signal, so far as I could tell. Certainly we weren't alerted to receive it. We were going at about twenty-five knots when that turn was executed, and it was almost a 180-degree turn. The carrier slowed down in the turn, and we came very close to hitting it. You can imagine the turmoil on our bridge as we tried to maneuver to avoid the carrier when it started turning in front of us. I can remember ducking as we got in close, because it looked like the fantail of the *Ranger* was going to take off our mast. Fortunately, our skipper was very alert and ordered right full rudder to take us the other way. I thought Captain Brown really handled it beautifully, and we managed to avoid a collision. A turn like that is the way some airdales run those things—the hell with the little guy behind you. But the destroyer is far more maneuverable, so it's the destroyer's job to stay out of the way, and we did.

Whenever we were operating with a carrier—in a storm or in any kind of intense operations—the skipper was generally on the bridge. I would go up to the bridge for most evolutions, and certainly I'd be up on the bridge when the captain felt it was a ticklish situation. We had a group of junior officers who were very good, very competent, but he felt that I, as a lieutenant commander, had more experience. Not in destroyer operations but in just plain old operations, and he valued my judgment. I was on the bridge just about all the time when he was there, and sometimes I took over when he needed some rest.

As exec, I was an administrator also, so I spent an awful lot of time in the ship's office or writing papers or going through inspecting the ship: making sure the bunks were made and people were up, the meals were served and on time, and those kinds of functions. I received the eight o'clock reports at night from the department heads and constantly kept the skipper aware of what was going on around the ship. I think one of the big problems with some ships is just simply morale. You've got to have your ears open to make sure things are going well. If you get any kind of word of dissatisfaction, you assess it, and if it's important enough, you tell the captain. "Hey, so-and-so is going on. Here's what I think we ought to do." Never keep the captain in the dark, and never let the poor guy get surprised.

It was often a judgment call. You want to keep the captain informed, but you also don't want to burden him with every detail. So you've got to sort out the items you hear about as to what is transpiring in the ship. And if you think the captain needs to know, then he ought to know. But you've also got to assess it and know which you can handle yourself. I think I was able to do that.

Actually, I had gotten a considerable amount of XO-type experience in the *Seminole*. I think it really stood me in good stead when I got to the *Theodore E. Chandler*. I knew how to handle men, and I knew the administrative details of the ship. My problem at that point was operating, and that's another reason I spent a lot more time on the bridge than some execs might have. But I had to be up there to see how things operated, see these fast maneuvers with antisubmarine warfare, as well as plane guarding and shore bombardment. I was up there watching and trying to learn.

The big test of operating ability was when we went on a deployment to the Seventh Fleet. The cruise, which began on March 5, 1960, included some time on the Formosa Patrol, and we went down to Okinawa, where we did some gunnery practice with the 5-inch guns. All my previous shipboard duty had been in the operations department. Now, day by day, I was picking up knowledge about the weapons and engineering departments. I got a lot of time going down to look at the engineering spaces.

My battle station was in the combat information center, so I got a chance to watch CIC in operation and to work with the radarmen. I knew how to handle telephone circuits or communication circuits and the maneuvering board and dead reckoning tracer. I picked up that kind of experience, knowing exactly what CIC had to do during various situations. We did some minor air controlling and other things to make me more proficient in that field. Along the way I had a glitch or two, but the *Theodore E. Chandler* was the ship that did it for me in terms of qualifying in destroyers.

In any event, during that deployment we went to Hong Kong as one of our liberty ports, and we spent a lot of time in Yokosuka, Japan. We had a unique happenstance when we left Yokosuka one time with an aircraft carrier. The carrier was off launching aircraft, and we were doing some independent steaming, trying to stay within visual range of it. When the carrier finished launching aircraft, the watch officer put the signal out for us to get ahead of it as part of a bent-line screen for protection against submarines. We started going over at about fifteen knots, because we didn't have very far to go. The *Henderson*, which was in our division, was running at about twenty-five, the *Duncan* was doing maybe ten, and somebody else doing about twenty.

Suddenly we took a wave, and the forward 5-inch gun mount caved into the chief petty officers' quarters. As the inhabitants came scrambling out, I saw some chiefs I hadn't seen in a week or so. They were all over the place. The captain stayed on the bridge, and I went up forward to supervise and make sure the damage control people got things squared away. Captain Brown seemed to be very happy with the way I handled my part. We were directed to go into Yokosuka for repairs, and we stayed about a month. Very shortly after that, the deployment was over. At the end of August, we arrived back in San Diego, where we began a normal upkeep and a rest and recreation period.

★★★

The *Theodore E. Chandler*, which was commissioned in 1946, was not a young ship. Previous to my coming aboard, the ship had had a FRAM InSurv inspection to determine whether or not it would be worthy of updating. Now, as I remember it, the destroyer program had two phases: FRAM I and FRAM II. A FRAM I destroyer went to a shipyard for a year and was completely rebuilt from just about the bridge to back aft. That modernization was designed to last eight years. The FRAM II ships went for a less comprehensive six-month conversion, and the modernization should last for five years.

As a ship of the *Gearing* class, the *Theodore E. Chandler* had been certified for a FRAM I conversion. Under a normal set of circumstances, the FRAM I ship went into the shipyard, and all of the officers except for the exec, the four department heads, and maybe one or two junior officers were transferred. The crew was cut down to about 125 sailors. In the case of the FRAM II, all of the people remained on board, with the CO handling the shipyard period.

During the time we had been approaching the end of the deployment, we began to wonder how this would work for our ship. I was probably more concerned about it than most people because I felt there was no way I would stay on board as the additional-duty CO. As exec, I felt someone would come on and relieve me, and I began to wonder where I would go next. I had that feeling primarily because, so far as I could tell from naval history, no black had served as a commanding officer of a U.S. Navy ship in the twentieth century.

After we got home, the orders began to hit for our people. The crew was being reduced in preparation for the FRAM overhaul. I contacted BuPers to see about my own situation. The detailer was an officer I had served with in the *Toledo*. I wrote him a letter that said I had been in the destroyer force for about seven or eight months. The commanding officers examination and qualification required, as I recall, eighteen to twenty-four months in the destroyer force with about twelve months as a department head or as exec. In my letter, I pointed out that I had been unable to do that, and so I would like to stay on the *Theodore E. Chandler* some additional time. That would enable me to meet the minimum qualifications and then take the command exam, or I could be transferred to another destroyer.

I got a nice letter from the bureau, which said, in essence, "We do not intend to move you." When I read that, I was overjoyed because I knew then that as soon as we got to the shipyard, I would relieve Captain Brown and have the responsibility for taking the ship through the shipyard. Well, we did that. The ship went into the Hunters Point Naval Shipyard up in San Francisco on February 15, 1961. That same day we had a very small relieving ceremony designed primarily to say good-bye to Captain Brown. It was not an official, formal change of command. We had the crew muster inside a machine shop or something. It was a big, spacious room, and we sort of passed the baton at that ceremony.

My taking command was a big milestone for a black officer, and I was delighted, despite the fact that I knew I was commanding officer of the ship now in commission in reserve. It wasn't going to go anyplace, but I've always been very, very pleased I got the opportunity to do that, for a couple of reasons. The first reason was that it gave me a chance to really, really learn a ship, because I watched the modernization from the moment the first shipyard worker came on, with all of the cutting and everything else, until it was completely rebuilt. That took about ten months.

Secondly, I got along really well with the shipyard people. I had very good rapport with Rear Admiral Charles Curtze, the commander of the naval shipyard. He became a personal friend of mine, and I really admired him. On a couple of occasions, at briefings, he pointed out things I was doing that he thought were productive. For example, I knew that no one liked to work in a dirty space. And then you suddenly wonder whose responsibility is it to clean up where the shipyard workers had worked. Well, the obvious answer was that every guy ought to clean up what he dirties. But we were paying that shipyard worker an awful lot of money just to repair and install items, and I didn't think we could afford to spend money to have this guy doing cleanup work a couple of sailors could do. So I established cleaning crews, which meant I got the shipyard guy for his full eight hours that day, and late that afternoon and evening I had a group of sailors who had nothing to do as a night job clean up that ship. And that just worked beautifully because those people were very pleased to come there. We weren't moving their tools or disturbing their work.

The other thing was that I spent an awful lot of time around there just looking at the ship, trying to make sure the work was being done right. I did not try to correct a shipyard worker, but if I saw something I didn't think was going along quite as it should be going, I would speak to the supervisor or somebody else in terms he would understand, and he would know I was not trying to interfere. If it was wrong, the supervisor would correct the guy and make him do it right. Or he'd explain to me why the workman was doing it that way. We also decided we would have a weekend picnic, to which we invited the shipyard workers. They came in droves, and when we saw them on Monday morning they were all at work with big smiles. In fact, Admiral Curtze came to our party. So things went well during our shipyard period.

Fortunately, during this period when I was acting CO I was able to make an arrangement that took some of the normal XO administrative load off me. I gave some of those chores to Lieutenant Mike Skubinna, the operations officer, who was a real sweetheart of a guy. For example, he took over the plan of the day and did it religiously. That change made sense because in a shipyard the operations officer isn't doing much other than getting the spaces done. He doesn't have the same responsibilities he would have at sea. I sort of prioritized what had to be done between my two jobs as CO and XO. I did some and gave others to someone else.

Mike's work enabled me to focus on the progress of the modernization work. We had a list of what jobs were being done and the completion dates for them. We made a chart of milestones on the various jobs, and we followed those very carefully. I would continually sit around and discuss how things were going with the department heads and about three other officers we had. Now, I'm convinced you don't run ships by committee. A ship is the responsibility of the commanding officer, but certainly we had wardroom meetings to talk in terms of jobs, and constantly they were apprising me of problems as they had them and letting me know how well work was going.

In the course of my moving throughout the ship one day, I happened to be going around right after we got our new signal bridge. I observed that the signal house was on backwards. The open space was to the sea side rather than inboard. The welder may have got it, say, Friday afternoon at about two o'clock. He probably just tack-welded it down so it would stay there and wouldn't blow off. Then it could be permanently welded later. But I was certainly chagrined when I went up there and saw it. A lot of little things like that happened, but we got them taken care of.

Morale was a continual concern, especially in the shipyard environment when you don't have the satisfaction you get from operating. A couple of factors helped. First of all, everybody had a certain amount of pride in the job he was doing on board the ship. Secondly, he knew that more than likely what was being done in the shipyard was something he was going to have to live with when the ship started operating. So he would try to make sure his spaces were taken care of and his work was done as well as it could be done. We also had softball teams and a number of other recreational opportunities.

The biggest thing that helped us was the BuPers policy of changing our home port, which meant most of the married guys took their families up to San Francisco, where they lived in Quonset huts. When you're with your family, a Quonset hut isn't the worst thing. So that facet of it was handled. We had a leave program. We also had a training program where we sent people off to San Diego every once in a while to various schools. I think morale was fairly good during that period. Part of it might have been that I do have a way with people; I enjoy working with people, and I think people enjoy working with me. So it was a little of me and certainly a lot of other things.

★★★

During the course of this time in the shipyard, I became concerned about my projected rotation date and when I might be leaving. I had a very dear friend who was in another ship in my division. He was in the same situation I was, as an additional duty commanding officer during a yard period. His ship was up at Mare Island Naval Shipyard in Vallejo, California, and he got pulled off to go to Brazil. I began to worry that something similar would happen to me. Would I be able to stay with the *Theodore E. Chandler* when it came out of the yard so I could then get my time in as well as take the command qualification exam?

At this time, I wrote another letter to the Bureau of Personnel. I pointed out that I had sufficient time on the ship, but as a result of being in the shipyard, I had not been able to meet the other qualifications for command, and I would just love to stay there to do that. I got another nice letter, and it basically said, "Your tour date has been extended." That was fine, and I happily went about my job.

That fall, perhaps around September, BuPers notified me that the destroyer-minecraft placement officer was coming out, and he wanted to talk in terms of the young officers the *Chandler* would be getting to build up the crew. The ship would be coming out of the yard around the beginning of 1962, and BuPers, in its normal way of thinking ahead, was going to tell me who would be coming on in the next four or five months.

The ship was in fairly good shape. It was fast approaching the date we would go through a recommissioning ceremony and the new commanding officer would come. Mike Skubinna, the ops officer, had been on there almost two years, and I expected that he would leave. I didn't want him to go through refresher training and the new guy take over without proper orientation and training. That was one of the concerns I had in mind to discuss with the officer from BuPers. But when he got there, he said: "Well, we really don't want to talk about those officers first. Let's talk about you."

I said, "Okay, where are you going to send me, sir?"

"You're going to command of—"

Then he started flipping through a few notes, and he said, "*Falgout*, DER out in Pearl Harbor."[1] And I must say that I was so happy I'm not sure I heard anything else he said after that, because I was really, really overjoyed. I was completely taken by surprise, and I certainly felt my efforts had all paid off. Here I was, going to my own command—one that would be operating.

What really surprised me was that this came about without my having been through the exam for prospective commanding officer. At that point in time, the practice of giving the exams had not been around long enough for everybody to go through these wickets. If I had stayed there and got back

1 A DER was a World War II–vintage destroyer escort that had been updated with enhanced radar capability.

into the operating for about three months, I don't think I could have been up to snuff to taking the exam. A new commanding officer would have to observe me a little bit, and then he'd have to recommend me. It would have taken him, certainly, through refresher training. Then there would have been a board of COs who would have given me this exam.

Before that time the selection of destroyer-type commanding officers was a matter that was handled in BuPers. Detailers and assignment officers looked at Joe Blow, who'd had certain types of duty, and not necessarily in the destroyer force, because I can remember destroyer skippers who'd never been on them before. But anyway, that was a wicket he had to have in his service jacket to make captain.[2] In this case, I assume someone in the bureau made the decision that my jacket was hot enough that probably I could handle a destroyer escort command, and certainly they'd give me the chance. That's the only explanation I can think of.

One other thing happened a little bit before the detailer came, and to some degree I felt quite pleased when I heard it. I'm not sure whether it was *Navy Times* or whether it was the orders to officers that you only got in messages, but a list came out, and it showed a new commanding officer coming to the *Theodore E. Chandler.* I happened to be up at a shipyard commander's meeting that morning, and Admiral Curtze said, "Sam, I just saw where there's a relief coming for you."

I said: "Yes, sir, that's fairly normal. The commanding officer of a destroyer is a commander, and I'm lieutenant commander at least a year or so away, and so I expected that."

He said: "Well, I do not think that's fair. Here you've been, working on this ship, and you've done a great job. I am going to call the chief of naval personnel." Admiral Curtze called the chief of naval personnel and told him about me. I guess that was the first time I had an inkling I might be going to command, because Admiral Curtze told me that in his talk with the chief of naval personnel he learned that some good things would happen to me.

The new skipper for the *Theodore E. Chandler* was Commander Joe Sperandio. He happened to be in the Hunters Point Naval Shipyard at that time.

---

2 In that era, it was almost essential for a surface warfare officer to be a destroyer skipper in the rank of commander in order to be considered for promotion to captain. The "jacket" referred to here is one's record of service and fitness reports submitted by his seniors. A "hot jacket" is one with many positive evaluations and recommendations.

He was exec of a destroyer that was going through about a four-month yard overhaul. I got a chance to meet with him, and we talked about how we wanted things to go. I had not really known him very well, although we had met primarily because the CO of his ship had been navigator of the *Toledo*. In my calling on the skipper there, I had met Joe, and, we saw each other at times while walking through the yard. When his skipper couldn't go to the shipyard commander's meetings, Joe would be there, and so we would talk in terms of when he'd be available to relieve and what our plans were.

He came over, and on October 21, 1961, we did have a full-blown change of command, with all the sailors in dress blues. I did my little talk, he did his little talk, and he took over as commanding officer. The biggest thing I can remember him saying to me was: "Sam, I've just heard such good things about *Theodore E. Chandler*, and I know you're doing the job I would want you to do on here. I'm the CO, and you're the exec. Just keep doing what you have been and keep me informed." So we went on that basis.

Now, it got to be a little bit difficult and a little embarrassing for both of us once he took over. For the preceding nine months, the young sailors on there had been saying, "Captain, should I do this? Captain, should I do that?" We were standing on the bridge about the time we were beginning to get under way, and a kid came up and said, "Captain, can I do this?"

I said: "Listen, son, do me a favor. There's the captain over there. Captain Sperandio is his name." Joe Sperandio took it all in good stead. He and I just became great friends with one single idea in mind—to do the best we could to get the *Theodore E. Chandler* ready to sail.

I went on one set of sea trials with the ship, and then I was relieved as exec and left the ship. My family had remained in San Diego during this whole time, and I had been going home about once a month while I was up there in the shipyard. So I went down to San Diego, and I packed. We decided we would take a trip across to Virginia to visit Alma's folks as well as mine, since we were going to Pearl, which was much farther away. We felt we would be over there eighteen months to two years and wouldn't get a chance to see them.

We had one of the most hectic drives across country we've ever had, and it was hectic in several respects. By this point in time I was beginning to expect more from civilian life than in the past. In my previous transits across country, I'd run into difficulties in trying to find places to eat and to stay overnight. Things had changed a little bit by this time because of the civil rights movement and the efforts by the Kennedy administration to see that things did change.

What we discovered was that even though things changed on paper, they didn't change readily in real life. For example, in Albuquerque, New Mexico, in trying to find a hotel room, we went to about three places, and whereas most of them would offer us two rooms, they wouldn't offer us two rooms together, which meant I'd be in one section of the motel with one kid, and Alma in another section of the motel with the other kid.[3] Something always seemed like a stumbling block, but somehow we managed it. I've forgotten what we finally did, but we did find whatever accommodations we needed.

When you come across the southern route, you pass through some real southern states. You come through Texas, you come through Oklahoma, you come through Arkansas, you come through Tennessee. I think we were in Arkansas when we stopped at one of the Tastee-Freez places. One of the kids wanted some ice cream, and I said, "Okay, I'll pull up here and get you some ice cream." When I walked into the place and asked for four ice cream cones, I was told to go to the back. They wouldn't serve me. I stood there for a minute, and then I just said, "The hell with it," and walked on out. I got in the car, started driving off. But the problem was trying to explain to the two kids there why they couldn't get ice cream. That sort of thing had happened to me before, but that probably was the first time they had ever had it happen to them.[4]

As I remember, Robbie and David were near four and two years old at the time. Kids that old are protected, number one, by their innocence and number two, they were fairly sheltered by being in the Navy environment. Certainly both kids had been in wardrooms where they ate with everybody, and they saw everybody, they walked over ships, and they enjoyed talking to people as much as four- and two-year-old kids can talk. Dad took care of everything. So the fact that Dad couldn't buy ice cream came as a shock to some degree.

---

3 By this time the Gravelys had a second son, David, who was born in June 1960 and adopted in November of that year.

4 Mrs. Gravely's recollections of this incident are contained in her afterword at the end of the book.

When we went through Tennessee, I am thoroughly convinced that the night we stayed in Memphis it was in the same hotel where Martin Luther King was shot a few years later. What I particularly remember is that we were traveling in the winter, with snow and ice on the street, and there was no heat. The only way we managed to stay comfortable was to get under about four blankets with four of us in the same bed. I was hugging one child, and Alma was hugging the other child as we tried to keep all of us warm. Eventually, we managed to finish the rest of the trip, but it was a reminder that racial progress still had a long way to go.

CHAPTER TWELVE

USS *Falgout*

Our new adventure began in January of 1962, when we drove all the way back across country. We caught a Navy transport and sailed to Pearl. Alma gets seasick, unfortunately, and we used up a lot of Dramamine on that voyage. The kids enjoyed the cruise. When we arrived at Pearl, the escort division commodore and a couple members of the staff met us and really took us in tow. They took us to a little place in the Waikiki Beach area of Honolulu, and we stayed there for several weeks until we got quarters. They made sure that everything we could possibly have wanted was taken care of. It was just a really great meeting. Captain John Newland was the commodore. He was another one of these truly great sailors. I had the feeling he didn't give a damn about my race. His view was that if BuPers had picked me to be the CO of the *Falgout*, then I was going to be able to hack it.

When I arrived, the *Falgout* was out on patrol. While I was waiting for the ship, I visited with Captain Newland two or three times. One of the things I discussed with him was the ship's mission. It was part of a group of World War II destroyer escorts that had been equipped with additional radar so they could serve as picket ships. Thus a DE became a DER. During the Cold War, they operated on the Distant Early Warning (DEW) Line that was designed to give advance notice if Soviet bombers were approaching the United States. A DER's typical station at the time was in the North Pacific. Each DER that went up there acted as sort of a lightship out there, a beacon that stayed within a twenty-five-mile circle of a spot in the ocean.

The commodore wanted to know if I felt I had any problems in approaching my first command. I told him I probably would not be his most outstanding ship handler because I had not had much close-in ship-handling work. As conning officer, I had guided the *Chandler* up against a pier two or three times, but I hadn't worked it to the point of being satisfied and confident.

He said: "Well, Sam, why don't you just take the *Falgout* as soon as it comes in? There's a mooring buoy out here in the middle of this harbor. Pearl Harbor is round and thin. Nobody's going to be watching. Just go out there and play with that thing as long as you want to." He did everything to make sure I would feel the confidence I really needed to command it.

One other thing happened while I was up at the commodore's office. The commodore had asked if there was anything else he could do to help me.

I said: "Well, Commodore, I hate to tell you this, but I was in San Francisco, where there were several DERs, and I tried my best to get aboard just to see one but never could. Is there some way I can see one?"

Another DER commanding officer was sitting in the office at that time: Lieutenant Commander Gordon Nagler, who later became a three-star admiral. He was then skipper of the *Forrester*, which was one of the finest ships in the division. Gordon said: "Hell yes, there's some way you can see one. I got one down here. You can come on down and have lunch with me. I'll introduce you to the wardroom and take you around the ship." Gordon did that for me, and I didn't expect that degree of kindness. Gordon Nagler and I are still tremendous friends today.[1]

★★★

The day the *Falgout* finally came into port, I was standing on the pier waiting for it. My predecessor brought the ship in and made a very fine landing. But, as I kept looking at the ship, there was something strange about it. Finally it hit me that the 3-inch gun mount up on the forecastle was cocked off to the side. I soon found out that this was the result of rough weather the ship had encountered on its patrol station. The ship had taken a beating, and this mount had been pushed over. My first chore as skipper would thus be to take the *Falgout* into the Pearl Harbor Naval Shipyard.

We had normal inspections and discussions before the change of command. On January 31, 1962, I relieved the skipper of the *Falgout*. I think

1 Vice Admiral Nagler died on July 11, 1998.

The future admiral's parents were Mary and Samuel L. Sr. They had five children, including Samuel L. Jr. (Courtesy of Alma Gravely)

Sam Jr., who was born June 4, 1922, was about six months old when this picture was taken. (Photo courtesy of Alma Gravely)

Gravely's first sea duty was in the submarine chaser *PC-1264*, which was virtually identical to sister ship *PC-1246*, shown here. (U.S. Naval Institute Photo Archive)

Alma Clark and Sam Gravely were married at her parents' home in Roanoke, Virginia, on February 12, 1946. (Courtesy of Alma Gravely)

The battleship *Iowa* is shown a few days before her recommissioning from mothballs in August 1951. Gravely reported on board soon afterward. (U.S. Naval Institute Photo Archive)

The heavy cruiser *Toledo* deployed frequently to the western Pacific during the 1950s. (U.S. Naval Institute Photo Archive)

Sam and Alma in the 1950s. (Courtesy of Alma Gravely)

The attack cargo ship *Seminole* was equipped with a large number of landing craft to carry supplies and equipment ashore during amphibious operations. (U.S. Naval Institute Photo Archive)

Alma poses in front of a Christmas tree with son Robert, whom the Gravelys adopted in 1958. (Courtesy of Alma Gravely)

Gravely's introduction to destroyer service came as executive officer and acting commanding officer of the *Theodore E. Chandler* in the early 1960s. The ship is shown here following the FRAM updates installed when Gravely was acting skipper. (U.S. Naval Institute Photo Archive)

The radar picket destroyer escort *Falgout*, home-ported in Pearl Harbor, Hawaii, was Gravely's first operating command. (U.S. Naval Institute Photo Archive)

Gravely commanded the destroyer *Taussig* during two deployments to the western Pacific. (U.S. Naval Institute Photo Archive)

An enthusiastic Alma joins her husband on the bridge of the *Jouett*. (Courtesy of Alma Gravely)

The guided missile frigate *Jouett* was redesignated a cruiser a few years after Captain Gravely's command tenure in 1970-71. (U.S. Naval Institute Photo Archive)

Captain Gravely and his phone talker on the starboard wing of the *Jouett*'s bridge. Gravely truly enjoyed being on the bridges of warships. (U.S. Naval Institute Photo Archive)

Shortly before being frocked as a rear admiral, Captain Gravely speaks to the audience on June 2, 1971, in turning over command of the *Jouett* to his successor. (U.S. Naval Institute Photo Archive)

Vice Admiral Ray Peet, Commander First Fleet, offers congratulations as Alma Gravely snaps on a shoulder board during the frocking ceremony on June 2, 1971. At right are daughter Tracey and son David. (U.S. Naval Institute Photo Archive)

The family, from left: Alma, Robert, Tracey, Sam, and David. (Courtesy of Alma Gravely)

As Commander Cruiser-Destroyer Group Two, Gravely often traveled by helicopter to visit his ships. (Courtesy of Alma Gravely)

During a break from operations by his flagship, Gravely goes fishing and shows off his catch. (Courtesy of Alma Gravely)

Vice Admiral Stansfield Turner, Commander Second Fleet, and Rear Admiral Gravely, ComCruDesGru 2, meet on the deck of an aircraft carrier. (Courtesy of Alma Gravely)

As commandant of the Eleventh Naval District, Gravely, shown saluting, often had ceremonial duties. He is shown here reviewing a parade at the naval training center in San Diego. (Courtesy of Alma Gravely)

On September 10, 1976, Vice Admiral Gravely became the first African-American fleet commander in the history of the U.S. Navy. His predecessor as Commander Third Fleet, Vice Admiral Robert P. Coogan, is at right. (U.S. Naval Institute Photo Archive)

Samuel L. Gravely Sr. and Jr. pose together in Richmond in the late 1960s. The senior Gravely lived long enough to know that his son had become an admiral in 1971. (Courtesy of Alma Gravely)

This family portrait was taken in the 1995, several years after David Gravely's marriage in 1987. Flanking David are his wife Beverly at left and sister Tracey at right. (Courtesy of Alma Gravely)

Sam and Alma Gravely during retirement, photographed around 2000 or 2001. (Courtesy of Alma Gravely)

Children and their relatives tour the school in Prince William County, Virginia, at the time of its opening. At upper right is the cartoon seadog that honors Gravely's naval experience. (Courtesy of Alma Gravely)

Festooned with bunting, the *Gravely* sits pier side at the Northrop Grumman shipyard in Pascagoula, Mississippi, prior to christening in May 2009. (Northrop Grumman Shipbuilding)

As prospective skipper Douglas Kunzman and Northrop Grumman shipbuilding president Mike Petters watch, Alma Gravely christens the destroyer named for her husband. (Northrop Grumman Shipbuilding)

The *Gravely* slices through the Gulf of Mexico during sea trials in late June 2010. (Northrop Grumman Shipbuilding)

every newspaper reporter on the island of Oahu was there. It went on the international wires, and I have copies of stories that were written in Spanish, as well as a couple of other languages, about my taking over command. I guess it's been stated that this was the first time a black had command of a U.S. Navy ship since Robert Smalls captured a small frigate out of the Charleston Harbor and turned it over to the Union forces during the Civil War. There was quite a bit of hoopla about my taking command. All kinds of press people wanted to come aboard and do interviews.

It was the first time I'd really had so much attention focused on me, although there'd been a couple of minor things. I can remember one when I was selected to go to the V-12 program. There were two or three minor stories when I graduated from midshipman school, because I was one of the first to do that. And there may have been a couple of other instances when there was some press attention, but I was not prepared for what happened in this case, nor did I welcome it. I was firmly convinced this wasn't what the Navy sent me there for.

Previously, I had received a request from a national black newspaper to interview me and take pictures. I'd already turned them down because they wanted to do it even before I got to the *Falgout*, and I said I would not even consider it before I got there. Then they put in their second request. I went down to see Commodore Newland and said, "I've got some requests for interviews here, and frankly, I don't think I should accept these things, because I don't have time."

He said: "Your job is to run that ship. If you think that is necessary, go ahead. If you don't, then turn it off." I didn't feel it was necessary. I got a little criticism in the black community for turning it off, but I didn't feel that was my prime mission.

Once I took command, my biggest concern was to get under way the first time. I had read a ship-handling book, and it told you how to handle the straight-stick destroyers, but it didn't tell you how to handle diesel engines that relied on compressed air for starts.[2] I had some butterflies my first time on the bridge of the *Falgout*, but moving it from the main pier to the shipyard was just a short trip. The butterflies had left by the time we got over there; I did it safely with no problem.

---

2 Typical destroyers of the era were powered by boilers and steam turbines.

Something that began to bother me a little bit was that the DER force, as far as I was concerned, did not get the cream of the crop among qualified ship handlers. You got a lot of good ROTC guys who were great at doing their specific jobs—as the engineering officer, as the communication officer, and so forth. The ship had maybe ten jaygees and ensigns who had really never done as much ship handling as I had, and I hadn't done very much at all. Fortunately, I had a good exec, and he knew how to handle the ship. But I always believed I had to be the best ship handler in the crowd, so I tried to handle it most of the time. I had some rough spots, but no major damage occurred.

In fact, I can remember that during another event when I was going into the shipyard, I lost one engine en route. I had a couple of choices: hitting either the side or the end of the pier. We hit the side. We had no damage, although we made a little bit more noise than you like to when you pull alongside. As it happened, my wife and my two sons were standing on the pier. As I began to move to get off the ship, Robbie said, "Daddy, you're fired." Can you imagine being fired by your four-year-old son for poor ship handling? I knew I had to improve.

★★★

Even though, as I said, the *Falgout* normally went on DEW Line patrols, my first few deployments with the ship involved a different mission. This was the time the United States was about to begin the high-altitude nuclear weapons testing in the Pacific. The DERs supported those tests, so we went down to Johnston and Christmas islands four or five times. The DER was suitable for that mission because the diesel engines gave the ship really long legs, that is, great range. We also saved fuel at times by lying to without the propellers turning.

A big part of the surveillance role was to keep ships and aircraft of other nations from getting too close to the tests. When someone would get a contact on an airplane, for example, we were to go over and give a warning that the guy was in a dangerous area. We had a five-hundred-mile circle drawn around Johnston and Christmas islands, and we patrolled one arc of the circle. In effect, the combat information center was the ship's main battery. The secondary battery was the Mark I eyeball on the bridge, because sometimes you could see things that CIC couldn't.

We had a fairly decent search radar. We also had a very, very good high-altitude radar—the SPS-8, as I recall—which we used for tracking when we sent up weather balloons. One of the things they needed down there was high-altitude weather, because the winds could have an effect on the weapons tests. We had on board a couple of aerographers who launched the balloons. One day they told me there shouldn't be too much difficulty in getting these balloons to one hundred thousand feet. From then on, I accepted nothing less. That kept them working a little bit, but a hundred thousand feet was what we aimed for and got most of the time. And we got fairly decent weather data.

Operationally, I can remember distinctly my first encounter with the Russians. Three Russian trawlers were in the area, and I was given a steer by Commander in Chief Pacific Fleet [CinCPacFLt] to go over and intercept them and give them the warning. I found what I thought was the guy in charge, and I gave him the order by flashing light, using international coded signals. He turned off, but that didn't mean he was gone. We bumped heads with him a couple of times down there, and we'd give warnings. He'd turn away then creep in from another side. So we continually watched for ships trying to do that.

One other experience, which I'm a little proud of, is that we were down there for a Polaris missile shot with a live warhead.[3] Certainly we were to keep everything out of that area. We picked up the submarine on radar, and we were in position when suddenly here came a small fishing boat just plowing down in there. The biggest concern was to get that guy out of there. When it was just about time for the shot, I went in and warned him, but he wouldn't move. So I decided I'd put the *Falgout* between him and the burst. We didn't get any bad effects, and we had satisfied my big concern by keeping him out so he couldn't start yelling for damages.

One thing I was initially curious about was why the nuclear tests went off at about five o'clock in the morning. After the first one, I knew, because we were given a set of dark glasses that everybody on the bridge had to use when the blast went off. I directed everybody to put on the glasses, and we all did it religiously. That was the brightest thing I've ever seen in my life. I can remember distinctly that with those glasses, I could light a match in front of me and still couldn't see anything. But when the nuclear warhead went off,

---

3 On May 6, 1962, a Polaris ballistic missile, fired from the submarine *Ethan Allen*, carried a live nuclear warhead into the atmosphere. It was the fifth of a series of nuclear weapons tests conducted in the Pacific test area near Christmas Island.

it was like daylight through the glasses. It was like a sun shining. We didn't have any problems, although I understand at least one guy in another ship developed a small hole in his retina as a result of looking at the blast with the naked eye.

Another concern we had was about the possibility of nuclear radiation coming to the ship. Radiation contaminates things when it hits, but I'm not sure what it does to the air, unless you've got a lot of particles in it. Of course, I didn't want any of my people contaminated. In fact, one of my biggest concerns occurred one night, after the ship had been told in the operation order to avoid rain clouds. I had a young officer on board who was a qualified officer of the deck. In fact, he'd just recently come aboard from a destroyer. I remember distinctly telling him, "Stay out of cloudbursts." I guess he couldn't avoid one, but he went into it, and we did get rained on.

We took out radiation meters of various kinds and went through the ship with a fine-tooth comb. Unfortunately, one of the meters pegged all the way over. It frightened us about half to death, and I sent off a couple of messages. We were told not to worry, that the radiac meters were probably malfunctioning. In the meantime, I made all those guys take off their clothes, take showers, and throw the clothes over the side. I wanted to make sure nothing bad happened. To the best of my knowledge, nobody got radiated.

★ ★ ★

In one respect, the operations in the *Falgout* were easier than those in the *Theodore E. Chandler* because generally, we were steaming independently. There wasn't another ship around. You didn't see very many ships transiting. The thing that concerned me most was a sudden shift in the weather, and I would make sure I was on the bridge for that, and of course, I was there when we encountered the foreign ships we had to warn away. Certainly you didn't think you were going to hit another ship. You were not maneuvering like you were in a destroyer in fast task force ops. You felt you had competent people for independent steaming, and that's all most of our people were qualified for.

The enlisted crew was fairly sharp. I can remember specifically a damage controlman, about a second class. He was seasick from the day the ship moved from port until it got back. But this young man walked around with a bucket and still did the job. You cannot ask for more dedication. Of course, he slowed down a little bit every once in a while when he upchucked, but he did the job for me.

I had a really, really top-notch signalman first class, someone you might have thought of as a typical pre–World War II sailor. Here was a guy who drank like a fish ashore. If there was any trouble, it was going to be ashore. He'd come back on the ship and do a competent job. One of the disciplinary tools was to reduce a man in rate and you could re-promote or essentially give him a suspended sentence and put him on probation. You would suspend the bust on him for his conduct ashore, and then get him on board and he'd work well for you till you gave it back to him. Then the next month you got in the same position. You're not really playing with the guy's career, but he would do some stupid things. Like he'd get over there and get drunk, and he wouldn't come back for two days. You had to have some kind of leverage. But most of the crew members were very, very good.

This signalman did surprise and amuse me on one incident. The op order required us to find crew members who spoke various languages, because ships of any nationality might be sailing through the area. On this particular occasion we were going alongside a Japanese fishing boat, and we wanted to make sure we had a guy who could speak that language. The signalman's service record indicated he could. Someone had put him down as a Japanese interpreter primarily because he had a Japanese wife.

We had a warning we could give. We had it written out in English on a piece of cardboard, and then our interpreter would give the message to the other ship in the language of its crew. The warning was: "You are proceeding in a danger area. Request you move south, or west, or north," depending on what it would take to get him out of there. Or steer course such-and-such. In the case of one Japanese boat, we flashed the sign out, and he just seemed to continue on. I was maybe a hundred feet away, yelling through this bullhorn to the crew in English. Finally, I said to the signalman, "Give it to him in Japanese," because, after all, he was a Japanese interpreter. His "Japanese" turned out to be: "Mushi-mushi. Get the fuck out of here." Well, believe it or not, the guy in the other ship understood that. He turned and went off in the direction we suggested. Maybe it took that kind of yelling to do it.

The nuclear tests were completed sometime in the autumn of that year, 1962. The Cuban Missile Crisis came in October. It affected us only from the standpoint that several of our reserve ships had been activated by then, so I found it harder to get a berth when we came into Pearl Harbor because there were many, many more ships in there. We got a little briefing by the commodore on the situation. We were certainly standing by in case anybody wanted us to move or go any other place or do any other thing, but we weren't called upon.

★★★

I got some really happy news around then; I was selected for commander at a time when only a couple of other black officers had reached that rank. A radio message came out and listed the names of officers who had been selected to commander. As the radiomen kept bringing the message to me page by page by page from the teletype, they missed a page. It was the page that would have had my name on it or would not have had my name on it, depending on whether I'd been selected. Figuratively speaking, some communicators sometimes lose their lives simply from missing messages. Fortunately, I did not kill my communicator.

While we were waiting to see if we could get a rerun on the missing page, I received a personal message from Vice Admiral William Smedberg, who was chief of naval personnel. He had been my skipper in the *Iowa*, and now he was congratulating me for making commander. Obviously, Admiral Smedberg sent messages to all of his former people, and I was particularly pleased to get it. My date of rank as a commander was October 1, 1962. The message from Admiral Smedberg arrived shortly before that.

★★★

It's worth mentioning what life was like in Honolulu for the Gravely family. We lived in government quarters, an area known as Radford Terrace in honor of a former commander in chief of the Pacific Fleet. Nearby were two or three other officers with whom I had served previously, so we had friends in the neighborhood.

On the other hand, we lived in a house that had a Marine family upstairs, and the Marine wasn't quite ready for this. He gave us minor problems, but nothing we couldn't handle. We were both going in through the same front door. He had to walk up a set of stairs, and I could just walk right in. But here was a guy who walked down the path from the driveway with me and wouldn't even speak. Unfortunately, he complained that my son Robbie was going into his mailbox. Well, Robbie was four years old and couldn't even reach the damn mailbox. The Marine created a little bit of a stink, so I took him out there. I showed him Robbie had to be standing on a rock on his tiptoes to reach the mailbox, so we got that one settled.

There were no major problems, but we did experience a couple of little incidents precipitated by some unthinking people. For example, one was a time when my kid came home crying, and he said, "Dad, why is it I can't get a little Mickey Mouse thing?" You had to send in a box top to get some kind of Mickey Mouse gadget. Some little kid had told him he was chocolate or something like that and this was only for white kids. These were little things that didn't amount to much in the long run, but at the moment they seemed big.

My set of quarters had a canvas over a terrace called the lanai. Most of the houses didn't, but apparently the guy who'd lived there before we did had put up this canvas and left the top there. One of my neighbors, a warrant officer, thought he was going to give me a hard time. His kid happened to come around when we weren't there, and he climbed up on this thing and was going to slide on it, but he slid through and fell on the cement. I got a frantic call from the warrant officer, who was going to call the authorities on me. I simply told him, "Hey, I kind of think I ought to call the authorities on you, because your son has no business on my back porch when I'm not there." Very shortly afterward I got a little note of apology, accompanied by a bottle of wine, so that ended that.

★★★

One sort of humorous incident occurred when we were in port in Hawaii. At the time, John F. Kennedy was president, and his administration was emphasizing physical fitness. Calisthenics became known as "JFKs." I didn't really grasp this emphasis initially, but I soon found out. We'd been back in port for only a couple of days, so it was time for some relaxation or whatever we were going to have there. Then I got a call from the commodore, who said, "Oh, by the way, Mr. Fay is coming out, and he wants to visit a ship and see how they conduct their athletic program." Paul Fay, who had served in PT boats with Kennedy during World War II, was by this time undersecretary of the Navy.

Fine, I made all the preparations. I determined that certainly I would have the ship cleaned, and I'd have my people ready to go out and show him how we did it. The commodore agreed. I didn't plan to take part myself because the instructions specifically stated you were exempt if you were over forty. I had just turned forty in June of that year. On the day scheduled for the visit, I was standing there all ready at the quarterdeck, everything all shining, and waiting for Mr. Fay. Up drove a big Cadillac with the undersecretary in it. I went out and saluted, shook hands, piped him aboard. I took him down to the wardroom and briefed him on our program. He was very happy with it, and he said: "Yes, but Captain, I want to see it. I want to see it in action."

I said, "Well, it just so happens, sir, we are testing our people this morning, and a few of them are out on the athletic field." The athletic field was far enough away that it was more convenient to go by car than to walk. As we stepped off the gangway, the Cadillac pulled up, and Mr. Fay said, "Well, son, shall we ride over?"

I said: "No, sir. I think maybe we ought to trot over, and we'll both be ready when we get there." Most people were pretty amazed to see me trotting alongside the undersecretary of the Navy over to this athletic field. He had changed into his shorts, sneakers, and skivvy shirt. We went over there, and he joined in each of these exercises with our people, and probably outdid most of them. Finally, it was about time for him to go to a luncheon he had scheduled. After I caught a high sign from my commodore, I went over to see the undersecretary.

I said, "Mr. Secretary, I think they're probably about ready now to take you to your next engagement."

He said, "Well, let me tell you, I'm not about to leave here until I see you do your exercises."

"Well, sir, you know, there's an out for me in that directive. It says if you're over forty, you don't do this. I'm over forty."

"Well, I don't care about that. I want to see you do your exercises."

"Yes, sir." So I got down, and I was doing sit-ups. As I came up, I looked, and there was a sailor running in my direction from the ship. When I finished the sit-ups, I looked and it was my corpsman. I said, "What the hell were you doing running over here?"

He said, "Well, the commodore told me he thought I better get over here in case you had a heart attack." He was pulling my leg a little bit. But in any event, I did my full set of pull-ups, and then we went to push-ups, and I had done about half of those when the undersecretary really did have to leave, and so we took him back to the ship. Unfortunately, when he left the wardroom going up to my cabin to change his clothes, he bumped his head on a ladder. Although he didn't get a gash, I'm sure he had a headache for a day or so. I felt kind of bad about it, but I almost thought he deserved it for making me do those damn exercises.

★★★

One of the interesting aspects of commanding the *Falgout* was that the officers and crew were almost all white. This was obviously a change from World War II, when black officers served only in ships or small craft that had black crews. I didn't lord it over anybody, but I was in command. The first executive officer and I got along fine, a normal CO-XO relationship. He was demanding, and he managed to get people to do the job. He was the type of leader who gets the job done without actually putting fear in people. There are a lot of leaders who can lead only by fear, and he went almost to that point. He stayed just far enough on this side of it that they weren't frightened of him; they performed well because they really respected him. Over the years, I met a couple of officers who relied strictly on fear as a tool. Man, that used to upset me a little bit.

After I'd been on board for a number of months, I got a second exec, Lieutenant Jim Eller. I think I was able to work much more closely with Jim than with his predecessor. And that was just a matter of normal turnover. The first exec was just as competent, but I think you have to train people the way you want them to be, and when you take over a guy that someone else has trained, he can see only one way for a long time. It is difficult to bring him around to your way of thinking. I think to some degree I had a little bit of that problem. Now, there were no disputes. Nobody was mad at anybody. He did the job as best he could and as he saw fit. And, of course, he showed me respect and did everything I asked him to do. I had no quarrels with that. In fact, I gave him a really outstanding fitness report. Since this was Jim Eller's first executive officer job, he was willing to do it my way from day one, and we had just a great rapport. Jim Eller was just a tremendous guy and really a fine ship handler too.

Earlier I mentioned the officer who ran the ship through the rain cloud while we were on the nuclear tests. I had another problem with him. One Monday morning I got a minor complaint from the squadron chaplain that we were not ready for church service when he had come aboard the day before. I listened to his complaint, and I went back to the ship to find out what had happened. Sure enough, we'd been a little remiss in that we weren't quite ready. As a skipper, I welcomed the chaplain so he could attend to the religious needs of the sailors. I was convinced some of them needed much more than others. All of them needed at least a little bit, and so it was good to have the chaplain come. To facilitate this I had written an instruction on what would happen for church service. The instruction directed the command duty officer to go back about half an hour before and make sure everything was set up for church services.

As I looked into the complaint, I wound up talking with my "rain-cloud" officer because he had been the command duty officer on the Sunday the chaplain was complaining about. This particular officer said to me he was very sorry that despite the fact he recognized that he'd been given orders to do things, this was an order he couldn't carry out. I said, "Why can't you carry it out?"

He said: "Well, Captain, I'm an atheist. I can't have anything to do with church."

"Well, I didn't tell you to have anything to do with church. I didn't tell you to go; I told you to be back there and make sure the thing was set up, and stay around to make sure it went off well."

"Well, I'm afraid that I can't obey that."

"Well, I understand you have the duty Sunday, and if you don't do this like I told you, I shall kick your butt off this ship, and I got to tell you I think I'm big enough to personally do it."

Now, this was a guy who had played football for the Naval Academy, but I was ready to do it. In fact, I told him if I ever told him to jump over the side of the ship, either I would see his heels as they went over or I personally would kick his butt off. We didn't have any more problems after that.

★ ★ ★

As I said, the cruise in the *Falgout* mostly involved the nuclear tests, but the ship did manage to make one northern barrier patrol, beginning in November of 1962. I had one of the roughest experiences on that trip I've ever had in my life. I sympathize with every CO who had to go up there more than once. I think everybody should have gone up there once, and once was enough. While we were there, we got into a couple of storms. I was sitting on the bridge at about two o'clock in the morning when I thought the ship was going to break in half. That's how much we were being beat up. We managed to get out of that one with a certain amount of fairly careful ship handling. I had on board an old quartermaster who'd been up there about a dozen times. He was constantly whispering in my ear, "Captain, I think you ought to do this." I thought he was right, so I followed his suggestions.

The next thing that happened to us was that one afternoon we began to hear a knocking under the hull. I kept sending the engineer and his people down to inspect the engine rooms. It sounded like a guy with a small hammer, and they heard it about once every thirty seconds or so. Then we realized the noise was coinciding with the roll of the ship. So we just kept inspecting and couldn't find anything. Finally, the next morning I decided I had to send somebody over the side to find out what this was, because the problem was obviously under the ship. We had the guys dressed in their diving gear. The weather was okay, but about that time a great white shark came through there, so we abandoned that idea in a hurry. Then, a couple of hours later, the noise just quit. As mysteriously as it appeared, it stopped, so we essentially forgot about it.

Later on that same patrol, we had a problem with our boilers. We had two small boilers that made the drinking water in connection with our evaporators. One of those was out already, and then the second one went out. With both boilers out, you don't have water for showers; you don't have water to wash the dishes. We had a little bit to drink. Nobody got really thirsty up there, but certainly we couldn't do the heavy things we normally did. So I decided I had to go into Midway Island. We got the boilers repaired there, and I also asked for a diver to look at the hull. He reported that a huge portion of the bilge keel had broken loose. It was scraping against the hull when we were on patrol, and that was what had made the noise we had heard. Then finally it broke off entirely, which was why the noise stopped. After we found out what it was, we just went without it during the remainder of the patrol.

The ship's biggest role during the patrol was communicating with the barrier patrol aircraft as they came by there frequently and checked navigation positions. You checked yours, and they checked theirs. Certainly we were also vigilant in watching for anything else that was coming in our direction. We would provide advance warning if the Soviets were headed toward the States. Our navigation was strictly celestial, taking star sights and working them out. We had to deal with overcast conditions an awful lot of the time, which made it a challenge to see the stars. When it was finally time to end the patrol, we had no trouble finding our way back to Hawaii, that's for sure.

★★★

When we got back to Pearl Harbor, mail call was a big event for the crew. The schedule called for the *Falgout* to go into the shipyard early in 1963. I'd been on continuous sea duty since '57, so I expected to go ashore someplace. I was expecting probably that I'd get transferred during the yard period. I thought I might get orders in the mail. Lo and behold, when we got the mail, I received three official letters. One was from the White House. It invited my wife and me to a cocktail party in celebration of the one hundredth anniversary of the signing of the Emancipation Proclamation.[4] Then I looked at my other two letters, which were from BuPers. One said, "You have been nominated for and will attend the '63 session of the Naval War College." The second one said: "Contrary to what I told you in my first letter, you are not going to the Naval War College. You will be advised later as to where you are going."

Right after that I reported to the commodore about the patrol we had just finished. This was Commodore Newland's successor, and he wanted to know why I had interrupted the patrol to go into Midway. I explained to him the problem with the boilers and that getting such repairs was at the commanding officer's discretion. Then I said: "Commodore, I want to tell you something. I really don't think that's my problem this morning. I think my problem is one of trying to say 'no' to the president."

He said, "What are you talking about?"

"Well, I've been invited to this Emancipation Proclamation celebration, and I really don't see how I can go to Washington."

"Well, let me see that letter." He took my letter and looked at it. He didn't say anything to me, but he went downstairs to check with Commander Destroyer Flotilla Five, the rear admiral who was his boss. I waited until he returned.

He said, "You're going to Washington."

I said, "Commodore, I really don't think I ought to go to Washington. There are a couple of reasons. Number one is that Washington is in blues. I am now a commander, and I don't have any striped blues."

4 On January 1, 1863, President Abraham Lincoln issued the Emancipation Proclamation, which declared an end to slavery in all areas of the Confederacy that were in rebellion against the United States.

"We'll fix that." He called the exchange and said, "Commander Gravely's wife is going to bring his blues by this afternoon, and I want them striped by Friday"—or something like that, because I had to take off very shortly.

"Well, what about my wife? My wife's going to want to go to Washington too, and I can't afford to take her."

"Don't worry about her; I'll talk to her."

"Commodore, I need at least a week. Who's going to come from Honolulu to Washington, D.C., and not stay Monday till Friday? Is that okay—five days' TAD?"

"Okay, great." I received temporary additional duty orders, but they weren't open ended. I had to report someplace. I was told to report to the Navy staff in the Pentagon for temporary duty in connection with a White House affair. My brother Ed lived out at Cheltenham, Maryland, at that time. After I flew to Washington, I rented a car and went on out to his house.

The next morning I reported to OpNav, and a female commander there gave me a rough time. She said, "Commander, you know you've got to report in here every morning."

I said: "Well, let me tell you what my situation is. I'm here for a week, but really I'm here to attend a cocktail party at the White House, and I'm currently staying out in Cheltenham, which is about thirty-five miles from here. I hope you don't want me to drive in to the Pentagon every morning just to check in with your office. Can't I call you?"

"Oh, no, you can't call, but let me see your orders." I showed her my orders, and she put on an endorsement stating when I had reported and when I would be detached. Apparently, she changed her mind after she saw the White House connection on the orders because after that I didn't have to go in there anymore.

As for the anniversary, I went to the cocktail party, and I wore my blues with the new commander's stripes. For about the first twenty minutes, I just sort of moved around in the group and looked to see who else was there. I saw Sammy Davis Jr., for example. I met the first black Army general, Benjamin O. Davis Sr. I saw several other people of that caliber, and I was taken aback to some degree by the company I was sort of associating with there. They were big people.

After I'd been taking things in for a while, I met up with Captain Tazewell Shepherd, who was President Kennedy's naval aide. I talked to him for a few minutes, and the impression I got was that I was to meet the president. That surprised me because there were so many people there. They took up a whole wing of the White House. Then suddenly I looked over, and there was Captain Shepherd giving me the high sign to come over and meet Kennedy. I thought, "Oh shit." But finally I got a chance to shake the president's hand. His greeting was, "How are you, Commander?"

That sort of set me on my heels a little bit. Here was a guy who really knew what a commander looked like. But then I realized he should know because he was an ex-Navy officer. We chitchatted for a bit, and then he had to move on because there were people all around. I was a little miffed at Tazewell for making me do that, but I guess I could see what his point was. He wanted to make sure the Navy was represented. I thought Kennedy was very cool, very coordinated. He knew what he was all about, knew what he was doing.

Subsequent to that I was over at one of the hors d'oeuvres tables, and here came Vice President Lyndon Johnson, who was a big man physically. He said: "How are you, Commander? Great, it's nice to see a naval officer here." Then he called his wife's name. "Lady Bird. Come on over here and meet the commander." Lady Bird came over, and I shook her hand, but I was sort of flustered by the experience. Obviously, I'd never been to the White House as part of a group that included the kinds of people there. I was really impressed by the big wheels at the party. It was a symbolic gesture during the time of the civil rights struggles in the South. Later that same year was when Martin Luther King Jr. made his famous "I have a dream" speech in Washington.

After the event at the White House, I returned to the *Falgout*, which was in the shipyard, and that repair and maintenance period went very smoothly. One of the big factors was that the ship's superintendent, my contact in the naval shipyard, was a man with whom I'd served in the *Seminole*. We had a fine relationship, which facilitated the process.

One of the highlights from that period was a visit by Rear Admiral Frank Virden. He was then Commander CruDesPac, our type commander. He was previously Director Naval Communications. I'd known him as a communicator for some time, and so I sort of looked up to him. He came aboard and inspected the ship, and I think he found it in fairly good shape, despite the fact it was in the yard. One part of the visit involved going through a compartment that was getting new tile on the deck. We got to a point where he could compare the appearance of the new tile and the old tile. He looked at it and he said, "Well, it seems like something is happening here, because I noticed that you're not tiling over here. This really looks good here, and that looks kind of beat up."

I said, "Admiral Virden, that's the point where I ran out of money." Sure enough, we got the money we needed to finish the tiling.

We finished the yard period, and by then I had my orders for the next tour of duty. This was another pioneering step, integration of the Naval War College for the first time. Previously, I had received conflicting letters about whether or not I would go there. When I had the orders in hand, it was easy to ignore the letter that told me I wasn't going.

In the spring of 1963, I wrapped things up in that job and turned the ship over to my relief on June 7. Looking back, there were just so many satisfactions from that first command. I liked being the guy in charge. Somehow, giving orders satisfied me. And I'm not a harsh guy with orders. I don't ask people to do impossible things, but just being able to assume and execute responsibility was satisfying to me. I appreciated the honors and other rewards that command provided. I didn't purposely have people make any special honors for me when I came aboard, or anything like that. But it was sort of a nice feeling when you came aboard and there were four side boys standing there and saluting. Things like that would have made anybody feel good. I said to myself, "Oh, if my dad could see me now." Because he was the guy who never thought I'd be much. By this time my horizons had gone beyond his suggestion that I work in the post office.

CHAPTER THIRTEEN

Naval War College

Because of the sort of haphazard way in which my career evolved, including my experience as a civilian between World War II and the Korean War, I didn't receive any postgraduate education for nearly twenty years following my commissioning in 1944. I'd had training courses in communications and amphibious warfare, but those were geared to specific shipboard jobs I would be filling. The fact that I was selected to take the Naval War College senior course at Newport, Rhode Island, in 1963–64 was a substantial milestone. This was really promising because it was clearly a preparatory step for more responsible billets to follow. Though my vision at one point had extended only as far as making lieutenant commander before retiring, I had now passed that step.

George Thompson, who was then a lieutenant commander, integrated the college's junior course at the same time I arrived there for the senior course. George was a young tiger, and I do mean tiger. I guess he finished the ROTC unit at UCLA, so we almost were friends from that standpoint, because I'd gone to UCLA. He was a big, outgoing guy—married to a beautiful woman—and gregarious. He was not a rival to me because I was somewhat senior to him. In fact, we used to go out to clubs together every once in a while, but our wives wouldn't let just the two of us get together too often. George had "command" written all over him. Not only that, he had the experience of integrating a ship's company of officers. He made captain, and I was later shocked when he didn't make admiral. Something else happened along the way that I don't know about, don't care to know about. But George was a great, great man.[1]

★★★

I was quite impressed with the Naval War College, with what the faculty was trying to do there in expanding our knowledge in a variety of areas. Even so, I came to the war college with a handicap in that my focus in the previous six years of sea duty had been relatively narrow: it was on the individual ships and their missions rather than on the Navy as a whole and on the other armed services. I'm a firm believer that the Navy makes a mistake in sending officers directly from sea duty to Newport without touching base with the Washington, D.C., community, organizations such as the Bureau of Naval Personnel and the Naval Operations (OpNav) staff. I'd had a two-year tour in Washington as a very junior officer in a recruiting district, but that was rather remote from the centers of power.

When you're selected for the Naval War College, they send you various materials to read, and they send an additional reading list as well. But there's no way that you can get as much out of it as Commander Joe Blow, who brings the practical experience of Washington jobs. So, I was a little bit behind the eight ball on that. It took one hell of a lot of reading. It took a lot of looking up things and trying to catch up—on politics, current events, military history, and so forth. I found it a little difficult at first, because the Navy and the defense establishment, so far as I'm concerned, are not easy ones to understand unless you've been there and you've worked in the environment.

In my efforts to get ahead, I tried to do even more than the course work required by the war college. I thought I should work on the master's degree program that was offered in Newport by extension from George Washington University. I started work on the master's program, but I took just one course. I found myself overwhelmed by the amount of reading I had to do for the master's program, plus the amount of reading I had to do for the war college, plus the amount of reading I had to do to catch up. I quickly realized I didn't have any time left over for my family. Alma and our children

1 George I. Thompson graduated from UCLA in 1952 and was commissioned through Officer Candidate School in 1953. His sea commands included the radar picket destroyer escort *Finch*, the destroyer *John R. Craig*, and Destroyer Squadron 25. He had several deployments in Vietnam War operations, including service on the staff of Commander Task Force 77, the attack carrier striking force. He was the first black officer on the staff of the Naval Academy.

had made sacrifices while I went to sea for six years, and now they deserved more of my time. So on weekends we used to go to Fort Adams, which was a former coastal fortification that dated from the eighteenth century. By the time we got to Newport, Fort Adams had been turned over to the Navy for family housing and recreation. Alma is an avid fisherman, so she had a lot of fun fishing there.

The subject matter in the course work and the reading ranged from plain old naval operations to the political and the strategic. I read a lot on political policy, current events, and material put out by the State Department. I was trying to get the big overall picture. For example, the Cuban Missile Crisis had occurred in late 1962. When I was driving a DER around in the Pacific, I didn't know any more about the confrontation with the Soviet Union than did the public at large—if that. But it wasn't till I got to the Naval War College that I really learned much about the why and what of all that went on. In trying to backtrack and get more information on that and how we got out of it, I read some of the various reports on the incident. I would call my year there just a general, all-around, practically brand-new education for me. On a number of occasions the speakers were individuals from outside the college—commanders in chief and other really top-notch men. It was a great introduction to the many facets of the government.

As for professional benefits beyond the required classes, I took a course in public speaking while I was there. I wrote my paper on amphibious warfare, which I thought was something I was probably more ready to do than, say, a subject in antisubmarine warfare or command and control, which I didn't know very much about. But I'd been in the amphib force in the *Seminole* and enjoyed the duty. I liked it, and thought that would be the place where I should take my paper.

While I was at Newport I had the opportunity to meet and talk with naval officers from across a wide spectrum. You got a broader view of the Navy. You got a broader view of people. You got a broader view of the world around you. It was just a broader view of everything. I met so many people, including the foreign students in the college, that it was a wonderful experience for Alma and me. We just thoroughly enjoyed it. No sweat on living accommodations. We were assigned a set of quarters just like everybody else. My neighbors became good friends; one member of my car pool was Commander Bill Thompson. Several years later, when Admiral Elmo Zumwalt became CNO, Bill was promoted to rear admiral and became the first public affairs specialist to serve as the Navy's chief of information (Chinfo).

In the mid-1960s era, the atmosphere at the war college was different from what came later. In those days, as I recall, it was referred to as a gentlemen's course. There wasn't a hell of a lot of competition among the students, and some students did just the minimum. I was on a committee with about eight or ten other people who sat around and discussed various problems, and, of course, we did papers and those kinds of things on our various discussions. To lead these discussion groups we had both a military guy as well as a civilian who was on the staff there.

As I remember, the kind of competition we had was just that there were always several guys who wanted to make sure they stood up and were noticed when the speaker turned to questions. There were a few guys who obviously were aspiring to become admirals. A couple of them made it, a couple of them didn't. But it wasn't nearly as competitive as it got to be when Vice Admiral Stansfield Turner became president of the college in the early 1970s and instituted a grading system and stiff requirements. In my time, you got to study in a relaxed atmosphere, and what you took away from the course really depended on how much effort you decided to put into it. As I said earlier, it would have helped in my case if I'd had more Washington time and more thorough preparation before I reported to the college. But I got what I came for and was very happy with having been there.

CHAPTER FOURTEEN

Housing Still a Problem

As I neared the end of the nine-month school year in Newport, I received orders for my next duty, which would be with the Defense Communications Agency in the Pentagon. The thing that got to me a little bit was the question of where we would live next. I'm not sure the Naval War College knew about what happened to us, because I'm not a complainer. Each year, when the orders were issued, they came out in the various publications, such as *Navy Times*. The next step was that many Realtors from the Washington, D.C., area went up to Newport and rented spaces. Then they invited the students to come see them about getting resettled around Washington. This was the summer of 1964, and even though Congress was passing important civil rights legislation that year, I decided I would not go see these traveling Realtors, who, of course, were white. I felt the only people who would find us a home were black Realtors.

I came home from the campus one day, and Alma told me she'd just gotten a call from this real-estate agent who knew I was going to Washington, D.C. He'd like to have the commander come over and talk to him. He thought he could find a house for us if we wanted one. Alma and I sat and kicked it around, saying, "Should we or should we not?" I kept telling her, "No, don't go." But she insisted. My wife is a very insistent person. She said, "They would not call you if they're not going to find a house for you."

We went over to see this real-estate agent; Alma and I walked in with our two kids. There were three guys in that office. I said: "I am Commander Gravely. You just called and told my wife you would find us a house." The first guy disappeared; he just escaped right through the place. I said, "We came to talk about housing." Then the second guy skipped out and left some poor guy in there to talk to us. The third man had to admit that he was very sorry, but they weren't in the process of renting houses to Negroes, as he put it. Alma is much more of a fighter than I, because I was ready to walk out right away. But she gave him a piece of her mind, and eventually we did leave. We had still not found a suitable place to live before we left Newport.

When I was stationed in Washington in the early 1950s, I had lived in the BOQ, and Alma lived and worked in Virginia. But now we had two kids, so we had to find a house. We drove down from Newport, and I had the whole family together while we shopped around, trying to find quarters. There was no place in Virginia where I could find a real-estate agent who would deal with me. There was nothing we could do in southern Maryland. The only thing we could do in Washington itself was to find a row house and rent a floor. I could pay to rent the whole row house, but it had stoves on every floor because the landlord had already divided it up into three or four apartments. Well, I didn't want that. After two weeks of this sort of run-around, we couldn't find a cotton-picking thing that would work for us. Finally, I told Alma the only thing I could think to do was that she would take the kids, go back to Virginia to stay with her folks, and I would then find a place.

At that time, there were fair-housing groups, and most of these were made up of both blacks and whites who were working toward improving these conditions. Somehow I got in touch with one of these groups. I remember several times going to the house of a woman who was part of this group. The effort finally paid off when we found a place over in Arlington, Virginia. The owner was a guy who had said he wanted to move back into Washington. He felt it was unfortunate that so many whites were moving out of Washington then. But he felt it was not his bag, and he didn't think they should do that. He and his wife were going to move back to Washington. However, there was a catch. He would not vacate his place until his mother died. She was an invalid who was living with him.

In the meantime, while I was doing all this searching, I was living in the bachelor officers' quarters at Fort Myer, which is close to the Pentagon. Alma was still down in Virginia, and it was getting fairly close to September when the kids would have to go to school. One day I got a call, and the guy said his mother had died. I was very sorry about that, but at the same time, as soon as the funeral and so forth were over, then I could rent his house.

I guess all the stress about the housing problem must have affected me to some degree. I began having headaches, and my blood pressure started acting up, so I went to the naval hospital out at Bethesda, Maryland, to check. I have a thing called central hypertension, and all the tests in the world don't tell why. They just say I have it. So I went on this bunch of pills, which I take even today. Anyway, as soon as I got out of the hospital, I went back to my job at the Defense Communications Agency. Once I had settled in again, I called Alma and told her I thought I'd found a place, and I'd like for her to come up and look at it. She got in there one Sunday night, and she looked, and she said: "This bedspread looks like mine. These curtains look like mine."

I said, "I've got to tell you, they are, because I just moved in here." The result was that we got a house there in Arlington, and we thoroughly enjoyed it during the time we were there.

CHAPTER FIFTEEN

Defense Communications Agency

When I got my orders to go from the Naval War College to the Defense Communications Agency (DCA), I was a little shocked. After damn near ten years in a variety of jobs, somebody was thinking about me as a communicator again. I had worked hard to establish myself as an unrestricted line officer, not as a specialist. But, obviously, I was picked for this because of my communications background.

Even though I was taken aback by the assignment, I prepared myself for it. The DCA was fairly new at that point in time. It was created in 1960 to consolidate the communications arms of the Army, Navy, and Air Force. I got hold of the organization chart and found out where the DCA fit in with the Joint Staff, the Department of Defense, and the other entities it served.[1] This involved a mental transition for me because I had served in only Navy commands up to then.

DCA was a joint agency with all the services there and civilians as well. I was assigned to an engineering group. I relieved a naval officer whom one could call the construction engineer for the building of the National Military Command Center (NMCC) in the Pentagon. He followed all the joint papers through the works until they finally made the decision they would build it. The Army funded it, and they were about ready to hire a construction agency to do it. My job as project manager then became one of being in on the selection process of the contractor, and after we got started, I would go

1 The multiservice Joint Staff comprises officers whose work supports that of the Joint Chiefs of Staff (JCS).

in there every day to see what the phase of the construction was and to report on it. Common sense would suggest that since the Army funded the project, it should manage it. At the least, there should have been an engineer as manager, but it was just my luck—or lack of it—that got me picked for the role.

Though I eventually headed the Defense Communications Agency years later as an admiral, I was disappointed in the way I was treated during that first tour. They just weren't used to me. I criticize them as of that time. I was one of the first black officers of any branch of the service to go to DCA and certainly the first black naval officer to go there. When I arrived, the staff in the office where I worked included another naval officer (a white commander), an Army colonel, an Air Force colonel, an Air Force captain, and then about ten civilians. All of us had desks in a huge open-bay area when I reported for duty. I mentioned earlier that I had been to the hospital for a short while around this time. Well, when I came back from the hospital, the big area had been divided up into individual cubbyholes. I had a cubbyhole; the colonel over here had a cubbyhole. These were not permanent bulkheads; these were temporary bulkheads, a lot like the ones that make up cubicles in offices today. I wondered if the change had anything to do with my race, so I simply asked, "Why have we done this?"

The answer I got was something like, "Well, okay, we did this for two reasons. One is that we felt the air wasn't circulating properly in this room, so now the air can roll under here and roll up above here, and blah, blah, blah. The second reason was the noise level; there's just too much noise." So I worked through that, and I've got to say that nobody snubbed me, nobody did anything to me, but that arrangement got to me a little bit. Even so, I did my job, and I had a civilian who worked with me and paid me the deepest respect. We got the job done.

Sometime later, probably two or three years after I had left, I went back to DCA for a visit and saw that all the temporary bulkheads had been taken down. I said, "Hey, I see you got a big bay again."

"Well, yeah, we discovered the air flows better if it just runs on an even keel, and there wasn't so much noise after all."

★★★

DCA was a really interesting experience. I worked for an Army general. The next senior in the chain was an Air Force brigadier general, with a Navy captain as his deputy. I'd never been in that situation before, with all these strange people, both civilians and officers from the other services. It took a little time to get used to it, but ultimately, I discovered they were people too, and we all got along fairly well.

The job in supervising the construction of the NMCC got to be very interesting because it's in the heart of the Pentagon, right on the second deck, and we had to tear out a lot of things. I was used to watching people tear things apart, including the shipyard modernization program on the *Theodore E. Chandler*. But I found nothing really fascinating about watching them tear down old walls and even less fascinating when they were putting up new ones. I had to make certain decisions along the way, however. For instance, the question came up, "Do we need a ladies' head?" "Head," of course, is the term the Navy uses for a restroom. Well, there were women on the Joint Staff, and we figured the time would come when they would be assigned to this space, so ultimately we decided to put a ladies' head in there.

Another example was the question, "How thick should these walls be, because, after all, certain classified information is going to be held here?"

I looked through the security manual, and I talked to people. Then I would decide, "Okay, you need an 8-inch-thick wall here; you need a 12-inch-thick wall here."

I made a lot of decisions on a lot of subjects, and we were proceeding along on the construction, but finally one day I just couldn't take it anymore. I went to the good Army colonel who was my boss, and I said: "Colonel, I've got to tell you, I have been doing this job to the best of my ability, but, frankly, I am not the guy you need. We have civil engineers in the Navy, and I really think one of them would be much more suited to supervise this job than me. In addition to that, I am currently working with a guy out of the J-3 [a section of the Joint Staff] organization. He's my counterpart, and he is a civil engineer, so why not get a civil engineer for that job?"

The colonel said: "Sam, I'm glad you talked to me about that. I don't know whether you know this or not, but we've just had a billet cut here." He explained that the inspector general had been through there, said they had too many people, so they decided to cut some billets. They had just lost the Air Force colonel who was running the National Emergency Airborne Command Post program. The colonel went on, "My intention is that you take that job." Since I was a surface warfare officer, airplanes were not quite up my alley either, but they sounded a hell of a lot more interesting than dealing with brick walls.

"Great, Colonel, I'd just love to do that. And oh, by the way, who do you want me to give this other one to?"

"No, I think you ought to do that job too." So I became the program manager for the National Emergency Airborne Command Post, and also I was still doing the Pentagon command center job. I'd been on the reconstruction job for about a year, and fortunately, we were fairly close to finishing up by then.

★★★

The concept of the National Emergency Airborne Command Post was that the inside of the plane was configured to take aboard the president and key members of his staff in the event of a nuclear attack. Presumably, with aerial refueling they could stay up there for one hell of a long time and make decisions on running the country. At that point in time, we not only had the three Boeing 707s that were the airborne command posts; we also had two Navy ships that were specifically configured for the role. The *Wright* and the *Northampton* were homeported out of Norfolk and were outfitted with command centers and the necessary communications. The ships were cut out of the budget several years later but in the 1960s, they were specifically set up to take the Joint Staff and any other high-level officials aboard, as well as the aircraft, during a nuclear emergency.

There was also at one time the idea of having a train for this mission. After all, if the Air Force had a mobile command post and the Navy had something, the Army wanted to have a train. We also talked in terms of big moving vans, and we talked in terms of various other ways of getting our prime officials to a safe haven to run the government. As I recall from the period when I was there, they had a response time of probably ten minutes or so to have the helicopter on the White House grounds, bring the president out to Andrews Air Force Base on the outskirts of Washington, and launch the 707.

As it turned out, I really enjoyed being involved with the airborne command post, especially because every Friday we used to take training trips out of Andrews. The training trip involved simply flying for a certain length of time—four hours or six hours—to make sure the system worked. They had one route during the Kennedy administration in which they used to fly straight up toward the Boston area. By the time I got into the program, Lyndon Johnson was president, and the plane had to go toward Texas. Sometimes they'd fly four hours, going part of the route. Other times the plane would take six hours and go the whole route. Every Friday I could fly in that airplane for four hours or six hours, and I really enjoyed it.

These flights basically simulated the missions the plane might fly in an emergency and tested the communications along the way. My responsibility was to make sure the communication equipment was set on the right frequencies and operating properly. Along the route we had a series of ultrahigh frequency (UHF) radio stations we checked into and checked out of on every flight. And, of course, these shore stations could then relay any messages they received right on back to the good old Pentagon or anyplace else in the world. But it was an actual check of the communications procedures and equipment as we flew along the way. So it was a real live test of the system. UHF was the primary means of radio communication at the time for aircraft because of reliability and compactness of the equipment. Things have changed since then, with the advent of satellite communications.

While I was on the command post airplane one day, an Air Force officer asked, "Commander, do you get flight pay or hazardous duty pay for flying as part of this aircrew here?"

I said, "Believe it or not, I don't get either one."

"Well, I've got to tell you, you rate it. Anybody who's flying as much time as you do rates flight pay or hazardous duty pay."

"Nobody's ever mentioned it to me."

"Well, if you go back and check with your service, you'll find they have an instruction out on it, and you rate one of those kinds of pay."

I went back, and I began to check. Sure enough, there was an instruction that told me how to put in for flight pay. I complied, including taking the flight physical, for which no flight physician would qualify me. But it didn't really make any difference whether you were qualified for flight training or not. It was a question of flying the missions, and I was doing it. I finally put together a letter to the Bureau of Naval Personnel in which I requested flight pay. About ten days later I got a call from the destroyer desk. "Commander Gravely, how would you like to go to sea? We have a destroyer out of San Diego that we're looking for a skipper for, and we've picked you. Now, we realize you have a three-year tour over in DCA, and it would be kind of hard to get you unless you want to go."

I said, "Just tell me where it is and when to go." A destroyer command was exactly what I wanted at that point. I chuckle every time I think about it, because I knew damn well they weren't going to pay a surface warfare officer flight pay for the job I was doing for Defense Communications Agency, but I had to ask, and it paid off. I got out of DCA after just seventeen months, not thirty-six months, which suited me fine.

★★★

There was an amusing side story about the NMCC. After we got it built, members of the Joint Staff began to move in and operate in the facility. When they did so, they discovered that there was a static electricity problem from the carpeting, and as project manager, I was required, obviously, to get the static out of the room. In the DCA system, each project manager had to write up a few brief paragraphs on what he was doing every day, and, you had to have a title for whatever you were doing. I came up with the title of "Project De-Static De-Rug." Every day I had to write up what I was doing on this thing. After all, you can't have generals knocked on their duffs by touching doorknobs for very long before people really get frantic.

In the course of trying to find out how to get the static out of this rug, I thought in terms of everything. Among other things, I called rug manufacturers, rug sellers, and rug cleaners. It was a frustrating process because even after all these calls, nobody really had a good solution. Finally one day, I talked with a guy who said, "Oh, I know how to do it." So I arranged to meet him and concluded he could do the job. The price seemed reasonable enough, and all I had to do was make arrangements to get him into the Pentagon.

Well, as serious as this problem was, it just really upset me no end because of all the people whose concurrence I had to get in order for this man to be admitted to the classified command center. That included members of the Joint Staff, the duty officers in the space, and so forth. But I made arrangements to get this guy admitted, and I rode with him in his little cotton-picking truck. The only piece of equipment he brought with him was a bucket. We got up there, and nobody would let us into the NMCC. So I explained to them again why he was there.

The duty officer said: "We have a joint exercise going on right now, and there are simply too many papers around here that this guy might get a chance to view, and we can't leave classified information unprotected. We've got to be very careful."

I said: "Gentlemen, I must tell you, I have ridden from Southeast Washington with this guy. He simply can't read, so he is not a threat at all." After all the discussion, they finally decided they could clear out their operation in a couple of hours. In the meantime, we would stand there and wait, and then we could get in and do what we needed to do.

The guy agreed, and I said, "Hey, how are you going to do this?"

He said: "They won't let me see their secrets. Well, I have secrets too."

"Okay, fine." We finally managed it. His method was very simple. He went to a water fountain, filled his little bucket, and he sprinkled that rug with water. That was his big scientific secret. Evidently, the air was just too dry in that space, and that's what led to the static. Adding moisture solved the problem. I'm not sure how they handled it once he had done his work, because I left shortly after that. I think the military people watered down the rug for a while themselves until finally they took it out. They had put the rug down over tile because they were concerned about a noise problem. The answer probably was that they could live with the noise as long as they didn't have to deal with the static. Anyway, that was one of the problems I solved: "Project De-Static De-Rug." I will never forget that one as long as I live.

★ ★ ★

As I reflect on that tour in the Pentagon, I realize it was something that I really needed in terms of my career, because the services were getting more and more involved in joint ventures. We did have officers from other services at the Naval War College, but that's not really an operating environment. My joint duty really gave me a new perspective on the Defense Department because my view up to then had been from the Navy's vantage point only. I'd see an Army soldier once in a while, but I didn't have much reason to think about what the Army did on a day-to-day basis. Working in the Pentagon certainly put me into the real world on joint operations. It really made me see that the Army has a job to do as well as the Air Force and everybody else. I learned a lot at DCA, and I had a lot of respect for the members of the other services by the time I left there.

Another benefit of working in that job was that I got much more into the planning function than I had previously. I learned, for example, about the color codes assigned to JCS papers—the red stripe, green stripe, that crap—which I didn't know that much about. That was one of the shortcomings in my knowledge when I was at the war college. A guy would say, "Well, this isn't green yet." I thought maybe he was talking about classifications, because we used green paper for confidential messages. They were actually talking about the stages of progress in approving a proposal within the JCS. My time at DCA really enhanced my education in the area of working with the Joint Staff, etc., in watching some of those guys move in that area who were very, very competent and knew what they were doing all the time. I enjoyed that.

I made a lot of friends too. In fact, some of the guys I met when I was there the first time were still there a dozen years later when I came back as head of DCA. I felt quite proud and happy to see them, and I think they were quite proud and pleased to see that I had progressed to the point where I commanded the whole place. That was something.

CHAPTER SIXTEEN

USS *Taussig*, 1966

In early January of 1966, I finished up my duty in Washington and flew out to San Diego to go aboard the *Taussig*. It was a 2,200-ton destroyer that had been commissioned originally in 1944 and twenty years later updated with the FRAM conversion. When I arrived, the *Taussig* had just recently completed a shipyard overhaul, and it was one week into refresher training for the crew. I relieved my predecessor on January 22, a Saturday morning, and I was simply overjoyed at getting a destroyer command. I had driven the *Falgout* for eighteen months, and I had enjoyed it. But this was a new facet of my life, because here I was on a full-fledged greyhound. It had speed, endurance, and guns; it had all the things you dream about when you take over a ship.

On my first day as skipper, after the change of command, I did what most naval officers would have done. I went home and began to think about things like the exercise schedule for the following week, moving the ship from the pier, and the channel we had to go through—because I knew I had to get under way on Monday morning. The more I thought about it, I decided, "Hey, I'd better go back to the ship and spend some time reading the op orders and familiarizing myself with antisubmarine warfare, which I will be faced with next week." So that Sunday afternoon, right after church, I went back to the *Taussig*, and I spent the afternoon there.

The next morning, we got under way, left San Diego, and began the exercise schedule. During the period of the refresher training, we went through gunfire support exercises, antisubmarine warfare training. We operated as a task group with a mix of ships each afternoon and night. If I'd had my druthers, I probably would have gone aboard two weeks earlier. In other words, I would have wanted to go through the week of in-port inspections and then handled the ship for the first week of the underway trials. I got only the second week.

One night during the refresher training we were operating with the aircraft carrier *Constellation*, and that really became a very, very hairy experience. While we were steaming along behind at twenty-five knots, I was listening to the aircraft land-launch frequency on the radio, and suddenly I heard the words, "Pull up. Pull up." About that time the *Constellation* turned off to the left, and we immediately knew a plane was in the water. Apparently, a plane the carrier launched had gotten what they call a cold catapult shot. There wasn't enough steam pressure to launch the plane at flying speed. It went off the bow of the ship and then plunged into the ocean.

At the speed we were steaming, we got there in a hurry. It was dark that night, and the minute we got close enough, I saw the pilot's helmet and began aiming for it. The pilot of the rescue helicopter apparently saw the thing at the same time I did. In trying to duck the helicopter and make a recovery, we hit the helmet. There was no damage to anything. We picked up his helmet, but there was nothing in it. Then we were detached and told to search. We steamed around until early the next morning but found nothing other than a lot of sharks. I finally went to bed, and then I got a call from the bridge because the people on watch had seen something weird that looked like an arm. It turned out to be a stick. That was my introduction to the good old *Taussig*.

★★★

Even though the ship had gotten out of the yard period in relatively good shape, there was a noise spoke in the sonar dome, an irregularity that prevented us from getting a complete picture.[1] So we were directed to go to Long Beach Naval Shipyard to correct that as soon as refresher training was over. The repair would be fairly simple, I thought, but before going into Long Beach, the ship had to go into the nearby Seal Beach weapons station to off-load ammunition, and it is quite a tight place. I had been in Seal Beach

1 If there is disfiguration of the surface of a sonar dome, the result can be cavitation, which produces a phenomenon known as a "noise spoke." The spoke compromises the performance of the sonar.

once before in the *Theodore E. Chandler*, and somehow we had bumped up against the pier. You learn from watching other people make mistakes, and I was not about to make that one.

Because the maneuvering room was so tight, I expected that a tug and a harbor pilot would be on hand when we arrived there, but they weren't. I guess when you're a young skipper, and you know your business, you're a little impatient when things aren't quite ready for you. After learning ship handling in the *Falgout*, I was cocky. I knew I could do it, so I just did it, and it worked out with no problem. Afterward, I talked with a couple of buddies who were in the area. One of them was a squadron commander. I went over to brag just a little bit, and he responded by saying, "Well, Sam, all I can say is, that was a stupid maneuver well carried out." We got a good laugh out of that one.

I did see another benefit of going in to the pier unaided. There's a tendency to be a little flashy so the crew will have confidence in the old man. You've got to know what you're doing, and you've got to make sure the crew is behind you. No matter how good a skipper is in other aspects of the job, the men are going to look down on him if he's not a decent ship handler. And the better you are, the better they're going to love you. Part of the destroyer tradition is to do it quickly, do it snappily, and then go do something else. I was not about to go against tradition.

After the ammo off-load, we spent some time in the Long Beach shipyard, where we got both the sonar and a steering problem repaired. We had to be dry-docked for the repair to the sonar dome, which took about thirty days. The upshot of the extra yard period was that the *Taussig* got out of the deployment cycle with the rest of the ships in its division. On April 20, we left the West Coast in company with two stragglers from other divisions, the *Boyd* and the *Rowan*.

★★★

As the ship was heading west, I had more on my hands than just running the *Taussig*. There was also a public affairs bit concerning my taking over as commanding officer, because the Navy recognized this as a milestone in its history. About two days before we deployed, I got a message from the office of the Navy's Chinfo. It said *Ebony* magazine wanted to send some people to interview and photograph me during the transit to Hawaii. I personally had decided I did not want to be interviewed. I didn't feel I had been on board long enough to undergo what to me seemed like a little pressure. Certainly when a guy is interviewed, he's got to have all the right words at the tip of his tongue, and I preferred not to do it.

But when I was talking over the phone with a friend of mine who was back in Chinfo, he said the decision had been reached. I should plan on them riding with me, and what they really wanted to know from me was simply what time the people should be on board. So I told the *Ebony* people I was departing at ten o'clock, and, sure enough, they were there. The magazine sent a writer and a photographer—very, very good people. They integrated into the wardroom quite well. No problem, because we had them living in officers' quarters.

We got under way without incident, and the three destroyers were steaming along in a sort of triangular formation. There was no plan for a big exercise or anything else, so I didn't hesitate to leave the bridge with the officer of the deck up there because he was quite qualified. I then went on down to eat lunch in the wardroom with my officers. When I got there, the officers were all standing and waiting. I noticed we had empty chairs there, so I asked them where the writer and photographer were. Nobody seemed to know, but they expected them at any minute. I sat, and the stewards began to serve. The minute the stewards came out of the pantry, I looked, and there was the photographer taking a picture.

They took pictures of me at every evolution I can think of. The interview included some hard questions, some easy questions, and some I really couldn't answer. But one of the questions had to do with how I kept in such good shape physically. I've always been fairly large, and I've long been overweight, but I didn't show the weight then as much as I do today. Then we began to discuss the calisthenics in the Kennedy athletic program, called "JFKs." I said: "Oh, I take my JFKs every morning. I go back to the helicopter hangar, and I do pushups and so on."

The photographer said, "Well, I would like to see that and take a picture." I agreed to that. The next morning at about 5:30 I got out of the bed. I went to the bridge for a few minutes, and then I went out on the fantail. I was out there hopping and jumping and everything else, and I did it for about a half an hour, and lo and behold, no photographer. I was angry because doing calisthenics wasn't really my normal routine. I was doing them for the photographer, and he didn't even show up.

A sort of amusing thing that happened in connection with the article was that I was reported as drinking a great deal of coffee. When you spend a lot of time on the bridge, as I did, every time the watch would change, a new messenger would want to get the captain a cup of coffee. Well, I did drink a lot of coffee, and I guess I said it was something like twenty-five cups a day, which came out in the story. After that I could not stand on the bridge for five minutes without somebody putting a cup of coffee in my hand. I never turned down one, but I don't think I ever quite got up to twenty-five.

The article appeared in the July 1966 issue of *Ebony*. I did, ultimately, get a copy of the magazine. Certainly those guys who had their pictures taken with the captain were very happy to see the article. There was nothing unfavorable about it, but to some degree I resented the publicity. It seemed that from about the time my command of the *Falgout* came about, every time I turned around somebody was sending me a copy of a picture of me being in the paper or something. I guess I felt a certain amount of pride that they were good newspaper articles as a general rule.

On the other hand, the publicity did bring on a little bit of uneasiness, because no matter how you tell the story of racial tension and segregation and discrimination, a bunch of people will disagree with you and say, "Hey, you really didn't tell it right." Or another group will say, "You didn't quite do it this way." You can't please everybody in those things, and I ultimately learned that, hell, it's not my job to please everybody. But sometimes I didn't even please myself in some of the interviews. Even though I guess I enjoyed the publicity, I really tried to avoid it, which was very difficult to do. I would not have agreed to have those guys ride with me to Pearl, for example, but the decision was not mine; it was made for me.

The upside, I realized, was that I had acquired a reputation that reached beyond the ship. This was an opportunity to influence all sorts of people indirectly. When you think about those times, the 1960s, we were trying to fight battles to win a degree of freedom for a group of people who had experienced a lot of discrimination. We were trying to make people more interested in education and progress in society. And they could look at me—the words finally dawned on me—as a role model. I felt proud I could be a role model, that people wanted to emulate me. The other big thing is that I think, to some degree, I probably did things a little bit better than I might have because I had the idea I was being watched. That was probably more my feeling than what actually occurred, but I think it had me a little bit more on my toes than if I had been just another destroyer skipper.

★★★

During the transit to Hawaii we spent some time on ships' exercises. We operated as a task group, playing leapfrog and tictacs;[2] the normal routine you would use for underway training. In making the landing at Pearl Harbor, setting the ship down onto the pier, I had some uncomfortable moments because the wind was blowing at twenty-five knots. First I was going ahead and then had to call for all engines to back down at emergency speed. I stopped the momentum at just the right moment and the ship slid into place perfectly. It was one of the best landings I've ever made, but also one of the most nerve-racking ones. It not only frightened me but also some of the Destroyer Flotilla Five people who were on the pier, because they thought we'd had it.

From there we went to Midway Island for refueling and to Guam for a period of upkeep. When we got under way from Guam, we had an exercise against the USS *Tecumseh*, one of the Navy's ballistic missile submarines, armed with Polaris.[3] The skipper of the submarine wanted to go out and play antisubmarine warfare (ASW) for a while, and I was glad to get the opportunity. He explained his rules of the game simply: "I am going to let you get contact, and you do all you can to maintain contact, but at five o'clock in the morning, I want you to back off, if you still have contact. And I don't expect you will. Then I'm going to shoot an air bubble through this missile tube."

I don't recall exactly what time we started, but let's say about ten o'clock in the morning. We did indeed maintain contact with the *Tecumseh* until five the next morning. Then I backed off as my instructions read, and he blew his air bubble. Now, how hard he tried to break contact, I don't know. I have no idea, but I assume he tried his damnedest because we did some violent turns in trying to keep up with him. I had a couple of things going for me: the variable-depth sonar on a cable and the big SQS-4 sonar. That boomer made a big mark on sonar scope.[4] I felt kind of cocky in my ASW because of being able to hold on to that big mother for so long. That was a good one.

---

2 "Tictacs" is a Navy slang term for tactical maneuvering exercises.

3 In the early 1960s the Navy began deploying nuclear submarines armed with Polaris nuclear missiles. The mission of those submarines—and their current successors, which are armed with Trident missiles—is nuclear deterrence.

4 "Boomer" is a generic nickname for ballistic missile submarines.

★★★

The next stop was at Subic Bay in the Philippines before heading to the war zone. The voyage from Subic to Vietnam turned out to be an eventful one. The navigation course was essentially 270 degrees, due west. We set out on the morning of May 26, 1966, traveling at a speed of fifteen knots and using one boiler. Suddenly, we began to encounter really rough weather out there. We learned that Typhoon Judy was to the south of us. We did have some advance warnings of the storm, but some of the navigational fixes on it weren't as good as they should have been, and it was a little bit closer to Subic than I had anticipated.

I'm not too sure now, in retrospect, if it was wise to get under way when we did, but I had made the decision to go because we were anxious to go to Vietnam. As we drove to the west, we began to realize we were taking a little bit more of a beating than I thought the ship should take. We were about ready to divert when I got a message that told me to go to the vicinity of Scarborough Shoals, where there were four sailors in the water. That's about all it said.

As soon as we got the message, I turned north and started in the direction of Scarborough Shoals at top speed. I had to make a decision, and I made it primarily because sailors are inherently curious. When they see heavy seas, they want to get to the highest spot in the ship that they can possibly get so they can get the best vantage point on these big waves. One of my radiomen slipped on the bridge and broke his leg. When that happened I said, "Well, I've got to come around and see if I can't come in behind this thing." So I made the change in course and slowed down. Then, as the storm went north, I turned around and went north too.

The next morning we arrived in the vicinity of Scarborough Shoals, and I had no damage to my ship at all. Unfortunately, as I read in a radio message, a destroyer coming down from the north had run into this typhoon and tried to push through it. That ship had lost one man, suffered all kinds of damage to antennas, and two or three other things. The storm had beaten up the destroyer quite a bit.

The men we were looking for had bailed out of a Navy A-3 attack aircraft that was forced down by the typhoon. We searched the first day and nothing happened. Didn't see anything. We searched a second day, and about that time the oiler *Cacapon* came up. The skipper took me under tactical command because he was a captain and senior to me. He sent me searching a couple of ways. We searched and searched. On the twenty-ninth of May we found a Mae West life jacket.[5] Written on the Mae West in grease pencil were May 26, May 27, May 28, and the guy was writing May 29 when something either pulled him out of his life jacket or he gave up. No one knows what really happened. But finding the life jacket certainly confirmed that there had been people up there.

About ten days after the *Taussig* was at the site, a Navy ship came through there and found the body of one of the missing sailors. It was quite a traumatic thing for me to look at that Mae West and wonder whether I could have found the man if I had gotten there earlier. It's one of those things you speculate about, you dream about. I will always remember the image of the Mae West, with those dates on it. I reported the finding of the life jacket and then, after going alongside the oiler for fuel, the skipper released me to continue on my duties assigned. I went on to the war zone.

★★★

Destroyers are versatile ships, and they had a mix of duties off the coast of Vietnam, including plane-guard duties with the aircraft carriers, shore bombardment, and manning search-and-rescue stations. Now, the beauty of this combat service, as far as I was concerned, was that on the *Taussig* I ultimately got to do at least one of everything. You name it, and we did a little bit of all of it.

Our first chore was to plane-guard for the *Constellation*. I stayed there for a few days, and I was given the mission of gunfire support. We had done some practice firing at San Clemente Island, off the coast of Southern California, prior to the deployment. I had a top-notch gunnery person on board, a fairly good navigational team, and a fine shooting team. We did harassment and interdiction (H&I) shooting an awful lot of the time. In fact, you could shoot H&I all night. There were a couple of times we were given an area in which to put some rounds. In many cases, we had aerial spotters to direct us onto specific targets. We shot at some of everything, including troop concentrations and moving vehicles.

---

5 "Mae West" was the nickname for an inflatable life jacket that fit over a man's head and chest. When not in use, it was rolled up into a pouch that he carried on his belt. The life jacket was named for the buxom movie actress of the World War II period.

One of my most interesting experiences came when we were given a mission of going up the Saigon River to shoot. The standing instructions said that under no circumstances were you to anchor in this river. But there was no way I could stay in position without anchoring. So I sent off a message to the operational commander, Commander Task Group 70.8, and said: "I have been told that I am to remain here for ten days, except for every third day or so come out and refuel and rearm. There's no way to successfully stay in this river for ten days without dropping the hook. Unless otherwise directed, I plan to anchor, taking all practical precautions in doing the job." I got no response, so I stayed there and anchored.

One particular mission while we were anchored in the river came about when we got a report from a spotter plane that there were some Communist sampans coming down the river. We were anchored at a point where there were two forks with a little island in the middle. The boats were approaching on the other side, and we couldn't really see them. We were being coached by the spotter. The idea was to shoot across the island, behind the boats, and thus drive them down the river and into the mouths of our guns. When the first boat came around, the weapons officer said, "Captain, I'm locked on and ready to go."

I said, "No, we'll let all three of them come around, and then we'll pick them off one by one." The second boat came around. The third boat came around. We were just beginning to pick up that boat, to lock on and get ready to shoot, when the weapons officer again asked for permission to fire. I said, "Just let him come around a little bit more." Just at that moment, the spotter's voice came over the gunfire support circuit and shouted: "Cease fire. Cease fire. They're friendly." I have always been just really undone in thinking about that one, because I'd been shooting behind those guys for half an hour, trying to drive them down there so I could really pick them off. I felt a sense of relief that I had held off until their identity was confirmed, because when they came around the curve of the island, they were less than a mile away.

In the meantime, as a result of shooting behind the boats, the *Taussig*'s lifelines were smoking. The cord that was wrapped around the lifelines was all burned up because in shooting at that range, the guns were essentially horizontal; the trajectory of the shots was almost flat. If not for the warning from the spotter, we would have bumped them off. Earlier that day, we'd hit a truck at about eight miles, because those kids in the gun mounts were getting good. We were shooting anywhere from an average of 400 to 450 rounds in a twenty-four-hour period. We shot as high as, say, 600 rounds in a day. During the cruise as a whole, we fired more than 5,600 5-inch rounds. That's a lot of bullets.

We had an unfortunate mishap amid all this firing. Because we shot so much, the ship was often in Condition II, in which only part of the gun battery was manned. That way we didn't have the entire crew at battle stations. During a break in the shooting, the gun captain of the forward 5-inch mount gave permission for his crew to come out and take a smoke. Unfortunately, he also made the decision at some point during the break to exercise the guns. In fact, he was raising and lowering the barrels, twisting the mount around. He was the only guy in there—so he thought. What he didn't realize was that one member of the gun crew was asleep and still in the mount. As the guns were being raised and lowered, they crushed the head of the sleeping sailor. I had a helicopter take him off for treatment. He was not killed instantly in the accident, but he ultimately died.

An investigation followed. I'm not sure what was in all of the documents that resulted from the investigation, but I don't think I got any disciplinary action out of it. Certainly I held mast on the gun captain, but that was about the extent of it. It seems that when some people got off duty, they sat up and played cards instead of going to bed. Then they tried to man their stations when they were very tired. That probably contributed to what happened in this case with the gun captain.

It was quite a traumatic incident for me, because I'd never really been involved in a fatal shipboard accident. The captain is responsible for whatever happens on board, even if he is not directly involved. Obviously, what I had wanted to do was to leave port with so many men on board and take every single one of them back. I really felt bad I wasn't able to take the sailor back to San Diego when the cruise was over.

★★★

I mentioned the search-and-rescue stations. This was in connection with the carrier operations against North Vietnam. The requirement was to be available to pick up a downed aviator if he had to ditch at sea. Normally, an all-gun destroyer such as the *Taussig* operated on the rescue station along with a guided missile destroyer, a DDG. The DDG typically had a squadron or division commander on board and it had superior antiaircraft firepower with its missiles, but the *Taussig* had more guns.

The routine called for the ships to operate within about a twenty-five-mile radius of a specified location in close to shore, ready to pick up pilots if necessary. During the daytime, you typically conducted tactical maneuvers on your own or in concert with the other destroyer; it was a good opportunity for training. Then at dusk, when the planes weren't flying very much, you steamed on back outside, and you stayed out in the open ocean and tooled around together out there. During all this time, we were constantly alert on radio communications so we could be ready to go to the scene if we needed to make a rescue.

Every few nights an oiler came into the vicinity to refuel us. The *Taussig* followed the DDG at maybe five hundred to a thousand yards as we ran along at twenty-five knots to catch the oiler. Finally, you'd pick up the oiler on radar, and at about five miles, as you watched the scope, you'd see him turn as both ships were barreling down on him. We went in on one side and the DDG on the other. You took aboard the fuel you needed as quickly as possible and then got out of the way because another ship would be coming in behind to get its drink of fuel as well. That was quite interesting. I loved high-speed fueling, and, boy, we did our share.

★★★

One of the highlights for me during the cruise was an encounter with a Soviet trawler, the *Gidrofon*. This was an AGI, a 700-ton electronic intelligence ship. The AGIs constantly followed the carriers around, listened to their communications, and reported on their movements. They had a habit of getting close to the carriers and, in some instances, getting in the way. Normally we sent a diesel-engine ship such as a fleet tug (ATF) to stay with these trawlers. When we ran out of those kinds of ships for a short period, we'd then send a full-fledged destroyer to watch and report on the trawlers.

On July 11 and 12 it was the *Taussig*'s role to stay with the *Gidrofon* for a couple of days. Unfortunately, in lying to in a destroyer and turning the engines over once every thirty minutes or so, you have a warping condition in your struts back aft. Engineers are very careful about starting back up again; they want to turn the engines over very slowly for a while until things sort of settle down, and then you can really get under way and move with no problem.

Well, in sitting there and watching the AGI, a condition arose wherein the engineer wanted to limit the speed. When an ATF came out to relieve me, I felt I should brief its commanding officer. I was all prepared to send my boat over to give him the current ops, tell him what had occurred, and everything else. But the skipper of the ATF was sort of a young wise-guy lieutenant who said: "I don't need all that crap. Just tell me what went on, and blah, blah, blah." We didn't really argue or anything like that because lieutenants don't argue with commanders. But I confess I was sort of flabbergasted. And while I was sitting there and nobody was really paying any attention, the *Gidrofon* slipped off. I had to turn him over to this guy who didn't want to accept the responsibility with the *Gidrofon* on the horizon. So I said, "All right, I'll get him again for you."

So I told my engineer: "I need to move this ship in a hurry. We've got to get going now."

He said, "Please don't go more than about twenty knots."

I said: "Screw it. I've got to go get that guy."

By that time, I could see the *Gidrofon* astern of the carrier. He got in to about a thousand yards and was trailing. Then I got a message from the flag officer on the carrier; it said, "Get him out of there." After a while we could make more speed. I maneuvered in fairly close to the Soviet ship, and then whipped across his stern, put on left rudder, and then started paralleling his course, coming in just slightly on him and moving on up his side. I got in there, and then I got just a little bit ahead of him—to the point wherein he thought we were going to collide. This was what we called "shouldering"—to move him out of the way.

The trawler sent me a message, "You're maneuvering like a wild man," or some such crap. Then the *Gidrofon* turned right and came under my stern. I whipped around hard to the right, and I had him trapped right between me and the ATF, which had come over to join us. We proceeded on like that for about ten or fifteen minutes. He couldn't get out one way or the other, and ultimately I felt he was far enough out of the area that I could turn him over to the ATF. I then proceeded to join the carrier as his plane guard and never saw the *Gidrofon* again.

★★★

During the deployment, I was blessed with having an excellent group of officers and enlisted men. There was the occasional disciplinary problem when

I had to hold captain's mast on a sailor, but overall I was very pleased. In the summer of 1966, after we'd been overseas for a few months, the ship got a few new officers, and one in particular stands out in my recollection. He was Ensign Tom Kimmel, the grandson of Admiral Husband Kimmel.[6] I think Tom was one of the most interesting and sharpest people I ever encountered in my whole career. Boy, he was just a sweetheart. He served in the weapons department and remained on board throughout the rest of my tour on the *Taussig*. In that time, he became a fully qualified fleet officer of the deck. In fact, one night I saw him make one of the most beautiful approaches on an oiler I've ever seen. He was a great guy.

In mid-October, not too long after he had come aboard, we got into the part of the schedule in which the *Boyd* and *Taussig* were directed to go down and join up with Australian forces for an exercise called Swordhilt. Since I was the senior skipper of the two, I was designated as officer in tactical command. Once we arrived, we moved into our slots in the formation and participated for about ten days in a very, very rigid and very, very high-class exercise. In addition to the Australians, there were also British and New Zealand ships. I was thoroughly impressed with every action they took.

I had operated with Brits before. I'd seen an Australian up in Vietnam before, but I'd never really been in a close tactical environment with those navies. I think we conducted ourselves very well. In fact, we were complimented at the hot wash-up discussions held at the end of the exercise.[7]

We went through varying evolutions there, including gunfire support and refueling from a British tanker. The connection of hoses between ships was about the same as in the U.S. Navy, but not quite.

In one instance, the ships of the different countries were bunched into a tight little formation so we could all be in the same photo. My position was right on the fantail of an Australian carrier, and there was another carrier astern of me, only about three hundred yards astern. If you're standing on the bridge of a destroyer and look back three hundred yards, you know that if you

6 Ensign Thomas K. Kimmel Jr., USN, graduated from the Naval Academy in the class of 1966. His grandfather, Admiral Husband E. Kimmel, USN, was commander in chief of the U.S. Pacific Fleet at the time the Japanese attacked Pearl Harbor in December 1941. After five years of commissioned service in the Navy, Tom Kimmel resigned and subsequently had a civilian career in the FBI.

7 The hot wash-up is a critique held shortly after an exercise. Participants compare notes and suggestions while events are still fresh in their minds. A more detailed written report often follows.

slow a knot, that guy's going to overtake you. I maintained a steady course and speed while steaming in formation and it went very well.

When the exercise terminated, we went into Melbourne, Australia, for a port visit. It was the first time I had been down under, and I found it to be a fascinating place. I had heard there was some discrimination in Melbourne. It was discrimination not so much against blacks or any other nationality as it was against their own aborigines, who are second-class citizens. And if you were dark, then you were almost classed as an aborigine. But I was invited to some of the nicest affairs I've ever attended, and nobody even looked twice at me.

We threw a party, as I recall, and invited some high-level Australians and other people in Melbourne, and they did the same. In fact, I went to a dinner down there with an organization that was similar to the Navy League, and I was sort of an honored guest and enjoyed it. We were scheduled to be there for about ten days. Unfortunately, that changed on November 4, a week after we arrived. Just before lunch, someone came in. I guess my ops officer had been talking to one of the Australian officers and he said, "There is a hot message coming in for *Taussig*." So we began to speculate on what it could be. The Australians didn't have any idea. I began to think the worst, wondering if we had done something that offended somebody, and they were kicking us out of port, but I couldn't recall anything like that.

We finished lunch, and about one o'clock here came a flash message from Commander Seventh Fleet: "Get under way immediately. Proceed to the vicinity of Frederick Reef. The *Tiru* is aground. Render whatever assistance you can." The *Tiru* was a U.S. diesel submarine that had been with us on this exercise. It had left port, gotten six or seven hours at sea, and on November 3 had run aground up in the Great Northern Reef area. Frederick Reef was a horseshoe-shaped reef, and the submarine was about halfway across, bobbing with each wave.

We left about 2:30. Many of our crew members had already gone ashore on liberty before we got the order to get under way. We tried every method we knew how to get the entire crew back, but I had to leave twenty-one sailors ashore in Melbourne. I knew full well the *Boyd* would pick them up, and since we were all going back to the States we'd join someplace, and the *Boyd* would bring my guys.

In retrospect, it bothered me for years afterward that the *Taussig* got called on for the job and had to cut liberty short. As the senior skipper, I thought the *Boyd* should have been directed to go after the *Tiru*. At that moment it didn't concern me. Hell, it was a job; go do it. Another aspect of the case was how long it took to get the message. I had all these inklings, but in that era, we didn't have satellite communications to the degree we have now. It took about two hours to receive a flash message, which you ought to get in maybe three minutes. If it took as long now as it did in 1966, somebody would be in trouble.

Anyway, we got under way and started moving on up north. For the most part, we were traveling at twenty-five knots whenever the weather permitted. I wanted to get up there in a hurry, but we had to tank up because we were at about fifty percent of fuel capacity. When we had finished fueling, someone told me he just heard over the news broadcast that the *Tiru* had been pulled off the reef. So I began to get in touch with some of the Australian authorities to find out if they still wanted me to continue to go up there.

The word I got was: "Yes, we do. We want you to go rendezvous with him, and release the Australian destroyer, who has another mission tomorrow. And you will escort *Tiru* back into Brisbane." Fine, I got under way from there and went on up and rendezvoused at first light. I relieved the Australian destroyer *Vendetta*, released it, and then escorted the submarine. Having enjoyed my liberty time down in Melbourne, I now wanted to see what Brisbane was like, and I began to calculate location versus speed and how long it was going to take. I had it figured out that if we continued on at the current speed, we'd probably be in there at about two or three o'clock that afternoon, which was just perfect. I could give the crew some liberty before anybody ever found out I was in the town, and then I'd get my instructions to proceed later on.

About that time the submarine suddenly slowed with no real reason given. I tried to get some explanation from the destroyer commander who was on board the submarine. He had already been flown in to start the investigation. I really got nothing from him, and then the *Tiru* slowed some more. The upshot was that it was about midnight by the time we got to Brisbane. I went over to find out the reason for the delay, to see if perhaps there was a leak or some other problem. No, they didn't have a problem; the commodore just decided he didn't want to arrive in port during daylight hours with the press there to do interviews and thus call attention to the misfortune. My guys wished they could have been there earlier, but they began their liberty at midnight instead.

★★★

After the mission was completed, I got a message from Commander Task Group 70.8; it directed me to proceed to Suva in the Fiji Islands. And the *Boyd*, which got under way at its regular time on Monday morning, was to rendezvous in Fiji with me, and then we'd return to the States together. Well, we stayed in there until Wednesday morning, so I did get a whole night of liberty there after most of the people had gotten a chance for liberty in Brisbane as well. We then sailed independently to Fiji, where later that day the *Boyd* came in and rejoined.

There was a celebration for some local event in Fiji. I viewed a big parade and drank some of the local liquor. They had a drink there that looked and tasted like muddy water; you drank it out of half a coconut shell. They almost insisted, and I didn't want to hurt a native's feelings by not drinking this good stuff, so I drank one. And one was more than enough. It was some real potent stuff. The main reason you didn't drink any more was because you heard the story of how it was made. Supposedly the older ladies of the village, toothless, chewed on this coconut pulp, and then spit out the saliva. They let that ferment for a few days, raked off the bugs, raked off the bubbles and everything else, and then you really got good liquor. Now, obviously they don't make it that way in this day and age, when they've got machines to crush it, but that's the way the natives told me they used to make it. My God, I'm glad I didn't have to do that again.

We then got under way after the celebration and headed east toward our home port in San Diego.

★★★

I must digress to explain that I was coming home to a family that had increased in size just before the deployment began that spring. In 1965, while I was still serving in the Pentagon, my baby sister died in her early thirties. She and her husband had seven children—five sons and then two younger daughters who were just babies at the time. The whole family was trying to decide for the husband what would be best for him.

In talking to him, I made the big pitch that he was a young man—thirty-three or thirty-four. I felt personally he needed some time to just get himself squared away, and I offered to take his family with me when I went to the West Coast. I made him a solemn promise I didn't want to steal his family from him, but I would like to do anything I could to help him. He declined the offer and said he felt it was his responsibility to raise his children, and he wanted to start fulfilling it as best he knew how, even without a wife. So he did.

As a result of that experience, I think I fell in love with the idea of having a girl in the family. We already had two boys then, Robbie and David. When we adopted the first child, I insisted on a boy, and then somehow every boy needs a brother, and so we got two. Then, shortly after we arrived at San Diego in January 1966, we started thinking in terms of a girl. Our home was approved for adoption about three weeks before the ship was due to deploy. The normal procedure is that if it's an infant, there's no problem about you going to the adoption agency, picking up this little baby, and bringing it home. But it's different for an older child, and our daughter, Tracey, was almost two years old when she was placed.

First of all, you've got to get acquainted. The child has a mind of her own, and she naturally doesn't take to people right away, particularly just picking her up and stealing her off. So the procedure was that she should come to the house, visit, play with the boys, play with her new dad and mom. And then she'd come there a second time, stay longer. And then the third time stay even longer, and finally she spent the night there. Well, we didn't have that kind of time. We'd made up our minds we wanted her, and the adoption people had made up their minds that this was the girl for us. She arrived to stay on the day before I deployed.

So here I was, going on a seven-month deployment, and Alma stepped on board with our new daughter. I saw Tracey one night and some time the next morning, and then we began our deployment. That was quite a chore for my wife, but she handled it beautifully.

★★★

As the *Taussig* and *Boyd* headed for San Diego, we were scheduled to get back on Thanksgiving Day, November 24. The commodore sent me a message that was not a direct order but told me in no uncertain terms he wanted me to arrive on Thanksgiving. I sat down with my officers, and we calculated it. We'd been running on one boiler, trying to conserve fuel, and the best speed we could achieve was about seventeen and a half or eighteen knots. That was the only way we felt we could make it unless we got a tanker. I sent him back a message that said, "I need a tanker at such-and-such a point south of Pearl, and then I'll need another tanker about four or five hundred miles west of San Diego."

Getting one tanker was pretty hard, much less getting two. We finally gave up on the idea and I said, "I'll be in there the morning after Thanksgiving." The commodore agreed. We got our tanker south of Pearl, topped off with fuel, and continued at our best one-boiler speed. When we arrived in San Diego on November 25, I discovered as we rounded North Island there were two boats sitting in the water to greet us. There were the commodore's gig and the admiral's barge, and they had on board the wives of officers from both the *Taussig* and the *Boyd*. Alma was among them.

Since I was the senior skipper of the two, the *Taussig* was in the lead as we arrived. That was quite a proud moment, as our wives waved at us. I spotted Alma on one of the boats, and I yelled to her: "Where's my daughter? Where is Tracey?" She couldn't quite hear that, and I was left wondering who was babysitting her. But anyway, the boats full of wives circled the *Taussig*, and then they went aft, and they circled the *Boyd*, and then they started to come up to go alongside the pier.

The commander of the cruiser-destroyer group there was Admiral Scott Goodfellow, who was just a great guy.[8] He was Commander Task Group 70.8 when the ship was out in Australia. Alma was on the boat with him and said, "Admiral, you know I wanted to be alongside the pier when my husband came in, but I think he's going to beat you."

Admiral Goodfellow said: "Alma, let me tell you something. First of all, I have never lost a wife over the side. And, secondly, no skipper's ever beat me into that pier yet." He turned up the speed, but then he said, "Whoops, Sam just did it."

That's because I was charging up there to get the ship into port. Although there's a ten-knot speed limit in that harbor, I stretched that as much as I could when we were coming home. Lo and behold, somebody was on the pier holding our new daughter.

As one might imagine, that was a really, really happy time for me. My whole family came on board and we all had a happy reunion. I got a chance

8 Rear Admiral A. Scott Goodfellow, USN, Commander Cruiser-Destroyer Flotilla Seven, 1966–67.

to talk to a daughter with whom I'd had virtually no contact at all between the time she joined the family and when we left to go overseas. I had some nice Australian candy and a Koala bear to give her. We just had a great time. When it was respectable to do so, we went ashore. I've never been a big one for being the first guy off of the ship, so we stayed there for a short while and enjoyed ourselves in my cabin, and then I took my family home.

CHAPTER SEVENTEEN

USS *Taussig*, 1967–68

Very shortly after the *Taussig* got home from the deployment, Alma said to me, "I guess you know that the ship is taking the wives to Acapulco."

I said, "No, Alma, the ship is not taking the wives to Acapulco."

"Well, the commodore says you are."

"Wait a minute, Alma. There's no way the commodore is going to make us take our wives to Acapulco. First of all, wives can't go on the ship."

"Oh, no, no. The wives are going to fly down to Acapulco, and they're going to meet the ships while they're down there."

"Alma, if we're going to Acapulco on a training exercise, that's a mission just like any other. If we're down there on a mission, and something happens and the ship has to leave, what are the wives going to do?"

"Well, I don't know what the wives are going to do, but the commodore's going to take us."

"No, you go back and talk to the commodore."

"You talk to the commodore."

The commodore was Captain Justin Langille, who was Commander Destroyer Division 213. He had indeed said that if he could get it approved the division would go south early in the New Year for an exercise. Included would be a five-day port visit in Acapulco, Mexico, and he told the wives they could fly down and meet us all there. Well, I, being all business about it, said there was no way this could happen because it was an operational commitment. And I couldn't back down. This issue set off quite a thing between my wife and me, as well as the commodore, because he had made the deal for the wives to come down.

In those days, destroyer crews were very close. As I recall, it was December when we had a divisional party, and somebody said to my wife, "Alma, are you going to Acapulco?" The question came up because she had first told them she was going, and then she said she wasn't going after I objected. I guess her answer at that party was, "I really don't know." This went on every time we were all together.

Finally, one time when we were together, Commodore Langille said: "Sam, come on over to the bar. I want to buy you a drink."

"Yes, sir."

"How about a cigar?" I lit up the cigar and took the drink. Then he said, "Sam, take your wife to Acapulco."

"Yes, sir." So the decision was made: we were to take wives to Acapulco.

★★★

In March 1967, we were almost ready to depart on the cruise. This would be my first opportunity to operate with all of the ships of the division, because our sonar problem had kept us from doing so the year before. This time a submarine was tasked to go with us, to provide ASW training during several days of exercises off the San Diego operating area. Then an oiler was to top us off with fuel before we steamed on down to Mexico.

Not long before we were due to sail, something came up that almost made it impossible for us to go. One of the young crew members in the *Taussig* spoke to his division officer and said, "Boy, did I get high last night." To make a long story short, we discovered we had a marijuana ring on board. The first thing I did was to call the Naval Investigative Service, which sent some people over. They started questioning people, and in the meantime, every time I turned around, they'd bring me a new suspect; the previous one was going to the brig ashore. By the time the questioning was completed, something like twenty-three of my crew members were hauled away to the brig. They were still interviewing the last one ten minutes before it was time to get under way.

By the time we left port, I wasn't worried so much about being shorthanded, but I was quite concerned about this drug thing. The worst part about it, I guess, was my decision to send them to the brig, because you couldn't keep people in the brig unless you filed some real charges. I didn't have time to do that before we left. The type commander, CruDesPac, investigated it very quickly. I got the word they were releasing a certain number of my men from the brig and the type commander would keep them. The men were not in confinement, but CruDesPac would maintain custody, which was fine.

That left me to concentrate on the training of the crew members who were still on board. En route to Acapulco, we had a tremendous exercise, played a little bit of everything. It was very helpful in ASW, because we hadn't had much opportunity to practice that during the previous year's cruise. One of the tools we had on board was a drone antisubmarine helicopter (DASH). The idea was that a controller on board the destroyer could fly the little helo remotely, and it could then drop a torpedo in the vicinity of a submarine. The idea was to extend the reach of the ship's weapons against submarines.

There was a requirement the DASH be flown for so many hours per month, and we did. Some ships had problems with the drone, but the *Taussig* had a very good operator on board, and it worked well for us. My experience was that having a DASH on board was just like having another friend, particularly during ASW training, but not everybody felt that way. I can remember being with one of our destroyers when the ship lost control of its DASH while in the midst of an ASW problem. The skipper had to crank up to twenty-five knots to go catch that thing because it was going in the opposite direction. He finally recaptured the drone and got it back aboard.

I was standing on the bridge once with my DASH officer. We were watching another ship, which was one of our nemeses, flying its DASH. This young officer said to me, "I wish that so-and-so would drop in the drink." Boom—it was almost as if he'd pressed a button and it did. It was to some degree hazardous flying, not from a standpoint that you're going to hit something or anything like that. But they lost a few of them because it had to be perfect from an airplane-handling part.

Subsequent to this Acapulco trip, we evaluated DASH as a spotting machine for gunfire support. The drone had a TV camera mounted on it, and we'd fly it off and take pictures of things, and it made a great spotting tool. I think what really killed DASH was being caught up in the controversy of a pilot-controlled vehicle versus the non-pilot-controlled vehicle. The aviators think if it flies, they've got to control it.

★ ★ ★

After we finished the exercises, we pulled into Acapulco on March 11. Commodore Langille called all the skippers over, and he briefed us thoroughly on his expectations for the destroyers' crews. He was bringing sailors and diplomats down there, he said, and not rabble-rousers. Well, we went ashore and went on liberty. Alma and I had a great time, as did many in the crew—but not everyone.

When I got back to the ship that night, I encountered a shore patrolman who was looking for a boilerman first class, one of the sailors in my engineering department. Then I began to see more and more and bigger people, like the naval attaché. Then somebody told me it was the deputy or one of the assistant ambassadors. Well, we'd had a sailor run amok down there. His problem was that he had been dealing with a girl, and he didn't get what he thought he'd paid his money for. In fleeing the scene, this girl was running from house to house, slamming doors, and he was going through doors without unslamming them. He'd created havoc down there.

When we finally collared him, he was going to face a court-martial and to have to pay for the damage he'd done. But there was more than the physical damage; we had damaged the Navy's reputation there. I was prepared to leave the next morning. I went over to call on the commodore to tell him that if he looked out his porthole, he'd see I had the steam up, and I was ready to go if I had to. I said: "Commodore, but don't forget now, my wife is down here. She's down here because you made me bring her."

He said, "Get out of my cabin!" He said it in sort of mock anger. I didn't have to sail. But anyway we had a very, very interesting time down there in Acapulco—a great liberty port.

Looking back on the trip, it was a good training exercise, a good liberty spot, but when I got home, I had to deal with the twenty-three marijuana users. The drug phenomenon hadn't really caught on in the Navy by then, and it wound up getting much worse before it got better in the early 1980s. In 1967, we didn't tolerate users; we got rid of them quickly. If a guy wanted to get out of the Navy, he said, "I smoke marijuana," and in short order he was in the brig and then out of the service.

My problem was conducting all the captain's masts on these characters. I went through every service jacket, every record of what the man had done—mitigating circumstances, the whole bit—and decided whether there would be a court-martial or whether it would be a straight mast. We had so many masts, and we had so many courts-martial, and I guess there were only two guys we really hit hard; they were the sellers. The real culprit was a recalled reservist who had been on board about a month or so, and he'd contaminated nearly two dozen members of my ship's crew. It took a long time to deal with the mess he'd made, but we finally got rid of all of it.

★★★

By this time, we were preparing for the next deployment, and CruDesPac began to form the ships up a little differently. We started as a group of multipurpose ships; in my division there were four FRAM IIs. Then CruDesPac came out with a new scheme, and we became part of an ASW squadron of six ships. Included were two of the *Dealey*-class destroyer escorts and a guided missile destroyer escort. The group was a mishmash, and we brought to the squadron different capabilities within the antisubmarine mission so far as the sensors and weapons were concerned. In addition to the DASH, the *Taussig* also had the variable-depth sonar, which was a great asset because it could be lowered through thermal layers that affect the sonar's performance.

In the spring of 1967, the squadron began to work together with the *Yorktown*, which was a CVS, an aircraft carrier specialized for antisubmarine work. My first meeting with the *Yorktown* was a little bit ahead of the rest of the group. We all knew this was the ship we'd ultimately deploy with, but even before then they needed an escort up in Long Beach because the *Yorktown* was going on a family cruise. They needed a destroyer to play with them a little bit and to show the families what ops the *Yorktown* would be undergoing.

During the course of this, the carrier had me do a couple of things. I plane-guarded for a bit. I went up ahead and set up a screen. Then, finally, I came alongside and took on a little fuel. Normal fueling speed was about twelve knots, as I recall, but we were getting a little late, and the *Yorktown* was a long way from Long Beach, so the skipper wanted to know if we could do it at fifteen. I said: "Fine. Step it up to fifteen."

"Hey, that's great. Can you do it at eighteen?"

"Hell, yes. Do it at eighteen."

"How about twenty-two?"

"Twenty-two, go."

The next thing I knew, there I was, alongside this guy, barreling back into Long Beach at twenty-five knots. He let me go after a while, and I took off and came on back to San Diego. It was an impressive show for the families, although they may have thought it was just standard routine. But the *Yorktown* task group became a favorite group to be with. That was because of the admiral on board, good old Ralph Weymouth.[1] He was just a great, fantastic guy, and I almost loved him, if you could love an admiral.

The time in San Diego became a series of inspections, and we did fairly well. We certainly did the ship exercises that were required as part of the competitive year.[2] I remember one night in particular, and this was a strange one. We were out with the division running exercises, and the commodore decided we ought to run a full-power trial. We lined up with the ships abreast of each other, and we started getting on up to maximum speed. After a while we were charging along at about thirty-four knots or close to it. I was sitting up on the bridge, and I guess I'd been there for ten or fifteen minutes when the CIC reported a contact dead ahead. As we were moving along, the contact kept getting closer.

Finally, our CIC said, "Collision course." On a full-power trial you do a little fishtailing no matter what, but you want to drive as straight and true as you can if you want to get maximum speed out of the propeller turns you're doing through the water. I said, "Hang in there." And suddenly we were close enough to the other ship that we could communicate by flashing light. We got a light from this ship, which turned out to be a Navy attack transport. The message said: "Request you stand clear. I am running a full-power trial. My speed sixteen."

I just said send him back, "My speed thirty-four." And it was obvious then that he changed course. Up to then I'm sure the skipper of the APA didn't believe it. It so happened that the ops officer on that ship was a young officer who was my protégé to some degree. He told me later he reported us as a surface contact running at thirty-four knots, and his skipper didn't believe him.

He said: "It must be a helicopter or something. You guys are all screwed up." But when he got "My speed thirty-four," he believed us and moved over.

---

1 Rear Admiral Ralph Weymouth, USN, Commander Antisubmarine Warfare Group One, 1967–68.

2 Each year, Navy ships within a given group compete with each other for honors, including the Battle Efficiency E. The standings are based on ship performance, inspections, and various exercises.

In the summer of 1967, we were involved with midshipman training, and we did more antisubmarine workups in the fall with the *Yorktown* and these other destroyers. We were always together after that time. One of the destroyers in the group was the *Chevalier*. The skipper of that ship and I were very good friends, but we had a slight problem because he was senior to me. One time when we were moored alongside the *Chevalier* my exec got a little bit overzealous. One of the notes he put in the plan of the day said, "We've got to clean up this ship, or else we'll look like all the rest of the dogs alongside." The skipper of the *Chevalier* was the only guy who really took offense. He called me over and showed me the note and said, "Don't we have enough problems keeping our sailors from fighting and all this?" I apologized to him.

Later he called me over there again, and I wondered what we had done now. This time he was on a telephone line back to Washington because he'd heard that the captains' selection list had come out, and someone in Washington was reading off the names to him. He was writing them down, and my name was on that list, which made me quite proud. I was fairly senior on the list, so I was able to put on my new insignia right away.

On the afternoon of the announcement, I went home and told Alma, "I'm sailing in the morning, and somehow I've got to get my blues striped by tomorrow morning." We went to downtown San Diego, but none of the tailor shops had any gold they could use. So I said, "Well, honey, I guess the only way we can do this is that you've got to do it." Bless her, my wife stayed up all night taking stripes off uniforms and matching the gold on the one I would wear. The next morning I went down to the ship, proud to be wearing four stripes, and got under way for Long Beach, where the *Yorktown* was based.

December 28, 1967, was the date we deployed. The six destroyers got under way from San Diego, rendezvoused with the *Yorktown*, and steamed to Pearl as a group. While we were operating off Pearl Harbor, we picked up a nuclear submarine. We tracked this guy for about half a day or so. Between the six destroyers and the aircraft from the *Yorktown* we managed to keep contact on him for a long time, but we did eventually lose him around French Frigate Shoal.

We stopped in Hawaii for a short rest and recuperation, and then we took off toward Yokosuka, Japan. In late January, we learned the North Koreans had captured the U.S. intelligence ship *Pueblo*. The Seventh Fleet ordered a large number of ships to assemble for a show of force off North Korea. So we went by Yokosuka at twenty-five knots, heading up to the Sea of Japan. We went up there and steamed around with all the rest of the ships for about forty-five days.

My thought was that two destroyers could get the job done—one of them to tow the *Pueblo* out of Pyongyang and the other to shoot up the North Koreans. I asked Admiral Weymouth, the group commander, to permit me to go in there, but he was much wiser than I. I really think it could have been done, but the political situation was such that we didn't do it. A U.S. attack might have led to a war with North Korea, and we already had one going in Vietnam.

That was a very, very interesting time for me. Previously, I had spent time off Korea in both the *Toledo* and the *Iowa*, but certainly not with the responsibility I had as commanding officer of the *Taussig*. In those earlier tours, I was inside the ships much of the time because of my duty stations. Here I was on an open bridge, and certainly I was seeing things I hadn't seen before. For example, I'd never seen it really snow at sea. In fact, I remember one time when some kid went up on the forecastle and made a snowman.

Day after day, we did that for a month and a half, and then the *Yorktown* group was detached and sent to other duties. We served as plane guard for the *Yorktown* on the way to Sasebo, Japan. Later the *Taussig* went into Kaohsiung, Taiwan, and down to Subic Bay in the Philippines. The individual ships in the group got out to Vietnam again, where we did more shore bombardment and some plane-guarding for other carriers.

Someplace along in there—and I'm not sure exactly when it happened—we were at sea, and one morning a *Taussig* sailor saw a small parrot on the lifeline. He asked me if I wanted him to go over and get the bird. I said, "Sure," because I had no idea he could actually do it. He brought the bird up to the bridge, and we let the parrot walk around on the gunwales there for a while. Of course, everybody was up there looking at the captain's bird.

Finally, I told my engineer officer, "Why don't we build a cage for this bird?" Then we started thinking of a name for it. The call sign for a helicopter is "Fetch," and the commander is "Fetch Zero Zero." So that was the name of our bird, "Fetch Zero Zero." We must have had him for three months or so. When we were under way he stayed on the bridge and took in some nice sunshine. When we got into port, I would keep him in my cabin. Members of the crew fed and watered him. He became sort of the ship's pet, and we really enjoyed Fetch Zero Zero. That was especially true for me because I've been a bird fancier for a long time.

We ultimately ended up in Malaysia for a port visit and were there when my relief, Commander Robert Adler, came aboard. On June 5, 1968, we had our change of command on the helicopter deck while the ship was en route to Vietnam. When the change of command was through and we swapped off, we opened up the helo hangar. In it were a big cake to cut and the cage with our crew member bird in it. Admiral Weymouth had seen Fetch Zero Zero previously, and he really admired him. The admiral came aboard the *Taussig* by helo for our change-of-command ceremony. Afterward, he sampled the cake and then changed back to his flight suit for the return to the *Yorktown*.

About then one of the sailors came up to me and said, "Captain, Captain, he's stealing our bird." Admiral Weymouth had reached into the cage, taken the bird, stuck it in his pocket, and walked on back to be hoisted into the helo. So when the kid told me the admiral had our bird, I said, "Son, go tell your captain, because I've been relieved, remember?"

As luck would have it, I was getting a ride to the carrier also, because I was going to be flown off the next morning to go home. I was hoisted up by cable right after Admiral Weymouth was, and the helo went on to the carrier. We got to the *Yorktown*, and the skipper greeted me saying, "You're going to sleep in my in-port cabin."

"Fine," and I started to leave.

Admiral Weymouth said, "Oh, no, come on up, come on up to my cabin for a few minutes."

I said, "Yes, sir." I went on up to his cabin, and he reached into his pocket and he pulled out the wettest and the maddest little bird you have ever seen. He set the parrot down on the table about the same time a steward came up and brought the admiral a glass of tea. The bird jumped up on the edge of his glass, took a big swig, let out a big turd, and then sat there a little while. Admiral Weymouth was just laughing and laughing. He said: "You know what? I liked your idea with him. I'm going to get me a cage."

I said, "Yes, sir."

He called up the damage control officer and asked him to build a cage for the bird. Well, this was a carrier, not a destroyer. On a destroyer you build a little cage about twelve by twelve by twelve, or something like that—great for the bird. The carrier damage control officer came over with a cage about three feet by three feet by three feet. Anyway, they took the bird, and I just sort of moved around the carrier.

The next morning I was going to fly off at about nine o'clock, so I was up and eating my breakfast. Then I went in to see Admiral Weymouth and tell him good-bye. He said, "When you get back to the States, would you check on the quarantine rules and write me a letter, and let me know what I've got to do to bring him in."

I said, "Yes, sir."

Before I left, I wanted to take one last look at the bird and learned he was in one of the ready rooms. I went down to the ready room and sort of said good-bye to Fetch Zero Zero. Then I went up and said to the captain, "I've got to tell you, that bird has to have sunlight. You've got a nice air-conditioned compartment down there for pilots, but it's dark. You ought to put him in a smaller cage, and put him up on the bridge."

He said: "Don't you worry about the bird. I'll take care of the admiral's bird."

"Yes, sir," and I got on my flight and flew back.

After I got home, I checked on the quarantine rules and found out it was no major problem. The bird had to be examined, but they'd let him in. Then I got a big long letter from Admiral Weymouth talking about how sorry he was he had stolen the bird, because the parrot had caught pneumonia and died shortly thereafter. That was a sad postscript to our adventure with Fetch Zero Zero.

★ ★ ★

That long flight back to the West Coast gave me time to think about my destroyer command. I really had mixed emotions then and I have mixed emotions about it even today. I spent thirty months in that destroyer, and I know I did a good job. But I'm more convinced than ever that thirty months was too long. I concluded that eighteen months is too short and thirty months is too long. So, about twenty-four months must be the right time to have command of a destroyer. There are just so many things that go on. I feel every time you get a ship under way, you lose a little bit of the one hundred percent luck you started with. I'm convinced that at about the twenty-four-month point you get down to less than fifty percent luck, and something's going to happen sooner or later. You can get too cocky. When everything's going to work right for you, you screw it up. Or you begin to get cautious, and you screw it up. I will also say I thoroughly enjoyed my time in command of the *Taussig*.

CHAPTER EIGHTEEN

Satellite Communications Program

After I was promoted to captain, I knew I was too senior for the *Taussig* billet, because destroyers didn't have four-stripers as skippers. By then, I'd been on board for almost two years, it was time to deploy, and I knew my time was fairly short. The officer to whom I reported resented the fact that there were two captains in the squadron—one as commanding officer of a ship, and he as the squadron commander. One day while he was crossing my ship, he told me he'd called the Bureau of Personnel to find out when they were going to take me off, because he preferred there be a young commander on board. Apparently, the bureau didn't give him any satisfaction.

What's interesting was that even though my boss wanted to get rid of me, I wasn't that eager to move. (This was before I got the insight I came to later—that two years was just about the right time to be in command of a destroyer.) At the time, I was very happy there in the ASW group. I really had found my niche there, and I had a good friend in the group commander. Admiral Weymouth liked me and trusted me, and he knew I was operating the ship as he wanted it operated. So I was not concerned about going on a deployment other than the fact that it was another six or seven months away from home.

Another factor about that time was the establishment of the first Naval ROTC unit in a predominantly black college—Prairie View A&M in Texas. Unofficially, I'd heard I was being considered as a commanding officer of the unit. Ultimately, Commander Jerry Thomas went down as exec and I was no longer in the running.[1] In fact, when I called the bureau, I couldn't get the detailer himself. The secretary told me that, yes, I was being taken care of back there, and I didn't have to worry. She said that the secretary of defense was looking into my assignment. That really upset me a little bit, because I knew something special was happening. I was the first black line captain, and I didn't want any special treatment.[2] I just wanted to be treated as another naval captain and get my next duty on merit. I don't know what all went into the process, but I did get a set of orders to be head of the Naval Satellite Communications Program.

There was no problem except for the fact that I really was not a post-graduate communicator. I'd had a couple of communication tours back in the 1950s in two ships, the *Toledo* and the *Iowa*, and ten years later, I had had that tour in the Pentagon with the construction of the command center. It just seemed to me I was being bandied around in the communications area, but I had not really been in communications enough to have a true grasp of the field.

Once I had left the *Taussig* and got back to San Diego, Alma and I decided we would go north, take the Trans-Canadian Highway across to the East Coast, and come on down to Washington, D.C. While we were en route from California, I became depressed. After we arrived in Washington, I had real difficulty in going to the Pentagon. I didn't understand it. Alma took me out to the naval hospital in Bethesda, Maryland, and I was admitted in a depressed condition. I stayed there for a couple of months, and ultimately I discovered the problem was a medication called Reserpine that I was taking for my high blood pressure. I never will forget that name because it really had me driven up a wall for a couple of months. And this was already a tough time simply because I was going into a new job, a very responsible job.

Finding a remedy for my hypertension turned out to be quite a challenge. It's unfortunate, but many of the medications you take for one kind of illness seem to have a side effect that gives you another one. Subsequently, I was put

---

1 Commander Gerald E. Thomas, USN, reported as XO of the Prairie View unit in April 1968. The first commanding officer of the unit was a white officer, Captain Francis X. Brady, USN. Thomas had been commissioned through the NROTC unit at Harvard University in 1951. He subsequently earned a PhD and in 1974 was promoted to rear admiral. He was the second African-American to achieve that rank.

2 U.S. naval officers are generally divided into two groups—line and staff. As previously indicated, Chaplain Dave Parham was the first African-American staff corps captain in the U.S. Navy. Parham's date of rank was February 1, 1966; Gravely's was November 1, 1967.

on another medication. Then one day I learned I had diabetic tendencies, and we discovered they were brought on by the second medication. So I went on still another medication. Then I discovered that the medication I'm currently on lowers my potassium, so I have to take a potassium supplement. But those are the hazards of high blood pressure and the medications that are supposed to treat it.

While I was hospitalized, Alma took care of the family and getting a place to live. Fortunately, the real estate climate had improved from the time in 1964 when we had such problems. She had no difficulty at all in finding the house we rented. We moved into a rather nice and quiet neighborhood in North Arlington. The owner was a political appointee in the federal government. As I recall, he went to Europe for a two-year tour, and I took his house while he was in Europe. We had good neighbors, and everything went fine with the house. My kids played little league football. In fact, I became one of the coaches of the team.

★★★

In getting into my new job, I had a lot of support from my boss, Admiral Fitzpatrick, who was just a top-notch guy.[3] He made sure I went to Norfolk to talk to the guy who preceded me in satellite communications, to follow the work he had done. I saw the comm station at Norfolk, and I had fairly good rapport with a group of people over at the Naval Electronic Systems Command (NavElex). In addition, we brought in a tremendous civilian by the name of Bob Langeleer, who was my deputy. He had come out of the Army as a captain and was very, very knowledgeable in the area of satellite communications. He made it quite easy for me to become familiar with the job. He was a good briefer who had original ideas and the whole gamut of capabilities. At that time, in the late 1960s, the area of satellite communications was relatively new for the Navy, so I was learning along with a number of other people. Trying to get the program through OpNav was probably one of the hardest things I had to do, and it certainly was a good time for me because I got an awful lot of visibility.

The first problem I had to deal with in that job was that the Navy had relied on superhigh frequency (SHF), and we had seven terminals that never worked. Not only that, they were huge, monstrous things. The antenna sec-

3 Rear Admiral Francis J. Fitzpatrick, USN, Commander Naval Communications Command.

tion weighed about twenty-five hundred pounds. It was tough getting the antennas to sea; in fact, they had gone on only the larger ships, and they constantly failed. A decision had to be reached as to what to do about this. I had the chore of circulating a message through OpNav, and I do mean carrying it by hand and getting all the approvals on it, to kill this SHF program. In the meantime, with Bob Langeleer there, we then went to the UHF satellite program, which is the one we have now. There were certain experiments being carried on with various satellites that were put up by Lincoln Lab, the Air Force, and two or three other groups. We began to join into those programs and managed to really get into the arena.

The people we worked with in developing the capability were in the laboratories. For example, at that time the Naval Ocean Systems Center had the Naval Electronics Laboratory Command. I met some really good people out there. The NavElex people worked as a team. We also dealt with a lot of private concerns, such as RCA and TRW, but you have to be very careful, particularly if you're on active duty. There's always the possibility of conflict of interest. Certainly, there's no conflict when you go out and see the program. But then you've got to watch the lunches and the cocktail parties and the other things that go along with it. In fact, I got some very, very valuable guidance from Admiral Fitzpatrick concerning that. One time a contractor invited me to an oyster roast. I went to see the admiral to ask if he thought it was all right. He simply said, "Avoid the appearance of evil," and I knew that accepting the invitation wasn't the right thing to do. I have never forgotten that.

★ ★ ★

There were really two jobs for the satellite communications office. One part had to do with developing the hardware and systems through research and development. The other part required selling the program in order to get the necessary funding. The money part was particularly difficult. I can remember briefing Vice Admiral Ralph Cousins, who was deputy chief of naval operations (fleet operations and readiness), and Secretary of the Navy John Chafee. All told, I briefed a couple of hundred people, and it was a very, very difficult program for the Navy to grasp. We could see it doing simply great things for communications, but I've always felt the problem was that communications don't go bang and don't make any waves through the water. Communication is an essential part of operating a navy, but it seems the only time communicators are noticed is when a message is missed, not when they've sent a message perfectly.

One of the hard things about a new program in communications is that you first must sacrifice the old to get the new. What do you do in the meantime? It was a case of trying to shuffle dollars from going into the repair and maintenance of old equipment to buying new equipment. We had some tough people in OpNav in those days. They were good people, and I think they sympathized with me, but at the same time their feeling was, "We've got to keep the ships armed, and we'll communicate as best we can."

Even though we were making progress, the Navy satellite communications program at that time was rather frustrating. I decided one morning I'd had enough. I'd served more than twenty years, so I should probably retire and try to do something else. I put in my retirement papers. At that time, I worked really for two admirals. Besides Admiral Fitzgerald, my other boss was Rear Admiral William J. Moran, director of the Navy Space Program Division. I was attached to his staff also, since satellites were under the space program, and to Fitzpatrick as a communicator. So I ran between two bosses.

I first handed my retirement letter to Admiral Moran, who said, "I'm going to keep this in my desk for a couple of days, and if you still think that way, we'll forward it on up."

He held it for two or three days, and then he decided to send it to Fitzpatrick, who called me down one day. He said: "Sam, I want you to go fishing. I want you to fish for four or five days, take leave, and then come back and let me know how you feel about this. And I want you to remember one thing: the purpose of fishing is not always to catch fish." I went off for the fishing and came back after about four days with renewed vigor.

I'm sure that was what he had in mind for me. I really admired Admiral Fitzpatrick, and I think he was fairly happy with the job I was doing, knowing that my physical and mental condition for at least the first part of the tour wasn't top-notch because of my health problems. In any event, I came back and I just went down there to Fitzpatrick and said, "Sir, if you don't mind giving me back that letter, I know what to do with it today." I threw it in the wastebasket.

I stayed in that billet for about fifteen or sixteen months. Then one day I got the magic call from the Bureau of Naval Personnel; it told me I had been selected for major sea command. I was overjoyed to get that news.

CHAPTER NINTEEN

USS *Jouett*

Learning from the Bureau of Naval Personnel that I had been selected for a major command was the happiest news I'd received in a long time. Soon I got a second call, which told me I'd been selected to go to the *Jouett*. It was then classified as DLG, guided missile frigate, and later in its career was redesignated a CG, guided missile cruiser. When I discovered I was going there, I became a little disappointed, because the *Jouett* was scheduled to go through a yard overhaul for a year. It was to be modernized as a flagship and would receive several other innovations.

I talked to my detailer, who said, "You were specifically picked to go to that job because we wanted a guy with a little knowledge of electronics." Of course, a little knowledge was about all I had at that point, but in any event I was quite pleased to be going back to sea. I eagerly awaited the day the orders would arrive.

When they came, the orders shocked me a little bit, although I can easily see now why they read the way they did. I was going to a ship that had Terrier missile, antisubmarine rocket (ASROC), and nuclear capability. Instead of going to the ship via schools that dealt with the weapon systems, I was ordered to attend damage control school. My concern was, "Here I'm going out driving this new vessel, and I know nothing about the main battery." But, after all, the *Jouett* was going into the shipyard for a year, and when I got there the major concern would be to make sure there were no fires, flooding, or other mishaps. I concluded I would have plenty of time to learn the weapon systems. So, after I looked into it, I was very happy about the arrangement.

The damage control course was in Philadelphia. Once I'd completed it, I headed out to San Diego, where the ship was homeported. I had a home in San Diego, but it was rented out at the time, so we rented a place in Chula Vista. To my considerable surprise (and pleasure), the ship's overhaul and modernization plans evaporated. The *Jouett* had gotten back from deployment to the western Pacific in mid-February 1970. Since the crew had been expecting to go into the shipyard in July, they made extensive preparations for that. I got to the ship on May 15, spent time in the turnover process, and took over command on May 22. The new schedule called for the ship to be made ready to deploy again in the autumn, which didn't provide much time to prepare for something considerably different from what we expected.

In addition, there would be a couple of fleet operations. In fact, we essentially had to complete our yearly schedule of exercises before we left, because we wouldn't get a chance to do many of those out in WestPac. So we put together a fast schedule to see what could we get out of the short time in which we had to work. We knew that a ship deploying in October would spend the months of August and September in port getting ready to go overseas. That gave me June and July to get the ship prepared. I was not disappointed the least bit that we would be skipping the lengthy shipyard overhaul, and I was not disappointed that we really had to do a lot of work during those coming months.

As events turned out, the next few months became a fruitful training period for me. We went in and out of San Diego, and I began to compare the maneuverability of the *Jouett* with the *Taussig*. I found the *Jouett* much easier to handle in all respects. Just a beautiful ship. I loved it. I loved the ship handling with it. I can remember the first time we came back into San Diego after being out in the operating area for three or four days. We were coming back in and had to go alongside a pier at the foot of Broadway. We took a harbor pilot aboard as normal and had a tug standing by. For some reason, the pilot and my exec began a conversation up on the wing of the bridge. I kept waiting for the pilot to say, "Well, do you want me to take it?" And he never said it. So I just drove it on in alongside, and boy, that really built up my confidence to where it should have been. The pilot complimented me as well, and I was very happy. As I said before, the captain really earns the respect of his crew if he's a capable ship handler.

To make up for the fact that the ship was going to miss the prolonged yard period, the *Jouett* spent about five weeks at the Long Beach Naval Shipyard. Among other things, we went to the dry dock. The shipyard people eliminated a spoke in the sonar dome—the same kind of problem we had to get fixed in the *Taussig* a few years earlier. The shipyard visit also meant trips into Seal Beach to off-load and reload ammunition. The only major exercise I can remember was one under the auspices of the First Fleet. At that point in time, First Fleet was based in San Diego, and Vice Admiral Isaac Kidd was the fleet commander.[1] The fleet exercise had in it, as I recall, at least two DLGs, and it also had a cruiser that was the First Fleet's flagship. Rear Admiral Art Esch basically ran the exercise for First Fleet.[2] Admiral Kidd wanted to go out and observe, but he did not want to be on board his flagship. I discovered that, so I put a bug in the ear of one of First Fleet's people and said we would be very happy to have the admiral on board the *Jouett*. He took me up on my offer, came aboard, and rode the ship for four days. I think I made a credible impression on Admiral Kidd because it was my understanding that a year later he sat on the selection board that was considering captains for promotion to rear admiral. So I didn't do things too badly.

Admiral Kidd was a very, very knowledgeable guy, and he wanted things done immediately. He also had a supervisory nature. I can remember once when we were transferring a missile, and I thought he was almost in the way of my people who were making the transfer because he was right down there on deck. He was not screaming or shouting or anything like that, but he was giving a few orders here and a few orders there. I liked the guy, I really did. He had a top-notch staff: very good people, very knowledgeable, never in the way, always just doing the job, and they did it well.

My favorite recollection from the exercise was a phase when we were shooting missiles. The other DLG unfortunately couldn't fire its missiles, so I got a chance to fire sixteen, which was about twice my allowance for the exercise. That was the first time I'd ever seen a missile go off. In a DLG-type ship, the captain typically conned the ship and ran the show from the CIC, where he kept track of the big picture electronically. In that arrangement, the

---

1 Vice Admiral Isaac C. Kidd Jr., USN, was then Commander First Fleet and soon thereafter was transferred to become Commander Sixth Fleet. His father, a rear admiral in 1941, was killed on board the battleship *Arizona* at Pearl Harbor.

2 Rear Admiral Arthur G. Esch, USN, Commander Cruiser-Destroyer Flotilla Eleven.

exec would be out on the bridge as a safety observer. But for that particular exercise, I changed places with the XO because I wanted to be out there to see the missiles launched. Later I did take up my battle station in CIC, but I didn't really care for it. I always thought the commanding officer had the best eyeballs on the ship, and he ought to be out there where he could use them. I spent most of my time on the bridge, and I think it paid off for me ultimately, but I'll get into that a little later.

There's one other thing I should mention from the period when the crew and I were getting acquainted with each other. When I got aboard, there was a picture of a bird called a jayhawk as part of the ship's insignia. I discovered one day just what it is—a little bird that preys on other birds. I didn't think that it was a proper representative for a proud ship of the fleet, so I changed it, and we became the *Jouett* Jaguars, with a flag and insignia to match. I thought the crew's spirit soared as the result of being connected with a beast like the jaguar instead of being a small jayhawker. And we had our little tricks of the trade when we would be in on an underway replenishment: make a nice fast approach, stay in until you were topped off, then you unhooked the lines, and you would break away at twenty-five knots, hoisting the flag with a little music for the troops on the other side. Little innovative things like that kept the spirits of the group going.

★ ★ ★

When the time came, we took off on October 2 and sailed to WestPac. We went independently, with a stop in Pearl, where we stayed for two days. I went up to Pacific Fleet headquarters and got various briefings. From there we went to Guam, Subic Bay, and on out to the line in Vietnam. Our mission was as a PIRAZ ship. That stood for positive identification radar advisory zone, which involved the Navy tactical data system. It was an early combination of radar and computers. The PIRAZ ship set up about medium way up north off Vietnam. The *Jouett* was responsible for the positive identification of any contact that came into the Tonkin Gulf. The U.S. carrier planes were bombing in Vietnam, and part of our job was to track the raids on the way in and back out again. We had to make sure that all the planes coming back to the aircraft carriers were American; that no enemy planes were tagging along.

Normally, you had a very senior destroyer commodore on board. He was responsible for the ops up there, but the ship's commanding officer certainly was his right-hand man. So whenever anybody had any kind of a radar contact, the information all came to the *Jouett,* which evaluated it and made a decision on whether it was friend or foe. We had a pretty sharp radar group on board and were also capable in ASW. We were the number-one ship up there, really, as far as I could tell.

The most unusual experience we had on PIRAZ station came in November 1970, when a force of U.S. commandos attempted to rescue American prisoners of war who were believed to be held at Son Tay, a city near Hanoi in North Vietnam. While the operation was in the preparatory stage, I was called over to the aircraft carrier that was flagship for Commander Task Force Seventy-Seven. I rode over in a helicopter, and while I was there, I developed what was called "Plan *Jouett.*" The basic idea was that the *Jouett* would go in as close inshore as possible, with all radars, everything, turned on. Then we would steam away in the dark, gradually cutting off things as the range increased to where nothing was heard. Then we would zip back and just let go. And, of course, we'd have the airplanes in there too. But the plan was never used, and I'm not sure why. As it happened, the raid did not bring about the desired result. When the Army's Green Berets got to the camp, they found the prisoners had been moved earlier by the North Vietnamese.

Normally on PIRAZ station, we had an all-gun destroyer with us. This was the same type ship as the *Taussig* I had commanded earlier—each armed with six 5-inch guns. We were refueling one day when we got word there was a contact sort of to the north and east of us about thirty miles away. The *Jouett*'s helicopter was already flying around, so I sent orders for it to investigate the contact. The helicopter reported on the radio that he was within about five miles of this contact. It appeared the contact had guns on it, and the pilot asked if we wanted him to go any closer. Instead, I told him to come on back, and as soon as we finished refueling we would steam over and investigate it ourselves.

I put my gun destroyer at five hundred yards astern of me and went charging over there at twenty-five knots. We discovered the contact was a Chinese merchant ship, painted completely white. I had my two ships at general quarters and we were all ready to go. I went close alongside, and we took pictures. I was apprehensive that there was something pointed at the *Jouett.* The Chinese ship had something that looked almost like a stovepipe with some guy standing behind it. What I saw was probably some kind of mortar. It was pointed at my bridge, and I could constantly see it aimed at my eyeballs every time I looked over there. We were ready for bear if anything had happened. In remembering the incident afterward, it always concerned me how things might have turned out. At the first clap of thunder, I think I would have let him have it. And I think he would have let me have it too.

★★★

The *Jouett* was a beautiful ship and a good deal larger than a destroyer. It was 547 feet long and displaced almost eight thousand tons. Because it was a major command, the ship was blessed with a great deal of talent, both enlisted men and officers. That was one of the most competent wardrooms I'd ever been associated with. In the 1950s, when I was on board the *Iowa* and the *Toledo*, it was during the Korean War and the phase-down of Korea. We still had a lot of reservists in the crew. With the *Jouett*, I had a larger proportion of regular Navy officers, men who were dedicated to being in the Navy and who were going to make a career out of it. I had two execs while I was skipper. They were both outstanding officers, and both of them made captain. One was Commander Nicholas Brown, who was just an outstanding officer. He was from the famous Browns of Rhode Island, the family associated with Brown University and so forth.[3] The other was Zeke Newcomb, who went down to Charleston to command a destroyer, and he did well.

There was a good group in engineering. Unfortunately, I had one officer whom I chose to fire. This guy had taken training to become a nuclear engineer. He had failed the program, but he was still a very good main propulsion assistant (MPA). But he had no leadership qualities whatsoever. He couldn't give an order like "Right standard rudder" or anything like that. He knew how to fix the valves, but that was about all he could do.

The major problem came up back when we were in Long Beach. This was in his purview really, because we were supposed to get a boiler inspection before we left for the western Pacific. He made arrangements for the CruDesPac boiler inspection team to come up and inspect our boilers. They arrived on a Monday morning, and they were there for about thirty minutes or so. I got word they wanted to see me, so I had them up to the cabin. One of them said, "Captain, we came up from San Diego to inspect your boilers, and the boilers are not ready for the inspection."

---

3 The father of the *Jouett*'s executive officer was John Nicholas Brown, who served in the Navy in World War I and was later assistant secretary of the Navy for air from 1946 to 1949.

I said, "Well, I'm sure if this is a surprise inspection, they're not."

"Oh, no. Your MPA scheduled this about three weeks ago, and we're going to have to give you an unsat."

"Well, let me find the MPA and talk to him." We couldn't find him. His boss, my engineer officer, normally would have been there, but he had been sent down to San Diego for a five-day training course. It would have been no problem for the MPA to hack it except the MPA wasn't there. I told them I had to accept the unsatisfactory assessment, but I assured them we'd have them back up in short order, and those boilers would be ready.

They left, and I guess it was about eleven o'clock; I began to take a routine stroll around the deck. And whom should I see but my MPA, who was walking a young lady around, giving her a tour of the ship. He came up to me and said: "Captain, I'd like you to meet my girlfriend. She came in from Brooklyn over the weekend, and she's staying so and so, and I'm taking her out to the airport to catch her plane back at about two o'clock [or something like that]."

I just said: "Yes. When you get back, you come in and see me." At about three o'clock he came back. By then I had all his bags packed and sent him on down to CruDesPac. He had scheduled this inspection and then forgot about it, and in the meantime his girlfriend was much more important to him than the ship. So I just decided I couldn't use him any longer. Not only that, I'd already given up on him on leadership and trying to get him up on the bridge. I sent him away.

My commodore, Captain Albert Stickles, sympathized with me, but I know he felt the guy should have been tried in another department. Well, your officers of the deck generally come from the weapons department, and he was not going to make an OOD; that was no place for him. The operations department didn't want him. Nobody wanted him, so even though we disagreed, I got rid of him.

★★★

Another milestone in that era was the advent of Admiral Zumwalt's tenure as CNO.[4] He took over about a month after I'd taken command of the *Jouett.* His office put out a series of policy directives known as Z-grams because of the first letter of Zumwalt's last name. They had the effect of liberalizing per-

4 Admiral Elmo R. Zumwalt Jr., USN, served as chief of naval operations from July 1970 to June 1974.

sonnel policies, and a number of them were controversial because they were viewed as undermining discipline. Z-grams, like any other messages generally, were interpreted by the officers and handed down or not handed down depending on where they applied.

Z-gram 66, which came out in December 1970, affected us more than any other. It had to do with racial discrimination and equal opportunity in the Navy. The commodore sent out a message to all of his ships asking what they were doing to implement Z-Gram 66. One guy sent back a message that just really upset me. I can't recall exactly what the tone was, but I do know that as a result I wrote a letter to the Naval Institute's *Proceedings* magazine, and it was published in the August 1971 issue. This individual's views on integration were just so contrary to what I thought the norm should be, especially for a commanding officer, that I took him to task.

It was no surprise that I didn't have any racial problems on board my ship. Nicholas Brown was an officer who believed a man was a man, and Zeke Newcomb, my second exec, felt about the same way. They wanted to carry out my policies, and as best we could discuss them, they did it. I was the commanding officer of the ship. Nobody doubted that. I didn't go around bragging about it, but I think in my walk and my way of doing business, people knew I was fully in charge. There was never, never any problem. I think most of the little fellows felt they were treated fairly on board the *Jouett*. I would hear of one or two minor incidents, and we'd investigate these things, and it was sort of a comme ci, comme ça thing. But never anything major.

One of the problems for COs of that era was the feeling the CNO was going around the chain of command rather than down through it. Some felt the Z-grams gave people rights that should ordinarily come from their own command, but I didn't get that feeling on board ship. I got that feeling more after I got onto the CNO's staff about a year later. I began to see it, I guess, from a different perspective, and I thought commanding officers were being trampled on a little bit. But then again, when your boss man says do something, you do it to the best of your ability.

On reflection, I think this method of instituting new policies was one of the problems for Admiral Zumwalt, even though he was someone I admired, especially for his stand on racial opportunity. The difficulty came because a lot of people felt they could drag their feet on implementing his directives. Then, when he sort of chomped down, they still dragged their feet, and it was just an impossible situation. If you as a four-star can't get three-stars to carry out your orders, you're in trouble. And as we all know, there was trouble during the regime.

I don't think the typical young black sailor was reading Z-grams. He might have heard this or heard that, but I don't believe the effect was as great as some people think it was. I do know there were race riots on board some ships during Admiral Zumwalt's tenure. I didn't have any of those on the *Jouett*, but a couple of ships did have them during that period. I think the impetus came from the new guys who'd had a certain amount of what they saw as freedom on the outside. They found it hard to adjust to the discipline and routines in the Navy. For example, at ten o'clock at night there's bed call. And at six in the morning there's reveille. You're free to do a lot of things in the Navy, but on board a ship you're not free to stay in bed after six o'clock in the morning. On board the *Jouett* there was no big uproar from men demanding rights as a result of these Z-grams. I continued to handle things through my officers, chiefs, and petty officers. The crew knew that was the way I wanted it.

In terms of leadership, I hark back to the situation I encountered when I first took command. At that point, the ship and crew had spent about three and a half months in San Diego after having come back from a deployment. In the first weeks after the return from WestPac, the crew had lots of leave and lots of liberty. In that kind of situation, a crew gets out of the habit of cleaning the ship daily. You think about that when you're operating out at sea, but you don't think about it so often when liberty begins every day at noon.

During my first three or four days as skipper, I didn't raise any fuss or stink. But things weren't just quite the way I thought they should be. I took about a day, and I inspected the entire ship. The next morning, right after quarters, I called all my officers together, from the exec down, and met with them in the wardroom. We had a long discussion about what I thought was wrong with the ship, where I thought people weren't doing the job. Then, after I finished, I went down to the chiefs' quarters and I gave them the same story. Then I said to myself, "I'd better carry this on down further." So I got all the first class petty officers together, and we discussed where I felt the ship ought to be going, what should be done, what the problems were.

It was amazing to me the number of people who nodded their heads in agreement. They'd been seeing these same conditions every day, but they hadn't really paid any attention to them. I think they were a little amazed that I came on there, a new guy, and in four or five days could find all this out. We got it squared away.

I remember one man in particular who was one of the most outstanding chief petty officers I ever saw in the Navy. He was a black guy, an electrician's mate. Everybody on that ship had a tremendous amount of respect for him. But I went down into his spaces, and I discovered that he himself hadn't been down to those spaces in three months. (The guy had a bad leg and couldn't move that easily.) You can imagine how embarrassed he was when I pointed this out to him, and how embarrassed the electrical officer and engineer officer were when they found this out. But they hadn't been down there either. So we got a movement afoot to clean that bucket up, in short order.

It is almost inevitable that a new commanding officer will have a somewhat different set of priorities from the previous one. The crew responds to his set of priorities when he lets it be known. Now, we could have continued on for four or five more months under the same set of directives as before. But I just had to let them know I expected better of guys who were being paid to do jobs, and they did respond. There's no doubt in my mind.

One of the bright spots of the tour was a young man, Ensign John Robinson, who joined the ship after graduating from the Naval Academy in the class of 1970. His father was Rear Admiral Rembrandt Robinson, who, sadly, was later killed in a helicopter crash off the coast of Vietnam in 1972. John was one of the finest and most impressive young officers I've ever met. He was the replacement for the main propulsion assistant who was more interested in his girlfriend than doing his job. After I fired the first MPA, we got orders on young Robinson, who was at engineering school.

When I saw the orders, I called up my engineer and said: "Hey, we have a new MPA coming, and he's right here in San Diego. I want you to go over and meet him, and find out what kind of fellow he is, and also tell him we're deploying the second of October. I want to make sure that if there's any gear he wants us to take out, it's aboard, and tell him we'll take it for him. And secondly, there might be a possibility for him to come over and watch you light off [the boilers] just before getting under way."

The engineer officer did that. And I guess we'd been under way for about an hour or so, and I happened to see the engineer and said, "Oh, how'd Robinson look to you?"

He said, "Well, he's a fine young officer, and I told him what you said about bringing his gear aboard."

"Did he bring anything?"

"Well, he sent his golf clubs."

"Oh my God, what am I getting?" But John Robinson did come aboard while we were out in WestPac, and I was most pleased with his performance. Within about three months after he reported, he was qualified as officer of the deck for all evolutions, including special sea detail. I had no fear whatsoever when that young man handled the ship. He was just that good, as I was happy to report to his father.

One other officer—not in the crew of the *Jouett*—should be mentioned because I became what he called his "sea daddy." Lieutenant Gordon Fisher had been an instructor in the first black NROTC unit down at Prairie View. In the fall of 1970, he was operations officer of a ship in San Diego. One day he came by my house for hot dogs or something, and he brought with him four ensigns who were new graduates out of Prairie View. They were reporting to duty in the San Diego area. We had a nice visit, but I never really expected to see them again.

Months later, while the ship was on the line out in WestPac, I got a message from a gun destroyer that was operating with the *Jouett*. It said that such-and-such young officer was on board, and he would like to come over and see my ship. He was one of the four ensigns I had met in San Diego. Well, the normal circumstance was that the PIRAZ ship, being much more modern than the old destroyers, which these guys were on, would send the helicopter over in the morning and bring over one or two officers, then let them stay on board all day. That gave them a chance to walk around, see things, and ask questions.

Since I had met this guy, I sent a message to his commanding officer and said: "I understand so-and-so is aboard. Would appreciate it if you would let him come over for a day as my guest. I'd be happy to take care of him and send him back the next morning." The CO agreed and sent him over. While I was on the bridge waiting for this young ensign to come aboard, I was wondering, "Now, what do I do with this guy?" Because I really wanted to do something special for him, and an idea dawned on me. I had a young white officer, sharp as a tack, who was my assistant CIC officer. I thought I'd put him together with this black ensign from the destroyer. I told my man:

"Listen, I want you to take this guy around, and I want him to be with you for the next twenty-four hours, except for a couple of times. He's going to be my guest, so for dinner tonight I'll have him up in my in-port cabin, and after the movie, then he can sleep in my in-port cabin. I'll sleep in my sea cabin. But the rest of the time I want him with you, standing watches, the whole bit." And he did.

Everything went along fine with that part of the program; the problem came the following morning. My habit was to get up about 5:30. I'd come out to the bridge, get a rundown from the command duty officer, talk to the CIC people, talk to my bridge people, and so forth. Then around six I'd go down to the in-port cabin and I'd read all the message traffic. Shortly thereafter, I'd have breakfast in my in-port cabin, and then I'd go back to the bridge. On this particular morning, I did my normal routine, and about 6:15 the steward came in, and I was reading. He said, "Captain, would you like your breakfast now?"

I said: "Well, I've got a guest, remember? I'll wait until he arrives." My guest was behind this closed door to the bedroom. Well, 6:30, he wasn't up; 6:45, he wasn't up; seven o'clock, he wasn't up. At 7:15 I just could not take it any longer. I didn't believe ensigns should sleep that late, so I went banging on the door. I called and told him it was time for breakfast. He got up and came on in after dressing.

Once he was there, we began to talk a little bit about his job, how he liked it, and what he was doing. It turned out he was the electronics material officer (EMO) for his ship. I asked him, "Do you have any gear down?" I'm not sure exactly how many pieces of gear this destroyer had on it, but his answer indicated that about ninety percent of his equipment wasn't working.

"My God, how do you guys operate over there? For Christ's sake, I've got two radio electricians on board. I've got three or four chiefs. I've got the whole works. I would have sent people over there."

"Well, we didn't want to worry you."

"Don't give me that. How about a MOTU [mobile technical unit]?"

Well, he didn't know anything about MOTU. He just religiously reported all this gear down every day. I gave him a little lecture. I told him I'd help him find a MOTU, and I'd send some people over to help him with his work. I said, "What's your routine like on that ship?"

"Well, what do you mean?"

"What time do you eat breakfast?"

"Well, I usually go in the wardroom about 7:15."

"Where's the captain when you get there?"

"Oh, the captain's sitting there about ready to finish his breakfast."

"What do you do next?"

"Well, I sit there until it's time for quarters, then I go out and muster my people and make my report to the department head. Then I go to the EMO shack, and I start whatever work I have to do."

"Well, listen. Why don't you change your routine a little bit? What I would like to see you do tomorrow morning is that when the captain comes down to breakfast—and I don't care what time the captain gets down there—I want you in there about ready to finish your breakfast. And when you finish your breakfast, I want you to get up and go to the EMO shack. And the captain's going to say to you, 'Where are you going?' And you tell him you are going back to the EMO shack to lay out your work for the day." I suggested a couple of other things as well. In short, I gave him some guidance on how to improve the way he was doing his job. I did everything but spank him, to be honest.

About three months later I happened to see his commanding officer in Subic, and he said, "What the hell did you do to that young man?"

I said: "I didn't do anything to him. I talked to him a little bit."

He said, "That guy is doing so well now that I'm thinking about sending him to comm. school when we get back, and he would be my communication officer."

My visitor from Prairie View was a guy who came from a small town in Texas. When he graduated from college and got his commission, he went back to his home and had on that gold bar of an ensign. He probably bought himself a car; he was the biggest man in town. So he became an overseer, and his idea of overseeing was: "Hey, I'll go down and see what the people are doing at about eight o'clock. I'll go back and rest a little bit, and right after lunch I'll go back down there again and check on them." And that was about the way he expected to do his job in that ship. I think I got across to him the idea that he was not just an overseer—that it was his damn job to make sure things got done. And with that change in outlook he really improved. This guy really got turned around as a result of the day he spent on board the *Jouett* with us and was a success until something else happened to him.

One day he was on board inspecting the ship. The captain sent for him and said: "I notice you are inspecting the ship. There are a couple of things I want you to do differently."

"Captain, I've been working this ship for two COs before you, and this procedure worked well for them. I think they'll work well for you."

"So change your procedure."

"Captain, I disagree." And the captain fired him. He was never the same after that. You do things the way the CO wants you to.

★★★

While on deployment, the *Jouett* visited several ports during breaks in the PIRAZ duty. Two in particular are worth mentioning. The ship got an interesting side job during a rest and recreation visit to Singapore from January 18 to January 26, 1971. The defense attaché there was an officer whom I had known for a long time. Apparently, some spy ships had been picking up radiation and messages from his office. So I steamed the *Jouett* around the south side of Singapore and surveyed the island with all my electronic listening gear up to find out if we could hear the same thing. We did, and advised him on the frequencies we thought the people were listening to.

The other one was to Australia in March and April. We received a message from CruDesPac, which said that for a couple of years ships had not been permitted to go down to Australia. However, they were planning on opening that up again, and if any of the ships would like to go down to Australia, they'd like to have the CO put in a schedule change request for the end of deployment. Well, I had been down to Australia in the *Taussig* and thought it was a great place for liberty. I applied for this, and it was approved.

One untoward thing happened while the ship was in Subic, just before we were to leave. I got a letter from my wife in which she said there were a couple of the wives of crew members who complained that by taking the ship to Australia I was keeping the men away from home an additional month. She wrote that these two women were even going to see the CruDesPac chaplain to complain.

During a phone call with Alma, I asked her if she had any idea who the wives were. She said, "Well, I really don't think I should tell you, but it was Mrs. So-and-so and Mrs. So-and-so."

I said, "Okay, I'll take care of it." When I got back to the ship after talking to her, I remembered there was a Z-gram that said 5 percent of the crew could be off the ship while we were deployed. I told my exec to make sure that 5 percent of our people went home early, and to make sure Chief So-and-so and Chief So-and-so were on that list. Now, they objected, because they wanted to go to Australia. They didn't really want to go home early, but we sent them anyway.

That was really some cruise, and I'm sure the crew enjoyed it. The ports we hit included Fremantle, which is adjacent to the city of Perth, and Melbourne. Then we went to Hobart, Tasmania, and then came on up to Wellington, New Zealand. We finally capped the cruise with a visit to Samoa, where I went for fuel, and spent a night in Pago Pago. We got under way the next morning and steamed to Pearl Harbor. We had only four hours there on April 27, just long enough to fuel. We didn't really care about liberty because we were on our way home.

That morning, for some reason, I began to think in terms of the flag list and wondered if it had come out. I didn't by any stretch of the imagination think I'd be on it because I was fairly junior at that point in my career. But at the same time, I was curious about who had made it. So I had made arrangements to call on Commander Cruiser-Destroyer Flotilla Five. I went over about eight o'clock and waited in his office until he arrived. We sort of discussed it, and I asked him if he had heard anything, which he had not.

In the meantime, I wanted him to do for me what Commodore Langille and Admiral Goodfellow had done when I came home in the *Taussig*. That is, I wanted to have a couple of barges come out and meet the ship on arrival in San Diego, with ten wives on board I believe: five in one boat and five in another one. Then we would steam up into the San Diego harbor. During this visit, I made sure those arrangements were made. Finally, after maybe thirty-five or forty minutes, we were through, so I came on back to the ship.

As I approached my ship, I noticed the quarterdeck watch rang the bell: "Bong-bong, bong-bong, bong-bong. *Jouett* arriving." It's one of the Navy's old customs to ring the bell and announce the imminent arrival of the skipper. But I rated only four bells as a captain, not six. I quickly thought, "My God, I wonder who that OOD is." I got out of the car, and I walked up the gangway, and there were all my officers lining the quarterdeck—along with six side boys. As I stepped up, my exec, Commander Newcomb, grabbed my hand and shook it and said: "Congratulations, Admiral. You made it, you made it."

I said, "What do you mean?"

"Well, we just heard that you've been selected for flag rank."

"Oh, no, no. You know I'm too junior. I don't really expect it at this point in my career, but thanks anyway."

"Well, come on over to the commodore's cabin. We've got something up there for you."

I went up, and in the cabin there were two bottles of wine. One of them was a bottle a guy had given me down in New Zealand to drink with my wife when I got back. I said: "Oh, God. Let me tell you guys something. First of all, you cannot drink on board a Navy ship. And, secondly, nobody's going to celebrate my becoming an admiral until I see it in print." So we broke up the gang, and they were all a little unhappy.

Then I got the story on what had happened. We had two officers who were due to leave the ship as soon as we arrived in San Diego and go off to new duty. They'd been over to the see the Pacific Fleet staff there in Hawaii to be briefed on their new clearances. One of the people there said he had heard that the first black in the history of the U.S. Navy has just been selected for flag rank. And they said, "Well, it can't be anybody but you."

I said: "Well, you're wrong. It could be Dave Parham." He was a senior Navy captain and a chaplain. And, obviously, it could have been Dave. But in any event, we made preparations and got under way. We had been under way about fifteen or twenty minutes, I guess, when I got word that both CinCPac and CinCPacFlt wanted to talk to me. I went down to the radio shack, and, as normal, communications at a critical time failed, because I could never talk to either one of them. One was the cigar-smoking admiral, John S. McCain, who was CinCPacFlt and the father of later Senator McCain. CinCPacFlt was Admiral Chick Clarey. They both wanted to congratulate me because the message had come out, and it was official. I was told at that moment that was why they wanted to call me. In the meantime, while I was in the radio shack, I was looking at the incoming message file, including the list of new rear admirals. I was simply overjoyed.

Then I started thinking about a lot of things, like: "Why did I deserve this? Why have I been selected?" I guess the person I thought about most was my mother, who had died in 1937. She always had great aspirations for me, and she was *the* biggest influence in my life. I just wish my mother could have been there at that time. My dad was still alive, but I didn't think about him very much. It was my mother I thought about.

After seeing the message in the radio shack, I went back up to the bridge, and I said: "XO, you remember that wine you guys had down there? Well, it's official now. Maybe we ought to go back down there and drink it." So we broke out the two bottles of wine and had them. I left one guy up on the bridge and said, "He can drink his a little later."

As we continued to steam toward San Diego, I got a couple of messages that concerned me a little bit. One said I was to be interviewed by the press the moment I arrived. Rear Admiral Doug Plate, who was ComCruDesPac, warned me in a message to remember that the most important thing about the ship was not that I had been selected for flag rank, but that the ship was coming back from a deployment. I wrote him back and said: "I agree. And, let's face it, I am also coming back from a deployment and haven't seen my wife and children in seven months."

Well, despite that, the press briefing had to take place. The second thing was that somebody got the wise idea the press should be flown out about twenty-five or thirty miles before I got into San Diego. According to this plan, they would come aboard at sea, and then we'd start the interview. I just totally objected to that and told them I did not want to be bothered with the press while I was bringing my ship back. I would agree to an interview afterward, but certainly not during that time.

I guess the third thing was that I was to send off a dispatch on my feelings on being selected the first black flag officer in the Navy. And it is quite interesting how that occurred—not so much what was in the message as the writing of the message. Because when the message came in, my exec said, "Captain, why don't you and I go down and we'll do it?"

I said, "Well, how about the PAO [public affairs officer]?" He thought that was great. The PAO was a Jewish officer. And I said, "Oh, by the way, bring down the weapons officer too." The weapons officer was an Indian. So the message Sam Gravely put out as being from the first black officer was written by four people, really: an American Indian, an American Jewish type, an American Caucasian, and the American black who got selected. We put the message together and sent it out.

We finally got to San Diego on May 1, and the wives came aboard. Alma was one of the first. She came on up to the bridge. I showed her how to handle the ship, because I handled it all the way in. My time as a skipper was about to come to an end, and I wanted to do it myself on that last lap. I just pushed the pilot aside.

I was quite amazed at the crowd of people standing on the pier. People were holding signs to welcome us back, and our daughter, Tracey, was holding one of them. Then I had to deal with the reporters, which wasn't easy. I've never gotten used to reporters for some reason, and I'm not sure why. They just overwhelmed me, and obviously they were an intrusion on our homecoming. The media people try to be as nice as possible, and they try to put you at ease, but I just am not one of those people who fare well in interviews. But I got through it, and I was eager for it to be over, because I had told my wife and the kids we were going up to my cabin for a few minutes, because I had some candy for my daughter and presents for the boys.

Lo and behold, after I thought we had gotten rid of the press, here was some guy in my cabin, and he wanted to get a special interview. I booted him out of there. And then, to top it off, a guy followed me home to get an interview. I guess I obliged him, but the press was overwhelming.

Well, now I was about to be an admiral, and the mail started coming. I have never, never in my life, even when I commanded the *Taussig* and the *Falgout*, gotten as much mail. It came from everybody. It came from old friends; it came from interested people; it came from foreigners. People sent me clippings, including one from Cuba. I had so many letters I couldn't answer them all, even though I tried. I started a program that I would answer about twenty-five letters a day. Since the ship had just gotten back from a deployment, people were taking leave. I decided I didn't want to be in the first leave party. Let the exec go first, and I'd take something on the tail end. The exec was gone, as were half the officers and half the crew.

During this period, we got some new crew members aboard, and I got a really, really sharp yeoman. In trying to write about twenty-five a day, all I was doing was writing two or three lines, thanking people. But I wanted to let them know I had heard from them. This yeoman had a great solution. He said, "Captain, I can help you with those."

I said, "Oh?"

"Yes. I've been here for two or three days now. I know how you're going to write, what you're doing and what you're saying. Why don't you give me that bale of letters, and I'll write a rough for you, and then all you have to do is initial it off, and I will then smooth it for you to sign." I thought that was a bang-up idea, because for the most part they were people I didn't know anyway. In case of any really old friends, then I could smooth up the rough letter he'd given me with some special words in there.

Well, this program went on through Friday, and on Saturday morning, I guess, I came down thinking there'd be a couple of letters, and there were no letters. Then Monday I got back, there were no letters. Monday afternoon I called the yeoman up and said: "Hey, what are you doing about writing these letters? If you're not going to write them, give me the mail bag."

He said: "Captain, I put those letters into a burn bag [which is what we used for classified material that was to be destroyed]; that was the only thing I had to hold them. I had it in the ship's office, and we were cleaning up the ship for inspection on Friday. And damn if the bag didn't get thrown out with the trash."

So there went the end of my letter writing. But during the time I had been so diligent about it I got quite a surprise. Out of this whole batch of mail, which I would guess probably amounted to fifteen hundred to eighteen hundred letters, only one was derogatory. It supposedly was from some electronics type over in Northern Ireland. He said that I certainly wasn't the right guy and blah, blah, blah. After I had answered him, I turned his letter over to the FBI or to the Naval Investigative Service people, and that was the last I heard about it.

All this attention coming my way was not something I craved. In fact, I didn't really enjoy it. I thought I had already paid the price when the people rode the *Taussig* as I went out to Pearl several years earlier. But I guess every new venture requires new attention, and certainly they considered this an accomplishment they wanted to write about.

The change of command ceremony was on June 2, 1971, there in San Diego. Part of the change of command ceremony was a frocking. That is, even though I hadn't yet been officially promoted, I first wore the rank of a rear admiral the day I left the *Jouett*. The man who officiated was Vice Admiral Ray Peet, who by then had relieved Admiral Kidd as Commander First Fleet. He was the guest speaker and snapped on one of my new gold shoulder boards. Alma snapped on the other one. Our daughter, Tracey, put my new admiral's hat on me. It was quite a day.

CHAPTER TWENTY

Director of Naval Communications

The first step for a new rear admiral was to go to Washington, D.C., for a five-day indoctrination course affectionately known as "charm school." One thing I especially recall about the trip wasn't really related to charm school. I got a call from Rembrandt Robinson, who was then on the Joint Staff in the Pentagon. As I mentioned earlier, his son John had come aboard the *Jouett* the year before as my main propulsion assistant. Naturally, Rembrandt wanted to find out something about how John was doing, and I was happy to tell him.

Besides that, Rembrandt also brought up an incident that had occurred while I was in the *Jouett*. During the course of our WestPac deployment, we had gone into Hong Kong. We had no problem about getting in there; we had to come in, turn around, and then moor to a buoy. While we were making our maneuvers and coming up to the buoy, the Kowloon ferry came up, and in sort of trying to see what was going on, the captain of that ferry wanted to get close to my ship. The ferry came too close, and scraped my stern. We moored, no damages, nothing.

The tug people came aboard *Jouett* very shortly after that to say, "Hey, if there are any damages, we're willing to pay." The last thing the guy said was, "You know, nothing really happened here, other than the scraping incident, but I can assure you this afternoon it's going to be in the Communist paper that American warship sinks tug in Hong Kong Harbor."

The first thing that came to my mind was that this incident needed to be reported to the chain of command. Lieutenant Pete Deutermann was my operations officer. He and I sat down, wrote out the proper message, and got it off in good order. We soon got a message from Commander U.S. Naval Forces Marianas, who had area coordination for the region. He wanted to know if there were any damages or injuries. I'd put in the original report that there was no damage and no injuries. I just repeated that in answering his questions.

What I found out in this discussion with Rembrandt was that the report of the incident had reached the White House situation room. Somebody wanted to know, "How could that dumb captain hit a Chinese ferry going into Hong Kong?" Robinson told me he was very happy he was there—not so much for me but to explain to people how things like that happen, and to make sure they all knew I had done everything possible. It wasn't my fault. We had the pilot on board, and we had the flag showing. The guy came too close in trying to look, and he was probably looking while he should have been steering. I got over that one with no problem and no investigation, but it's an example of how things can be exaggerated.

★★★

During the charm school portion of the trip, we incoming flag officers were briefed by the highest authorities in the Navy, the other services, and the Department of Defense. Their purpose was to acquaint us with the jobs we were going to do on the flag level, tell us how to do it, bring up some new policies, and those kinds of things. It was very good, and I needed that, and I enjoyed it.

During one afternoon of that week, we went to a party the CNO hosted for all his new flag officers. The party was held at Admiral Zumwalt's quarters. At that time, the CNO lived in a house on the grounds of the Naval Observatory; subsequently, it became the vice president's official residence. By mid-1971, I had probably been to only one or two flag officers' quarters in my entire career. I didn't have a whole lot of background, but I was determined I was not going to do anything wrong. In addition, I was in civilian clothes, just like we were told to be, and I didn't want to have any problem about getting in the gate.

That afternoon, about fifteen minutes before the party, I parked outside of Rock Creek Park, just across Massachusetts Avenue from the Naval Observatory, to watch people go in. I wanted to make sure my arrival would be just like theirs; I wanted to do it right. After seeing two or three cars with new flag officers in them turn into the place, I turned in also. It was a simple procedure. You went to the gate and showed your ID card. Somebody checked you off on the guest list, and then you would be told to go on. After the initial approach, I got to a circular driveway.

I was behind about four other cars, and I noticed a car pulled up and stopped in front of the place. There were two sailors near the door. One let out the new admiral's wife; the other let out the new admiral on the other side and gave him a little piece of paper. Then a sailor drove the car away to park it. This went on for three cars ahead of me. But the minute I drove up there, one of the sailors said: "Move it. Move it. Take that car to the rear. Take that car to the rear." I was about to get out of the car, and I thought: "Well, I really don't want to create a disturbance in front of the CNO's house. There's no sense in explaining." So when he said, "Take it to the rear," I drove it around to the back. When I pulled into the parking lot, a chief petty officer came up, and he said, "You're Admiral Gravely, aren't you?"

I said, "Yes."

"Well, you're not supposed to do it this way, sir. What you're supposed—"

"Wait a minute. I've tried that already, and it doesn't work. Now, if you have no objection, I'll leave the car here, and I'll come back and get it when I'm through."

"Okay, fine."

I left the car there and started walking around to the front, and this little sailor who had given me the high sign about moving the car was standing there, and he was talking over this walkie-talkie. I imagine at that point in time the chief was really giving him down the country, because he was beginning to get a little redder in the face. I stepped up, he looked me in the eye, and with a nice sharp, snappy salute, he said: "Pardon me, sir. I didn't know you were Admiral Gravely. I thought you were a chauffeur."

I took my first step, and I started thinking, and I turned and said to him: "Well, son. Please don't worry about it. But I want you to always remember; chauffeurs wear caps."

★★★

That week's briefings were very well done. I enjoyed them, and I got a lot out of them. We ended on a Friday, and then it was time to go back to San

Diego. About that time, my orders hit, sending me back to OpNav, the staff of the CNO. I discovered I was coming back to relieve my former boss, Admiral Fitzpatrick, as director of naval communications. I had mixed emotions about it, but I was quite pleased. I felt that my earlier job in the Pentagon, even though I was there only about fifteen or eighteen months, had prepared me. I was in much better shape than I would have been if I had not had the job there.

I got the family together, and we prepared to come back. Despite the fact that things had eased considerably in terms of housing in the Washington, D.C., area, I was a little bit concerned about coming back and finding a place for my family.

I guess a day or so before we left our home in San Diego, I heard from an Army major who was a neighbor we had lived near in North Arlington when I was in the Pentagon previously. He wrote me a letter in which he said: "We are planning to go to Texas, and we're taking all the children. My house is vacant for the next month, and you're certainly welcome to use it." One can imagine how helpful that was. So we moved into his place and started to look for a house. We bought a house in Falls Church. It was owned by the company that we had tried to deal with when I was at the Naval War College. The people from that company had just sort of disappeared when they discovered that we were black.

There was an irony there, and it also shows how fast things turn around. This was seven years later, and the process had completely reversed in that time. Our new home, which I really enjoyed, was in an integrated neighborhood. Of course, this was unheard of in northern Virginia in the old days. We kept the house for about ten years before we finally sold it

★★★

The job in OpNav was a very, very interesting one, because at about that time the Navy had decided to reorganize from the communications division to what they called command and control, or C^2. If I'm not mistaken, the Navy had probably the first C^3I business—command, control, communications, and intelligence—because on that staff we had the communications, intelligence, and cryptologic people—all those things that are elements of command support. Admiral Fritz Harlfinger was in charge of that.[1] He was a

1 Rear Admiral Frederick J. Harlfinger II, USN, Director Command Support Programs, OpNav.

former director of naval intelligence, and he was just simply a wonderful guy to work for—easy to work for. You did your job. He did his job. He became the first czar of the command and control group and really did a bang-up job. He was a two-star admiral when he came there but got the third star very shortly afterward.

The job I went into was a little bit tougher, I think, than it became later. The main reason I think it was a little tougher was simply that the flag officer was double-hatted. I was not only the director of naval communications from the OpNav side of the house but also commander of the Naval Telecommunications Command from the other side. The OpNav job had to do with the policy aspects of communications, and the ComNavTelCom job basically had to do with the operation and maintenance of the comm stations, and also making sure the shipboard equipment and so forth could carry out the policies I set in my other hat. It was quite interesting that once in a while I would find myself writing a message in one hat to myself in the other hat. Then I had to go over to the other side of the house and answer that message. Sometimes I couldn't answer it as easily as I could ask the question. But it was quite an interesting job, and it kept me hopping. I had plenty of good talent on the staff. I had three chiefs of staff while I was in that job. All three of them made admiral within the next year or so. I had good people to work with.

There were some interesting situations in being double-hatted. Generally, there were info addressees on the messages, so no matter which way you answered it, you would upset somebody. Another facet of the job, which was a little bit disturbing for me, was that I couldn't devote full time to either one of them. And they were far removed. The OpNav job was in the Pentagon, in Arlington, Virginia. The other job was up on Nebraska Avenue in Washington, with quite a distance between. Since I felt the OpNav job was the more demanding, I spent most of my time in the Pentagon, but I spent anywhere from one to two days a week out at Nebraska Avenue.

Part of my role was looking out for the interests of the Navy, trying to make sure we were foremost in the communications world. We also had our joint programs, working with the Army, Navy, and Air Force. In improving communications, we decided on a couple of routes. One was we appointed a committee called the CIACT, CNO's Industry Advisory Committee to Telecommunications. Some very, very big guys were on that committee. They were big wheels in the civilian community as well as a couple of retired folk. When this group finally submitted its report, it came out with several recommendations.

One of the best ones, so far as I was concerned, was that the director of naval communications should always be an upper-half rear admiral, a two-star. At that point I was a one-star, lower-half rear admiral, which said I was too junior for the job, really. A second recommendation was that the director of naval communications should be able to go to sea after that billet, because historically our communicators had come into the communications jobs and then sort of got locked in. That was about as far as they went. Normally, when it came time to cut people, these were the easy guys to cut because they didn't have the sea experience as flag officers. So when the report said I needed to be upper half, that was fine with me, and that I needed to go to sea was also fine.

I can remember going with Admiral Harlfinger, who decided he would take his bearings, as he called them, to see the fleet. A group of us went to McGuire Air Force Base in New Jersey and flew to Rota, Spain. We went on from there to Naples, Italy, where we met with Vice Admiral Ike Kidd, who by then was Commander Sixth Fleet. He made some remarks, and I talked with him personally. He struck me as someone who really didn't understand communications. He said, "Sam, let me tell you about communications."

"Yes, sir."

He said, "The problem with communications is you send too many messages."

Not trying to be smart, I simply responded: "Well, Admiral, I don't send them, I carry them, and the bag is heavy. I've read your op order, and the guys who require the messages are the fleet commanders."

When you get right down to it, that's true. Every guy who wrote an op order would put in it that he'd want to hear from you if you were away from the task group. He'd want to know where you were at eight o'clock in the morning, noon, and at eight in the evening. Or he wanted to know your fuel capacity: when you were down to eighty percent, seventy percent, sixty percent, fifty percent, so on and so forth. In this search for how to stop sending so many messages, we've got to look to ourselves, because we as fleet and group commanders are the guys who are requiring as many unnecessary messages as there are. In the course of the discussion, Admiral Kidd and I both lectured each other. Obviously, he won because he was senior, but that's the way I felt about it.

★★★

There was more to being in the Washington area than just the Navy jobs. I began to get a lot of demands on my time from outside activities. Even though I've never really been a great speaker, I was certainly in demand for speeches with various black groups, NAACP groups, high schools, and those kinds of things. I tried to honor as many of those as I possibly could. One of the things I regretted was not being able to be involved when President Tubman of Liberia died right after I got to Washington.[2] I was offered the chance to fly over as part of the entourage the United States sent for the burial. I had to respectfully decline because I felt I was brand-new in my job, and I'd better stay there and learn it. I regret that to some degree now, because I have never been to Africa. I don't know why I want to go, but I have a feeling you ought to see a little bit of everything in this world, and one of these days I'm going to have to take my wife and go.[3]

One of the by-products of my becoming well-known was how others perceived me. Even though I viewed myself as a naval officer, other people saw me as a symbol. I can't think of a thing to which I wasn't invited. One of the things that happened to me practically every year I was a flag officer was that I was decreed to be one of the one hundred most influential blacks in this country. *Ebony* magazine published a list each year, and I made the magazine for about ten years in a row. Nobody cares about me now that I'm retired, but I hope I'm as influential today as I was then.

Fortunately, I think I was able to maintain a proper sense of humility while all this was going on. My head didn't get too big. I guess that was just something ingrained from birth. I'm sure I might have appeared at times to let it get too big, but I tried not to. I remember I was criticized in a newspaper for not attending a certain event. The writer said it was because I felt I was too big for it. I sent a letter to the reporter who wrote that in her paper. I told her I was very sorry I had to decline, but I did so primarily because I had to go to

---

2 William V. S. Tubman served as president of Liberia from 1944 until his death on July 23, 1971.

3 A few years before his death in 2004 Admiral Gravely made a trip to Africa as an election observer.

my stepmother's funeral. I never heard anything from her, but I can imagine how bad she must have felt after reading my letter.

In one sense, race was a nonfactor. I guess the question I was asked the most concerning that tour was, "How often did Admiral Zumwalt call you up to discuss racial problems?" Well, he really didn't need to, number one, and number two, he didn't call. For example, there was a racial revolt on board the aircraft carrier *Kitty Hawk* in October 1972. I wasn't involved at all in the Navy's response. Admiral Zumwalt had other individuals who advised him, Bill Norman being one. He was a black lieutenant commander who was the CNO's special assistant for equal opportunity, his right-hand man.

When things went on racially, I was never involved in helping the CNO make a decision. He had people there who could help him make decisions. I didn't feel a bit left out. If I had wanted to make an input I had no problem with being able to do it, and I could have done it. And I guess Bill Norman and two or three of the other young officers who were around came to me periodically to ask questions and to see how I would go on certain things. But the biggest one was the *Kitty Hawk*, and I just simply had no part in it. In several of the other incidents I saw the reports, but that's about as far as I got. I certainly applauded Admiral Zumwalt for everything he was trying to do in the area of race relations.

If I were to be critical of anything he did, it would be in his methods rather than his objectives. In trying to hammer things down, it almost seemed to me as if he sat in a little corner someplace with some junior advisers who gave him advice contrary to the way these old sea lords had been doing things for years and years and years. Then he just suddenly hit the Navy with a message, rather than getting a group of admirals together and sort of coordinating things and seeing what you could work out. I don't think he did enough of that. Now, I may be wrong, but that's my view of it.

He did hold a famous meeting that almost came across like a rebuke of senior flag officers rather than an attempt to win them over and persuade them to follow his leadership on the issue. There were two things that were to some degree rebukes. Certainly that was one of them. I sat in there and listened to all of that and wondered what the hell I did to rate this kind of a whipping. The second one was the sensitivity training sessions, and they were pretty hard for me to swallow. They were hard from the idea that they had a young group up there telling me that I, as an admiral, was to blame for all of the Navy's problems. Well, frankly, I thought I was the *result* of the changes in the Navy. It got to me a little bit. In fact, I wondered why I even was sent.

There were a lot of things that might have been much more successful if handled a little differently. You had two or three different types of people. You had an old group that had been in the Navy and seen how the Navy had been working for years and years, since before World War II, and they weren't about to change. Some of the World War II senior officers, first of all, couldn't tolerate reserves being part of the Navy. Nor did they want blacks and other minorities being part of it. At the other end of the spectrum, you had a group of young black officers and men coming up. They had been parties to the sit-ins and those kinds of things and were going to make the people change, no matter what.

The kind of discipline the Navy had wouldn't permit those two factions to sit side by side, and so that brought on some of these revolts. I think it should have been explained better. I don't think the young group of racial reformers was necessarily right when they came in insisting that theirs was the only way to do things. I don't think they realized how hard-core that group of senior officers was. The older group said you couldn't do it any way but their way, and they weren't right either.

It was not the most pleasant of times, but then again, it was not the worst of times either. The thing we'll never know about the Navy's racial climate in the early 1970s is whether things might have been even worse if not for Admiral Zumwalt's approach. Somehow there's been a meeting of the minds within the last few years, and I think things have improved tremendously.

CHAPTER TWENTY-ONE

Cruiser-Destroyer Group Two

John Chafee was the secretary of the Navy who selected Admiral Zumwalt to become CNO, and he did so in order to foster change. In May of 1972, John Warner, who later became a senator from Virginia, relieved Chafee as secretary. The spate of racial disturbances in the fleet broke out in the autumn of that year. Warner tried to get Zumwalt to go slower, and he has been accused at certain times of impeding racial progress. I'm not sure he impeded racial progress as much as he was trying to do it cautiously. But caution was not the name of the game in those days, so they were both wrong.

On the other hand, it has always interested me that it was John Warner who told me I was going to command Cruiser-Destroyer Group Two. Most of the good things that happened to me in the Navy I learned about from somebody above me in the chain of command, not the normal detail route. In this case, Alma and I were guests at John Warner's apartment in Georgetown. He said to her, "I see Sam is going to get a little salt water sprinkled on his tail."

Alma said something like "I hope they're not going to send him on another deployment." I was so mad I could have clobbered her because I think any naval officer worth his salt, when he gets to be an admiral and is a group commander, wants to go out and operate. I had spent an awful lot of time in the Pacific Fleet, and I really wanted to get a group out there, but the one Warner mentioned was in the Atlantic. I had no problem with going to Group Two other than the fact that Group Two did not deploy. I was a little upset from that side. Certainly training is one thing, but operating is another, and I wanted to operate.

In any event, in the summer of 1973, after I completed my tour of duty in OpNav, I relieved an old friend, Ralph Wentworth.[1] Vice Admiral Jake Finneran was the Second Fleet commander, just a tremendous naval officer.[2] I knew of Jake Finneran's reputation from destroyers. In fact, it's quite interesting that you didn't necessarily know everybody individually, or know them well, but you heard about them, and you felt you knew them. And that's the way it was with Jake. I knew of him very well.

Group Two up to then operated out of Newport, Rhode Island, but it was about to move. The shore establishment was being cut back in size, and Newport's role was reduced dramatically. When I got there, the ships were in the process of changing home ports from Newport to Norfolk, Virginia; to Charleston, South Carolina; and to Mayport, Florida. I guess one argument was that we'd be closer to the training grounds. Another part of the rationale was that the Northeast was really a tough area in which to operate during wintertime. Instead, you'd move more ships down closer to the sunny South. In the case of Group Two, the staff was to move to Charleston.

In its role as a readiness and training group, my new command ran a number of scheduled exercises at sea. First the staff wrote up the operation order, and then we generally flew to Charleston or to Mayport or Norfolk for the exercise itself. We went down and held a quick briefing, and then we went to sea. The result was that I didn't get a chance to see the ships daily, which was what I would have liked to do. Suddenly I had a bunch of ships, and they were out at sea operating. We operated not only with American ships, but a couple of times we were with the Standing Naval Force Atlantic, a multinational group of five ships that operated together under the auspices of NATO. In some of our various exercises we had amphibs and replenishment ships and even submarines.

I was the officer in tactical command on all the exercises except for those when Admiral Finneran was along, because I was generally the senior flag officer out there. In preparing for an exercise, my staff would write up a proposed op order, and then I would make changes as I saw necessary. As far as

---

1 Rear Admiral Ralph S. Wentworth Jr., USN.

2 Vice Admiral John G. Finneran, USN, commanded the Second Fleet from January 1973 to August 1974.

the actual handling of the ships was concerned, if there was task force maneuvering, I generally was either on the bridge or in CIC, where we had our little cubbyhole. I would issue directions when we made our turns or when we did various other maneuvers. One of the staff officers would come up with those recommendations, and I'd either follow them or do as I thought best. But a flag officer is quite busy at sea.

Even though I was officially in command of a cruiser-destroyer group, the cruisers had nearly all been decommissioned by that time. So generally I had either a straight destroyer or a guided missile destroyer as flagship. At various times I had DLGs like the *Standley* and the *Wainwright.* The regular flagship was a destroyer tender, and I left the administrative staff there when I went to sea. I took along maybe four or five officers and a few enlisted types. Usually in a destroyer you ate your meals in the wardroom just like anybody else. You were always a guest of the captain. He, of course, sat at the head of the table. It is quite unfortunate that a guided missile destroyer, because of its size, is really not capable of handling a flag and his staff, so somehow you make room, double bunking and those kinds of things.

In addition to the training at sea, in-port exercises became a big thing at that time. This was dictated by the fuel crunch that came along after the Yom Kippur War in 1973. By the following spring, Americans were sitting in gas lines, and the Navy increased the amount of training it did in port. I did some pioneering work in going down to Norfolk, for example, with five ships, all alongside the pier, and conducting a full week of training. I think we accomplished much, but certainly when you are simulating rather than actually operating it's difficult to imagine that you've got a collision when you're in port and you can't see a hole in the side of a ship. It's also difficult to say I'm going to get under way and leave but not make any preparations.

Another reason for the in-port exercises was that the size of the fleet was dramatically reduced in the early 1970s as ships from the World War II era were retired. We were getting down in the number of ships but still maintaining a fast tempo for the ships that were operating out in WestPac and in the Med. You had to give the crews some time in port, not only to repair and maintain their ships but also to have some leave and liberty. Conditions dictated a different kind of operation from what we'd known earlier.

Certainly I enjoyed it when we could go to sea. We had routine ops down in the Caribbean. I worked with Jake Finneran down in the Caribbean. After Vice Admiral Stan Turner took over from Jake as Commander Second Fleet, I flew to Rota, Spain, to work with a group that was winding up a Sixth Fleet deployment.[3] Stan Turner decided they should have training on the way home. I brought the group back to the States.

Another chore involved an outfit called the Destroyer Development Group, which was up in Newport. A decision was reached that when Cruiser-Destroyer Group Two went to Charleston the Destroyer Development Group would become a part of my assets. In that outfit you were looking at destroyer tactics, writing tac notes, and those kinds of things.

Moving to Charleston was not easy for lots of people for lots of reasons. The Newport group of destroyer types really didn't want to leave there. They loved Newport, and Newport loved them. Blacks generally didn't want to go to Charleston because of the racial conditions they felt would be there. I personally didn't want to move at that moment because I'd just got to Newport, had the children established in schools, and preferred the racial climate there. There was really no need to hurry to Charleston, so I remained in Newport for my first year in that job and then moved.

Anyway, we went to Charleston, conducted a couple of exercises. One of the things I decided to do was to go see the naval district commandant down there and talk in terms of possible quarters for my family. With the changes that had taken place in this country over the previous decade, I didn't realize quarters would be a problem. The commandant told me he had a reserve destroyer squadron commander who had a set of quarters; he had planned to move him someplace else and I would take over those quarters.

Well, at first note that sounded fine, but I went down there and took a look. On the base were six stately old homes that looked as if they had been built prior to the Civil War. They were designed basically as quarters for flag officers and their families. The quarters the commandant had in mind for me were in a fairly modern duplex, essentially for someone in the rank of captain. At that point, there were only about three flag types down there who had these big antebellum-type quarters. Commander Submarine Group Six had a set, Commander Mine Warfare had a set, and the commandant had a set. The other big ones were occupied by the shipyard commander and the supply type, both of whom were captains. There must have been one other.

3 Vice Admiral Stansfield Turner, USN, commanded the Second Fleet from August 1974 to July 1975.

I talked to the commandant about getting quarters that were rated for an admiral. I told him I felt that if I went down there as a black officer, and the people in the community saw that I was getting second best, I'd be sort of laughed out of the community. I made my point and then went to see the shipyard commander, who, as I said, was a captain. Frankly, the guy made me a little angry. He told me he'd been there for seven years and lived in that set of quarters for seven years. Well, if you like shore duty, fine, but in my view I had moved seven times in seven years, and damn it, it was time for him to move too.

That was the set I decided I wanted. I made a statement, which I regretted later. I told the commandant: "I really want one of those sets of quarters. And I think I rate them." After all, I *was* senior to the mine warfare commander and the submarine group commander. Because the captain had made me angry, however, I told the commandant I wanted the shipyard commander's quarters.

He said, "Well, the major claimant for that set of quarters is NavShips [Naval Ship Systems Command], and we'll have to go to NavShips and do that."

I couldn't care less about that, but I said: "You know, Admiral, I would gladly move to the set of quarters you want to give me if there were six admirals down here already. But since there aren't, I want one set, and that's the set I want."

Well, that came back to haunt me a little bit. Somehow when word got to NavShips that those were the quarters I wanted, NavShips turned a flag officer around who was in San Francisco going to Honolulu to take a job. NavShips called him back and put him in that set of quarters. In fact, he was down there for the rest of my tour.

Finally, I simply said, "If it's that hard to get the kind of quarters I think I deserve down here, then I'll leave my family in Washington, D.C." So the year I remained in Charleston, my family was in Washington, and I commuted and lived in a BOQ. I've always regretted making that decision. I probably should have taken the other set of quarters, because my relief did take them. About three tours later, Admiral Harry Train, as Commander in Chief Atlantic Fleet, was the guy who really stood up and put the Group Two commander in the set of quarters he deserved.

Despite the fact that I'm sure there was racial prejudice down in Charleston, I didn't have any major problems. I can remember driving into the gate of the naval base about the first or second time I was down there, and I was called to pull over to the side. The sentry said, "You don't have a pass."

I said, "Well, that's right, but I've got stars on my car, and I didn't think I needed it."

He said: "Oh, no. Everybody here needs a pass."

I said, "Fine."

So I went on into the chief police officer there. And he said, "Well, you have to have a pass."

I said: "Well, let me tell you something. I'm Commander Cruiser-Destroyer Group Two, and I'm moving down here, and I'm going to be here for a while, so I'd appreciate it if you'd give me a pass." He gave me a pass that said "anytime, any spot," and two or three things like that. I was going to be there, and I didn't need a damn pass, but they said I did. I guess that was his way of being a little hard on me as the new boy on the block.

That was the sort of minor harassment, and the type of thing that would happen to the young black sailor in Charleston that he could never either handle or know why, and then that would cause some minor problems. As a rear admiral, obviously I didn't have any problems.

★ ★ ★

As a group commander, I had administrative responsibilities in addition to the operational ones. The commodores of the destroyer squadrons in the group reported to me. We used to have periodic meetings on board the flagship to let them talk about their problems and then see if we could solve them. And at least once a month we all gathered at a little officers' club right on the pier in Charleston, and we sat around and discussed things there. And I'd go aboard ships, sometimes for formal inspection, but most times just for informal inspections and informal chats with the various COs. So in that respect, I was quite busy. We also had a staff engineer who periodically went around and inspected ships' engineering plants. When he found problems, he'd come up to me, and I'd go to the ship's captain to find solutions.

We didn't do a lot of scheduling because the type commander, Surface Force Atlantic Fleet (SurfLant), basically handled schedules. But when we thought modifications were necessary, I sent off a message to SurfLant to see if we could get a guy's schedule changed to suit his needs. I also did an investigation or two. In one case a young skipper ran his ship aground up in the Baltic Sea. When he got back I had to conduct the investigation on him. It was quite unfortunate, but I think his career was wrecked as a result. He was a young charger, made commander early, and probably had made lieutenant commander early. But that grounding was a career killer, and he didn't make captain.

★★★

Working for Stan Turner was very interesting. He was probably one of the smartest naval officers we've ever had. He went on to become Commander in Chief Allied Forces Southern Europe and later director of the Central Intelligence Agency. I admired him. He was fair. He directed the job to be done, and he expected it to be done. I remember an exercise called Solid Shield we held down at Camp Lejeune, North Carolina. We got together a group of amphibious ships and Marines. I was the destroyer group commander for the exercise. Stan was a strong advocate of good communications, and he wanted to talk frequently with his group commanders. So we were constantly sitting up in the radio shack there sending messages back and forth, telling people how to do things.

If I had any problem with Stan at all, it was in his effort to consolidate commands. Stan Turner directed me to find out how we could integrate my command, CruDesGru 2, with the Navy's South Atlantic Force (SoLant). Vice Admiral Robert Adamson was my type commander, SurfLant. SoLant was as much an asset of SurfLant as it was of Stan Turner's Second Fleet, and SurfLant didn't want them integrated. I worked for both: operationally under Second Fleet and administratively under SurfLant. So here I was, a two-star working for two three-stars who wanted opposite things. And no matter what answer I came up with, I really was caught in the middle. I had to tell Stan, "It can't be done." And he was quite upset with what I had to tell him.

But I don't think Stan would have said, "Do it," knowing full well he had to coordinate it with the other guy first. Unfortunately, Stan Turner and Rojo Adamson didn't really talk. Stan gave me the chore of taking over SoLant, and when it didn't come about, he would say, "What the hell are you doing, Sam?" I felt that wasn't handled quite right, and it was difficult. Shortly after the issue came up, I was transferred, and so was Turner. As a result, we simply didn't solve it while I was down there. That was the only problem I had with him.

At one point in 1975 I happened to be in Norfolk, so I went by the Second Fleet flagship to see Admiral Turner, and he congratulated me. He said, "I just saw something on your orders, and you're going to Third Fleet." I was quite overjoyed, and I reminded him it was my understanding that before you got three stars you were normally interviewed by SecDef and two or three other people. He said, "Well, I don't know about that, but I just saw your orders this morning, and you're going to Third Fleet." That would mean a promotion to vice admiral.

I was quite happy with the news, and I went to my home in Falls Church before going back to Charleston. I told Alma, "Hey, don't tell anybody, but we're going to Honolulu for our next duty, and I'm going to command the Third Fleet." She was obviously pleased, but the happiness faded quickly. The next morning I got a call from the flag detailer, who said: "Admiral, I want to offer congratulations. Your orders have just been approved by SecNav, and you're going as commandant of the Eleventh Naval District."

This really took me aback because I was thinking: "What about the Third Fleet? What about the third star and the whole bit?" But he wasn't the guy to ask, so I didn't ask him. I just got off the phone and told Alma: "Hey, change that. We're going to San Diego again where I'll be commandant of the Eleventh Naval District." Well, I was a little disappointed, but I liked San Diego, so that made up for it. Rear Admiral Bruce Keener, who got selected that spring, came down to Charleston and relieved me as group commander.

In looking back, it was certainly a pleasure to have a sea command as an admiral, but you don't have the same control as when you have your own ship. There's nothing like being on a bridge of your flagship and watching a young commander not do it right as skipper. And I say that with a smile, because you think nobody does it right unless he's doing it your way. As much as I enjoyed being a seagoing flag officer, there was not the personal satisfaction I'd had when I commanded any one of the ships I had. Being close to the individuals and working directly with them was what I really enjoyed. You just don't do that in flag rank. And you have to be very careful because despite the fact that you've got a seat on the bridge, and you're ready to jump up, you've got to remember it's not your ship. So that was kind of hard, but I lived through it.

CHAPTER TWENTY-TWO

Eleventh Naval District

After we wrapped up things in Charleston, I made preparations to do something with my house in northern Virginia and to move on out to San Diego. I knew I wouldn't face the same housing problem I had in Charleston, because there was a specific set of quarters designated for the naval district commandant. There was a minor problem, and it wasn't San Diego's fault. It wasn't anybody's fault, I guess. I was detached in June and ordered to relieve Rear Admiral Fillmore B. Gilkeson, who wasn't retiring until August, so I came home. I needed a little time, but I certainly didn't need sixty days, which was almost what it amounted to. But we sold our house and drove out to San Diego, and I mapped a route on which we could hit guest quarters or bachelor officers' quarters all the way across country. It was a lot easier traveling as a Navy admiral in the 1970s than it had been as a young officer in the 1950s and 1960s.

San Diego was probably the most interesting place I've ever been, and I've always liked it, so I was pleased by that part. I did have a feeling I was probably being sent out there to retire. This was my third two-star job, and certainly my contemporaries—even some junior to me—had been selected for three stars. In looking into it, I learned that the job as commandant had been in place since 1921, but not a single Com Eleven had gone on to three stars. A couple of them had been nominated for vice admiral, but for different reasons, they didn't make it. I decided that, okay, if this is where I'm going to retire, fine, but at the same time, I'm going to do this job the best I know how and make the most of it.

San Diego became one of the busiest jobs I've ever had from a social aspect. That was basically the commandant's job out there. I was an interface between the military and the civilian community. I certainly knew all the big people out there, went to all the right affairs. Hopefully did all the right things. I was giving something like a speech a month. I had lots of good friends out there and made new ones. Mayor Pete Wilson, who later became governor of California, became a good friend of mine. So did Robert Wilson, who was the congressman from there. From a Navy standpoint, Vice Admiral Bob Baldwin and Vice Admiral Emmitt Tidd were there as type commanders. So it was a really, really enjoyable tour.

As the district commandant, I was area coordinator for naval activities in the state of Arizona and in Southern California. Long Beach was under Com Eleven, so I spent time up in the shipyard and at the naval station, checking on how they were doing things. I was very closely aligned with the commander of the naval base in San Diego. We used to have area coordination meetings about once a quarter. We got the COs all in and laid down policies. Among other things, we set the uniform of the day. For San Diego most of the year it was whites anyway, so that was a minor issue.

There was some tie with the Naval Reserve in the area. There was a reserve destroyer group commander out there during my time. I really didn't do much in the way of functions with the reservists except attending a change of command or making a speech at some other reserve function every now and then. This group commander really ran the outfit so far as I was concerned. There was also a reserve training center in San Diego, and I used to go there once in a while to talk to the commanding officer, find out if he had problems, and things like that.

A big part of the job was that it required me to be constantly alert to problems in the community. I heard about one situation through a minister there, as I recall. He told me about a woman whose son was about a second class petty officer in the Navy. He had been stationed on the East Coast and had been transferred to San Francisco. When he went through Atlanta, Georgia, where his mother lived, the mother let him bring a seventeen-year-old boy out with him. They stopped in San Diego for some reason, went down to Tijuana, and got thrown in the pokey for buying marijuana. In fact, the guy from whom they bought the marijuana was probably the guy who fingered them.

The boy's mother apparently worked for an airline and periodically got flights to the West Coast, so she was out there quite often. One night my wife and I were discussing this case, and I said, "Well, my God, you can only go down to Tijuana and visit a son just so often. What does she do the rest of the day?" We thought we ought to at least meet her and see if there was any help we could offer. One night I located her and brought her up to the house. She and Alma became really fast friends. The mother told me she had a plan to break her son out of jail. She had come up with an idea of somewhat dubious legality because she had already used every legal approach she possibly could. Apparently about all the Mexican legal types were doing was just taking her money and doing nothing.

Somehow the seventeen-year-old boy got out, but they just kept the other kid down there. Ultimately this woman came up with a plan that she would go down there dressed as a prostitute, along with two other women, and they would spring him out of there. The plan was the three women would go down to the shore patrol headquarters, get a pass, and then about halfway to the jail one woman would get sick. So the mother feigned illness and turned back. When they carried out the plan, the other two women continued on, taking with them the pass that had been issued to the mother. When they got to the jail, they were admitted.

The Mexicans were probably chuckling because here was this guy who had two women down at the jail at the same time. They had conjugal privileges there, so you can guess what they imagined. Actually, one was his sister and another was a friend of the family, and they had brought in enough clothing for him under their clothes. When they got into his jail cell, he immediately changed into the women's clothes, and, now he had a pass. I guess the watch changed or something, but anyway, two women went in there and three came out, and they all got back. They managed to break out this kid who had been in the Mexican jail for about two or three months.

As a result of all this, the mother was not very popular with a lot of people around there. The Mexicans swore that the shore patrol had more or less instigated this. But ultimately it was proven it was just the mother's plan, and she got him out. And then he went on back to his naval duty station up in San Francisco. He had been held unlawfully, really, and so there were no problems with him. He reported to his assigned duty station and didn't face any retribution from the Navy. When you're caught like that, there's nothing you can do about it as far as Navy discipline. You can't say he didn't want to come back because he had wanted to get back.

★★★

The other big thing that I remember about San Diego was the annual sailboat race from Newport Beach, California, to Ensenada, Mexico. Each year the commandant goes down to Ensenada to present a trophy from the secretary of the navy to the one class of winners of the race. I was granted the opportunity to do that.

There was nothing really unusual except for a couple of funny incidents. My aide had been down the year before with Admiral Gilkeson. He told me, "The way we did it last year was that in order to ensure that we didn't have any problem down there, we went through each city en route, and we paid a visit on the mayor and the chief of police and usually presented them with a plaque." So we decided to do that. The mayor of one town, as I recall, wasn't there, but we left the plaque for him. The chief of police was apparently a guy who was appointed, and not a full-time policeman like our people are. He was a businessman in the normal chain of events, but he was a police chief on the side.

We went down and met him at the police station, and he was so pleased with the plaque that he decided he wanted us to see his business. We agreed. He operated a jewelry store, and he had watches galore, rings galore, and everything that glittered. He was so happy he decided he'd present each of us with a watch. He gave me a watch, and he gave my driver a watch, and he gave the aide a watch. I was quite grateful, and I put the watch on. When I started winding it, the stem broke off in my hand. Being diplomatic, I just quickly covered it up and went on from there.

The boat race went on as scheduled. Alma wanted to go fishing, so the Mexican Navy put the two of us on a minesweeper, and she and I went out fishing. They probably thought they were going to have a larger crowd. They supplied enough Cokes and sandwiches for about twenty people, but there were only the two of us. We went out there and had a good time.

★★★

I didn't get involved in handling many of the judicial cases in the naval district because most of them were the responsibility of the operational commanders. Inadvertently I got into a couple of things. One involved a young black officer who was assigned to the SOSUS station on Midway Island.[1] Vice Admiral Jim Watkins, who was the chief of naval personnel, asked me to look into this situation for him. It turned out this individual had been an enlisted man. Through the Navy Enlisted Scientific Education Program, the young man got his engineering degree at Purdue University and then a commission through Officer Candidate School.

Once he got out of school, he decided he wanted to be a race-relations expert, but that wasn't why the Navy paid for his education. The Bureau of Personnel sent him to serve as an engineering officer on board a destroyer as his first duty station after he was commissioned. That was the finest set of orders a young man could have. Instead, he constantly said, "No, I want to be a race-relations expert."

When he attended a short course at surface warfare school, he dragged his feet. Finally the people there decided he wasn't trying, so he ended up getting orders out to the SOSUS station at Midway. Apparently he was there for about a month when the commanding officer said to him, "You know, in the next two months or so we're going to have an operational readiness inspection, and I want you, along with two or three other officers here, to be qualified watch officers by the time this team comes off. Personally I don't think you're working at it hard enough."

The young man said, "Okay, sir, I'll do what I can," or something like that, but he just continued to drag his feet. Finally the commanding officer recommended him for a court-martial, and I guess ultimately he was dismissed from the Navy. I got involved in the review process, whether or not they should try him someplace else. As far as I was concerned, he had used up all of his chances at success. We had to do without him, despite the fact that here was a guy who by this time had about six or seven years in the Navy and a college degree. I guess the Navy wasn't the best spot for him.

We had another strange incident. The commanding officer of the naval communication station had his office right above the commandant's office in San Diego. The young man who commanded the station had worked for me at NavTelCom and was just really an outstanding guy. I admired him, and so occasionally I'd go up and have a cup of coffee with him. They had a problem in that a young black girl reported she had come back to her desk one day and

---

1 SOSUS is a network of underwater sensors that pick up the sounds of submarines.

there was a cross burning on it. I got into that one and did some investigating. It's hard to believe, but we discovered that she had only imagined she saw a cross burning on her desk. It was just the strangest thing I've ever seen. It did not really happen. Once in a while you get involved in things like that, and you don't know why or how they take place.

★ ★ ★

I really enjoyed that job in San Diego. My principal role was to be a good-will ambassador for the Navy in the area. We had all kinds of visitors out there. One I remember was William Middendorf, who was then secretary of the Navy. We hosted a cocktail party for Secretary Middendorf, and Mayor Pete Wilson was at the party. Being commandant was a fun tour, despite the fact that it was historically a retirement billet. I don't regret going there one bit because I met so many good people and was able to do so many things I'd never done before in my life.

The other good news was that I didn't have to retire then after all.

CHAPTER TWENTY-THREE

Third Fleet

When I went out to San Diego for the commandant's job in 1975, I figured I would get perhaps a two- or three-year tour. As it happened, I was there only eleven months. In the late spring of 1976, I was going around to visit various reserve training centers. I happened to be up in the San Francisco area on one of these trips when I got a call from the office of the CNO. By then Admiral Jim Holloway had taken over from Admiral Zumwalt.[1] I was surprised by the call in the first place and even more surprised when I talked to Admiral Holloway himself. He told me he wanted me to come to Washington because I was to talk to the secretary of defense concerning my next job.

My first thought was: "Well, okay, it'll be a communications job someplace as a two-star," because there was no hint at all it was to be a three-star job. But then I thought about it and concluded it might be, because he mentioned that I had an interview with the SecDef. I knew that normally if you went to the three-star level you were interviewed first by SecDef. Even so, I remained cautious. I'd had my hopes up the previous year when Stan Turner told me I was in line for a third star, and that hadn't come about.

Naturally, when the CNO called, I told him I could certainly go to Washington at any time. I quickly went back to San Diego, got on a flight to Washington, and went in for my interviews. Admiral Holloway told me he had nominated me to become Commander Third Fleet, which was then

1 Admiral James L. Holloway III served as chief of naval operations from June 29, 1974, to July 1, 1978.

based in Hawaii. He told me I had done an outstanding job at Com Eleven, so he felt I rated a look for possible promotion. Whether I got the job would depend on my interviews. For some reason, I felt the secretary of the Navy would interview me, but he did not. After I spoke with Admiral Holloway, I went up to the office of the SecDef.

When I went in, I was interviewed first by the deputy SecDef, William Clements. We talked in general terms about what the responsibilities of the job were. He was a little bit pleased, I believe, by my answers, although there were a couple of times when he said, "Well, the responsibilities are greater than that." I had thought more in terms of the training aspect than I did the aspect of the defense of the continental limits of the United States. I had focused on training, because I knew Third Fleet trained the ships for the deployment out to the Seventh Fleet. He wanted to make sure I was aware that it was more than that. So fine, I was aware of that, but I thought it was a secondary mission. Really, it's the primary mission.

In any event, after that interview I went in to see the secretary of defense himself, Donald Rumsfeld. That interview was rather straightforward, and some of the same questions were asked. He talked a little bit about my having been director of naval communications, and why hadn't I solved the secure voice program problem, which nobody had really done.

Then he asked me one question that made me think a little bit: if I had been promised the job of Commander Third Fleet, and then was told I would not get it, how would I feel about it. I simply said: "Well, I'm not sure, but I know I wouldn't go out and shoot myself." I didn't think that much about the question at the time, but shortly afterward I discovered the reason for it. The problem was that another officer, Rear Admiral Al Whittle, had been told he would get the job, and then the leadership had to backtrack. The reason I knew that was because I subsequently got his mail for about three or four weeks after I was selected for Third Fleet and got settled in at Pearl Harbor.

Al Whittle did get a three-star job, as chief of staff to Admiral Ike Kidd, who was NATO's Supreme Allied Commander Atlantic. I later talked to Admiral Whittle about it. He said he would have liked to get the Third Fleet job, but it really didn't make any difference as long as he got the third star, which he did, and later got four stars. He and I were selected for flag rank the same year, so we knew each other. And whereas I guess any two admirals who are two stars are sort of fighting each other—in other words, trying to get the three stars first—we weren't enemies. I guess you would say we were good friendly competitors.

About a week or ten days after I'd been in Washington, I got another call from Admiral Holloway. This time he said the Navy expected to announce I would be the next Commander Third Fleet. By then I was back on the West Coast and was up in the Long Beach area. He told me the announcement would be that day at one o'clock in Washington and ten o'clock California time.

There was an interesting side note. That day in Long Beach I happened to be attending a luncheon with the commander of the San Francisco Naval Base. He wanted to have the Third Fleet Commander in the San Francisco area for Navy Day in October. His real concern was that he was not able to ask the fleet commander and get a commitment out of him because he didn't know who it would be. And there I was, sitting and talking to him. I knew I would be in the job by then, but I couldn't tell him. The Navy's announcement came just about the time we were finishing up our luncheon. I said to him, "Okay, I'll do it for you."

★ ★ ★

The news of my promotion provided a great deal of pleasure and satisfaction for my entire family. We had been out in Hawaii before, at Pearl Harbor, and we were quite happy and eager to get back a second time, certainly with the third star. In order to get a job like that, there is an element of luck involved. It's a matter of being at the right place at the right time and, of course, having the right experience in your background. I was at the right place at the right time, and hopefully had the right experience. Whatever factors were involved, I successfully got it.

The ceremony at which I was relieved as Com Eleven was quite nice. It was on July 26, 1976, a few weeks after the nation's bicentennial celebration. We had a really, really nice crowd because I had made a lot of friends in San Diego, and friends from all over came to that. The biggest thing was that the ship on which I was frocked for two stars in 1971, the USS *Jouett*, was used for the change of command ceremony for Com Eleven. I was frocked with my third star on *Jouett* as well, so I have always considered that quite a significant happening. Vice Admiral Bill St. George was Commander Naval Surface

Force Pacific Fleet, and he was the frocker. I guess you'd call me the frockee. It was a thoroughly enjoyable ceremony.

In September of that year, at Pearl Harbor, I relieved Vice Admiral Robert Coogan, a naval aviator, as Commander Third Fleet. Admiral Thomas Hayward was Commander in Chief Pacific Fleet. I had known Admiral Hayward, so that aspect was fairly easy. Even so, I got involved in something I really didn't think was mine, despite the fact that Admiral Hayward thought it was my bailiwick. Since early in World War II, the Navy used the island of Kahoolawe as a target for naval gunfire support training. That was still taking place when I got there, but a group of Hawaiians was against the Navy using the island for our purposes. There were all kinds of concerns, including bird migration. The racing pigeon fans wrote an article that said the shooting was interfering with the homing pigeons' instinct, and they weren't coming home on time.

These protesters formed an organization called Protect Kahoolawe Ohana (PKO) and sued the Navy. They contended that the island should be cleaned up, and somehow it should be turned over for use of native Hawaiians, and probably the Navy ought to pay reparations. It was basically the same situation that came up years later in connection with the Atlantic Fleet's target range on the island of Culebra, near Puerto Rico. Originally the Commandant of the Fourteenth Naval District, with headquarters at Pearl Harbor, had been the biggest defender of the Kahoolawe range. He was the guy who had gone to court when PKO sued, but then the people from Com Fourteen were transferred over to Commander Third Fleet, and as the user of the facility, I became the defender of it.

The people who opposed the Navy's use of Kahoolawe wanted a meeting on the island, which I had to arrange. We were also to take Congressman Cecil Heftel there for the meeting. The agreement was that there'd be no press; only the Navy, Congressman Heftel, the councilman from Maui, and the proponents for the island would be taken over there. But when we arrived in Maui, the councilman was not there. It turned out that he could not go, which meant there was an extra seat on the airplane. There were two press people. One was a reporter, and she had a photographer with her. They decided the open seat then belonged to one of them. The young lady went over to Congressman Heftel while I was standing out sort of waiting to see if the councilman was coming. She demanded from the congressman that she be given the seat.

He promptly told her that, no, this was a Navy helicopter, and she would have to get her seat from the admiral. Knowing full well the agreement was that there would be no press, I refused to take her. I went over to where she was climbing into the airplane, and I said, "I'm sorry, Miss, but I cannot permit you to go in that airplane." The woman turned around and slugged me. She was about ready to slug me again when I just sort of put both hands on her arms and lifted her off of the step of the helicopter. Again I said, "I'm sorry, Miss, but I can't let you on there." She then sat underneath the airplane to prevent us from taking off. We promptly got the police to get her out of there.

Everything would have been okay, I guess, except that her photographer took a picture that made it look like I slugged her. In fact, I got a call from my brother when he saw the picture in the *Washington Post*. He said, "Hey, you don't slap women." And, of course, I had not done it. I think the whole thing was staged. In any event, we went on to the island and did our business. The only thing I really objected to was the publicity, including the picture.

I guess the Honolulu news types were a little unhappy with me, because the first thing they wanted when I got off the helicopter back at Pearl Harbor was an interview. But I just slipped off the airplane and went on home. I guess I should have satisfied them, but I'd had my fill of press people by then, so I did nothing. The minute I got home, the reporter's lawyer called and wanted to find out if I planned to sue. But I personally felt it would look kind of strange for a 250-pound admiral to be suing a 100-pound woman because she slapped him.

Among the irritants were the PKO people who would sneak onto the island. Sadly, one of them drowned. On another occasion, two of them, Noa Emmett Aluli and Walter Ritter, got on the island and managed to elude capture for about two days before being removed. When he left, Ritter got off with some little goats in a knapsack. That upset the commander in chief, Admiral Hayward, but there wasn't much we could do about it. In virtually all my dealings with him, he was very pleasant. But he was a strong enough individual that he knew how to snap up a guy who was a little lagging. I can remember that he was quite unhappy when Ritter came back with those damn goats, and he let me know. "Hey, you didn't quite do the job here. Don't let it happen again." I was mad that it had happened. I felt I had let him down; however, I'm not sure I could have counted the goats in the bag either.

I should add that Admiral Hayward was a tremendous naval officer. He was obviously very sharp. He was later selected in 1978 to be CNO. He was an active guy, and he wanted things done. He held various briefings and conferences for his type commanders. In fact, we went to Guam a couple of times when there were meetings in which the Third Fleet and the Seventh Fleet commanders got together with CinCPacFlt. He was very nice to me, and when I wanted to take a trip, he usually made available to me one of his aircraft so I could take my staff and we could all go together. That made it quite easy, because if you took an airplane, then you could obviously relax and study and work on the airplane, whereas you couldn't do it very well on a commercial airplane.

I guess the thing I'd like to say is that Admiral Hayward really had it all together, and I was quite impressed with how well organized he was, how he was able to meld things together and make things happen.

To wrap up the discussion of Kahoolawe, despite the meetings and the continuing concern about the issue, I wasn't able to bring about any resolution during the time I was there. The Navy continued to use the island for its training purposes after I left.[2]

★★★

Obviously there was much more to my job than dealing with Kahoolawe. As I mentioned, Deputy Secretary Clements had talked about the responsibility for protecting the West Coast of the United States. We executed that responsibility through the commanders of the various naval bases. In fact, it was the whole Pacific Coast, really, so I had a two-star Canadian officer with whom I worked. I met with the North American Air Defense Command on one occasion, and I also went down to Phoenix to meet with Air Force people. There were no special exercises devoted to continental defense, but certainly when an exercise was in the area, that was among the things written into the op order as goals to accomplish. In years gone by, that had been

2 In 1990, President George H. W. Bush directed that the Navy stop using the island as a target for live-fire exercises. In 1994, the Navy transferred the title of Kahoolawe to the state of Hawaii.

handled by the Commander Western Sea Frontier, based in San Francisco. But that command had long since been disbanded, and now the job belonged to the Third Fleet.

The basic role as fleet commander was the readiness and the training of all the forces that belonged to Third Fleet. That included scheduling and monitoring the various training exercises. My staff kept track of them, and occasionally I went out to sea myself, riding one ship after another. Third Fleet placed considerable emphasis on antisubmarine warfare readiness and arranged for lots of ASW training. The Seventh Fleet in the western Pacific was the one that did the forward operations. Our role was to put the ships through their paces and make sure they were well prepared before they deployed. That didn't require me to go aboard every ship, but I did get a number of opportunities. Often I'd catch a ride to an aircraft carrier and then visit a number of ships while they were at sea.

From the time a ship began its workups for deployment, it was under my operational command. Certainly the Pacific Fleet commander in chief could take it away from me, but I didn't have any problem with anyone else, and the fleet CinC wasn't likely to intervene. The ship belonged to me, and the skipper took his orders from me until he moved under the control of Commander Seventh Fleet at an appropriate time when he was going west. I had absolute control until then.

The one thing the Third Fleet commander always wanted, and any other guy in that position wanted, was that when a ship was turned over from the type commander, SurfPac, the ship was ready to operate rather than having to go back for repairs. Every once in a while there was some concern that the ship really wasn't ready for Third Fleet ops, so you had to look at it very carefully and decide whether or not you wanted to turn it back. The staff and I would get together on those kinds of things and decide, okay, he needs another four weeks in the yards, or four more weeks under the type commander to work up to the point wherein he's ready for multi-ship Third Fleet operations. Third Fleet ops were the fast-paced things, faster than the slow things a ship would do in refresher training under the type commander.

We conducted three or four major fleet exercises a year. Several of them were multinational in that we worked with the Australians and the New Zealanders. We also had the French in on a couple of exercises; they came up from Tahiti. In fact, I went down to Tahiti and Australia on a couple of occasions to brief on upcoming exercises in which their forces would be involved. We had Canadians in on our exercises. I don't think we had any British participation during my two years out there because most of the Brits were on East Coast exercises, but there had been times when we operated with them as well.

The biggest exercise was a multinational one called RimPac. That is normally run on a two-year cycle. We had the first one and then were able to schedule another for the following year because we knew the Australian carrier would not be available two years later. So I was fortunate in being able to conduct two in a row.

The scheduling and permission for these multinational drills came from Commander in Chief Pacific Fleet, but it was the officers on my staff who planned the exercises and the various series of events that would be involved. Obviously, there was appropriate coordination with representatives from the other navies. After the staff had put together the operation order, I reviewed it and signed off on it to make it official.

Another one of the functions was that the Antarctic Support Forces were under the cognizance of Third Fleet. So I went down to Antarctica, and I also came up to Port Hueneme, California, the site of the support force's headquarters. I once participated in the Rose Bowl Festival and was crowned as one of the honorees. And incidentally, getting back to it, the thing that Commander San Francisco Naval Base had wanted was Commander Third Fleet to be there for Navy Day in 1976. I used one of the DLGs as a flagship for the event. It was a special celebration because of the bicentennial year. We had probably about twenty ships in there, which is many more than normally go into a place at the same time. I was there for about a week, as I recall, and during that time I hosted a dinner.

I made a fair number of public appearances in the job, lots of speeches and lots of events up and down the West Coast. I attended Navy League functions. And there were other organizations that wanted to hear from me as the first black admiral. The American Battleship Association had an event in Honolulu, and I was the speaker, because I'm an ex-battleship sailor. An enjoyable part was that for the first time in many, many years I got to visit with retired Rear Admiral Edward Stephan, who had been the executive officer when I served on board the *Iowa* during the Korean War. He was a great guy, really; I enjoyed working with him.

One of the pleasant side trips from the job came in 1977, when I attended the first reunion of the Golden Thirteen since they had been commissioned in 1944, the same year I was. They got together in California, and I came in from Hawaii. Admiral Holloway was there, and I think I came as much for that reason, because I wanted to hear what Admiral Holloway was going to say, as I did for the fact that the Golden Thirteen were there. I hadn't seen them for years and wanted to touch base with them again. I had been closely aligned with many of them. Dalton Baugh was in my company as a recruit and also in my service-school class down at Hampton Institute. Johnny Reagan was in Hampton, in service school, as an electrician's mate. And then he was in San Diego when I got here. George Cooper was on the staff down at Hampton when I was there. It was great to see them again.

★★★

The most lasting memory of our time in Hawaii is a personal one. Alma and I lost our son Robbie out there. He was killed as the result of an automobile accident on Ford Island, which is where we had our living quarters and the fleet headquarters. It's the island in the middle of Pearl Harbor, and it's where the battleships were moored in 1941 when the Japanese hit.

What was really traumatic about the stay out there was not just the loss of our son; there were three other deaths on Ford Island in those two years. Ford Island is not that big a community, so it has quite an impact on you. What happened to Robbie involved a strange set of circumstances. When we left San Diego in the summer of 1976, Robbie came back to Virginia Union, my alma mater, to go to college. He spent a year there and he didn't do very well. I was all set to take him out of school and bring him back home. The administrators at the university said he just wasn't really mature enough to be on his own. But Alma convinced me we ought to try giving him more time, and we did. So he started his third semester there, his second year, and attended school until he came home for the Christmas holidays. By then he hadn't done any better, so I said: "Give me your ticket. I'm not going to send you back anymore."

While he was in Hawaii he went to work, and he bought his first car. He had a little problem with it in that the wheel bearings had to be repaired. When it was ready, he picked up the car, and that night he was driving it for the first time after the repairs. I can imagine that he was running around Ford Island, sort of checking it out. Unfortunately, he got to a curve he couldn't make, and the car went over into the water. He drowned rather than being killed in the crash. The car went upside down in about three feet of water, and he perished. It was just a real tragedy.

It was even more traumatic for me because it happened when Alma was in the Tripler Army Hospital, having just had her feet operated on. Then we had a whole weekend when we couldn't do anything as far as arranging things. I guess even more traumatic was that it was my birthday. Three of us were born in June: my birthday is June 4, my son David's birthday is June 9, my daughter Tracey's birthday is June 13. It turned out Robbie was killed on my birthday, buried on my other son's birthday, and only four days away from my daughter's. So once a year we're constantly reminded of these things. After talking it over, we decided to bury Robbie at the National Cemetery in San Diego. The three of us—David, Tracey, and I—brought the body back to San Diego and buried him there. Alma wasn't yet able to travel.

Our faith provided a source of solace in the aftermath of Robbie's death. One of the ironic things was that he was getting kind of religious at that time, because there was a Bible in the car when it was recovered. I think back to the night of the accident. I got the news about 1:30 on a Saturday morning, and then I had to get off Ford Island and go to the hospital to tell Alma. Word of the accident obviously got over to Tripler by the time I did. While I was in there waking Alma and telling her, and we were both trying to console each other, in walked a minister. He gathered us together, and we said the Lord's Prayer, and he prayed a bit. That did me as much good as anything else did. There are times in life when you need to be comforted, and that was certainly one of them.

CHAPTER TWENTY-FOUR

Defense Communications Agency

The accidental passing of Robbie set me to thinking about the future. Losing that boy was just such a blow for me that everything in the Navy reminded me of him. I felt, "Okay, it's time to get out of the environment and go home." The Navy hadn't done anything to me, but his untimely death really demoralized me. But then, when I discovered I'd been nominated for another job, I felt I really owed the Navy something. The Navy had given me an opportunity in the Third Fleet command, one I really enjoyed. I felt I'd done some good there, and I said to myself, "Now the Navy is offering me a chance to do them some good here in this joint arena in the Defense Communications Agency. The Navy really needs to have a guy in the DCA job. I will come back and do that one, and I'll stay at least a couple of years anyway." And I did.

DCA is a multifaceted job, really. The first thing is that this agency runs the defense communications system. It provides all of the strategic and the long-haul communications for the Joint Staff and for the services. Historically, the services have had all of their own communications arrangements, but in 1960 the secretary of defense decided there should be one agency to provide the long-haul connections and thus get rid of duplication. The services continue to provide their own tactical communications. The defense communications system (DCS) has different forms. For example, it has satellite communications, and it uses the telephone company's commercial communication systems.

The other mission is that the director is the manager of the National Communications System. The various departments of the government, such as the State Department, all come together, and they meet periodically to decide what their communication requirements are and how to keep from duplicating. There are also administrative service-related communications. For instance, when you're talking in terms of an administrative message that goes from the CNO out to Pearl Harbor, it goes over a DCS line until it gets to Pearl Harbor. At some point it goes through the main frame, and then it becomes Navy again.

The establishment of the DCA was done by edict and has succeeded in meeting the objective of eliminating the duplication. There's always been a certain amount of disagreement, because the services would like to do it all themselves. There's always been an argument between the services and Joint Chiefs of Staff, for example, or any joint agency. The services feel they can satisfy their individual needs much better. The services feel they are unique, and so they have unique requirements. And when it is determined that their unique requirement would be satisfied by this big monster called DCA, the Army might say, "He can't do that, because he doesn't know what my real requirement is." The real issue is that the services no longer have the degree of control they would like to have. So you've got a tremendous job of coordination and patience. It calls for diplomacy. It calls for skills in negotiating. And it calls for being able to put the fist down, too, and say, "Hey, that's where the crap ends."

The hardest job for me came when the Defense Science Board met and decided that the Defense Communications Agency should be more in the acquisition business. Basically, in the long-haul communications, DCA is responsible for them—with a budget and everything else—but there are certain communications they don't really acquire and pay for. But anyway, they wanted DCA to become DC^{3}A, which would also put DCA's nose a little bit under the camel's tent in that it was getting a little bit into the tactical communications area.

Dr. Gerald Dinneen tasked me to come up with a plan for doing that.[1] But, of course, any plan that is going to do something new will cost somebody people and dollars. I thought we put together a plan to carry out that function at a minimum cost and with a minimum number of people. But you've got to remember where your dollars come from. They come out of the individual

1 Dr. Gerald Dinneen, principal deputy undersecretary and assistant secretary of defense for command, control, and intelligence.

service budgets, and the people come out of the services' hide. So there was quite an objection to that. Ultimately what really happened, I believe, was the establishment of JC^{3}S, a group of people on the Joint Staff who were formed to do the function that the Defense Science Board felt should be done, without giving that power to a separate agency or the DCA.

There was another problem. The services have all yelled and screamed about their requirement for secure voice communication. And we got into that one. It was a problem we just have not been really able to successfully coordinate with the National Security Agency (NSA) types. It's not the fault of the NSA, because NSA people feel they were satisfying a requirement that's been laid down to them. The services and DCA always felt it wasn't being done fast enough or as completely as it should have been done.

I stayed in that job for two years, and about six or eight months away from the end of the two-year period I decided I would retire. I would be fifty-eight years old in the summer of 1980. I knew that under any set of circumstances, no matter what happened to me, I probably would not get a fourth star. I had devoted thirty-four years to the naval service, and that was enough. So I put the letter in, and I retired officially as of August 1, 1980. Then I came on out to the next phase of my life.

CHAPTER TWENTY-FIVE

After the Navy

When I first took off the uniform after all those years of active duty, I didn't plan to do anything in the line of work. I had purchased a mini-farm, as I call it. It's about three acres of land in Haymarket, Virginia. I didn't plan to do much more than have a garden and some fruit trees. I did plant a lot of pine trees, and they've grown quite large over the years. Another pleasant diversion was keeping chickens and pigeons; pigeons are a hobby of mine, and I need to reach way back to cover the origin of that.

I became interested in pigeons as a youngster. A young man and his mother moved into my neighborhood in Richmond because his parents were divorcing or something. They lived very close to us, so I was brought into the picture to show him around the neighborhood. I went to visit his house, and he had a bunch of pigeons out back. They were a type called rollers, generally fancy, beautifully colored birds. They fly and flop and roll, which is the reason for the name. I just became utterly fascinated. Somehow I got a couple of males and some hens. I also found out you could eat them, and squabs are a delicacy. My mother could really fix them well, but there was not much meat. I picked all the feathers off one, and by the time I got done, the bird was about the size of a robin.

Then I got fascinated with homing pigeons. These are a little larger, fly, and return home after a while. And I could fly them around. One of my neighbors had some, and we had chickens as well. My father was a big one for chickens. In those days baby chickens came through the mail. If the mailman couldn't find the guy's house where the chickens went, then they'd raffle them off at the post office. And dad would say, "Well, son, I've got another hundred chickens for you to feed. Twenty-five cents." Twenty-five cents for one hundred chickens! Boy, oh, boy. I took care of them.

One day we went out there, and about half of these hundred chickens were dead. I noticed they were all wet. My baby brother had been trying to teach them to swim, because he thought they were ducks. Oh, Lord, I wanted to skin him alive.

Another hobby of mine was learning about the role of homing pigeons in the armed forces. I've read all the fascinating stories about the pigeons that were used by the U.S. Navy and Army in World War II and before. The Army had a pigeon place up in Fort Monmouth, New Jersey, where they bred and trained them. In my last tour of active duty, I once went to Korea as part of the DCA contingent, and a guy said, "Oh, I hear you're a pigeon man."

"Yes, sir."

He said, "We have a pigeon corps too."

I looked, and there, standing beside us, was a guy with a pigeon in a cage. He said, "When you take off in this helicopter, I'm going to let him go." He let him go, and when we got to our destination and got off the helicopter, the pigeon was sitting on the roof, trying to get in. So I've always contended (with tongue in cheek) that pigeons are going to be my backup communications system.

In any event, for the first nine months off active duty, I just sort of took care of the birds and worked around my yard. But after a while I got kind of frustrated, a little bit tired of doing nothing. I didn't actively go out and seek work, but a guy who knew there was a job available came out one day and told me about it, and I went to work for a defense contractor. The job required an individual who had a background in intelligence more than communications, although communications experience was certainly an asset.

My new employer was a small company called CTEC. CTEC had been in the OSIS business—ocean surveillance information systems. It had designed and built a system I knew and had used previously; even as a ship driver you use it to some degree. But I kept having this conflict-of-interest feeling. When I first retired, I went over to see a member of the Judge Advocate General's Corps, a Navy lawyer, and said to him, "I want you to explain to me what I can really do and what can't I do."

The first question he asked was, "Do you like to go to the Pentagon?"

I said, "Yes."

"Well, don't."

"Oh?"

"Well, I know you want to go into the Pentagon, and you've got friends there and you're just going to visit them. But then that's going to be interpreted as selling. And you can't do that."

I guess as a result of that, every once in a while I was asked what was going on in the Navy, and I would go to the Pentagon and find out. But I kept getting this conflict-of-interest feeling, so I quit.

But, just before quitting, I had met the president of another company, which was a small minority company, and he said he needed some help, and I could certainly help him. I quit CTEC and went to work for Automated Business Systems and Services. As it turned out, this was much more of a conflict because of the kind of help he needed. I worked there for a year, and I finally decided I just couldn't live in an environment in which I felt I was in a potential conflict. Nobody was going to interfere with my retirement pay, so I decided I would leave that type of life.

In December of 1983 I began working for the Armed Forces Communications and Electronics Association (AFCEA), which is a nonprofit. I'd been in the business of education and training, and certainly there was no conflict there. In this job I had three basic functions. One was to run a professional development center in which we taught one- to five-day continuing education courses. I scheduled about twenty of those courses a year. I didn't do the teaching myself, but I used course coordinators who put them together. Each coordinator lined up the instructors, and then I made the arrangements for locations, got the material cleared, and facilitated the process.

The customers were three types, and we had three different price ranges. One group was made up of military-government people, who came in large numbers. We had the AFCEA members, which came from the 750 corporations included in the association or affiliated with it. Then we got a considerable number of other types; they were not members of AFCEA, but they were people interested in our courses. In some instances, they were from defense contractors, and in some they weren't. So we had both civilians and military-government types to the courses.

The courses, depending on the value of them to various groups, would run anywhere from, say, 40 to 150 students. I maintained the budget, so I needed to know what my revenue was going to be. The most difficult thing was to predict how many students we'd get. Even harder was the breakdown of students within that number because of our different price schedules.

The second function in my job was certainly of much interest to me—the AFCEA Educational Fund. That part involved soliciting money from the corporations and members of AFCEA to fund scholarships for ROTC students. Each year we selected fifteen Army, fifteen Navy, and fifteen Air Force recipients. That included five each incoming sophomores, incoming juniors, incoming seniors in the ROTC schools, and we gave them scholarships of $500, $750, and $1,000, respectively. The really rewarding part of the experience was in the giving of the scholarships. It was another thing entirely to be asking people all the time, but that's an important program. We also gave out a certain number of awards to ROTC students, as well as awards each year to the top students in the field of electronics at the service academies.

My third function was that of running a career-planning center. I got the requirements from industry for the kinds of people they needed, and I also got résumés from the military people who were retiring. I tried to match those, sending the résumés to the appropriate corporations, and saying, "Here's a guy who's suitable for you." If they hired him, then AFCEA got a stipend of 5 percent of the new employee's first-year salary. So those were the three functions. In the case of the career-planning center, that is one of the things the Department of Defense says an association such as AFCEA should be involved in. This time, my job called for supporting the interests of the services rather than presenting any conflict.

I stayed with AFCEA for about six years. In the late 1980s, I began to have fainting episodes. I fell one time while I was working in the basement, and they found me lying on the floor. They rushed me to the hospital, and everybody checked my heart and the rest of it. I stayed in Fairfax Hospital for a few days. But I thought I had worked long enough, so I decided to give it up, and we have spent our time in our home in Haymarket ever since.

★★★

One of the organizations I continue to be a member of is the National Naval Officers Association, which exists to support minority officers in the Navy, Marine Corps, and Coast Guard. I get a call maybe once a year to speak to a group, to tell them a little bit about my experiences. I also get a call maybe twice a year from the recruiting command to do basically the same thing. They've got a big pitch for minority officers, and I'll go around. I guess the last one of those I did was down in South Carolina, where I went to each of the minority schools around there, the colleges as well as a couple of high schools, for a couple of days. And I got a call recently about going out to San Diego. I still know quite a number of young black naval officers whom I see and talk to occasionally.

Because of my own years of service in the Navy, I've developed a long-term perspective on how much it has changed. I think the service has done an outstanding job in providing career opportunities for blacks, especially when you consider that I knew a period when it wasn't doing any job at all. I get a little concerned that there are people who come in, see what the situation is, and then assess it as, "Hey, the Navy is not doing very much." When you look back to World War II, it has made a lot of progress. A critic will say, "Well, they should have done more." But you've got to remember with the Navy you're really assessing a history of more than two hundred years, and the changes have been remarkable in the recent past.

I agree with the concerns of those who believe still more could be done. I get a little concerned with a couple of things I see the Navy doing. One is the requirement that there be a black officer in all the recruiting districts—all stations, really. And I get concerned because what we're doing is we're taking the young officer who ought to be out learning his trade, and then putting him in two years of shore duty that doesn't really qualify him to be a naval officer. Okay, he's doing a vital job for the Navy, but doing vital jobs for the Navy doesn't really add up at the end when picking commanders of destroyers, aircraft squadrons, and submarines. You need to be in ships and aircraft to acquire the necessary skills and experience to get promoted.

I'm not sure there are many, many more things the Navy can do now to enhance opportunities. I'm not a guy who says, "Hey, give some opportunity over here to people who really aren't ready for that opportunity." I say, "Maybe you can do something to make them more ready and then give them more opportunity at that point in time." I'm not really sure what else there is we can do. We are constantly going out trying to recruit. We constantly get good numbers in. I'm curious why sometimes we get these numbers in and then, for example, potential aviators go to flight training at Pensacola, Florida, and fail. I do know the flunk out rate for blacks at Pensacola is just astronomical compared to other racial groups. What that's all about, I can't say, because I've never really been down there to see it.

I hear people complain about discrimination, but an awful lot of things are passed off as discrimination that I'm convinced are not discrimination. It becomes a convenient excuse in many, many, many cases. Don't get me wrong; I'm not saying in all cases, because I think discrimination does play a part. I remember something that happened when I was the Third Fleet commander. One of my officers, Commander Fred Bailey, left the staff and went to command the guided missile destroyer *Preble*. I happened to be coming back from San Diego. A young black officer, a lieutenant (junior grade) from his ship, asked me for a ride on the airplane, so we sat and talked. Then he went back to his seat. Ultimately, I had him in my little compartment on this airplane for one of the meals. I said, "What are your aspirations, Jaygee?"

He said, "You know, I think I'd like to be an aide."

"Hey, that's great. Let me tell you, I think an aide is a guy who probably has one of the best jobs in the Navy for a young officer who wants to learn. He's walking around with a flag officer, he's meeting them, and everything else. He sees how they comport themselves, and he can learn. He gets into high-level discussions, and all this. But, you know, I wouldn't have you for an aide."

His eyes bugged, and he said, "Well, why wouldn't you?"

"Well, first of all, you have a beard. You've got to shave your beard."

"Well, Admiral, I wouldn't shave my beard off for you or for anybody."

"Son, that's the reason you can't be an aide. Now, why won't you shave your beard?"

"Well, my beard connotes my blackness."

Well, damn it, if a beard has to connote blackness then there's something wrong. Because I could look at him and I could tell by the skin; I thought that connoted blackness.[1]

But we have some of those kinds of things, which I think are really against our being one people in this good country. The National Naval Officers Association is a good example, really a good group. They do things to help

1 This is now a moot point. The Navy subsequently issued an order that its personnel would have to stop wearing beards as of January 1,1985.

other black officers. But then it tells you that we're separated. It's that kind of thing that bothers me. And what else can be done about it? I don't know.

Equal opportunity is something I think this country has to practice. But I think at some point in time we've got to reach the place wherein equal opportunity is so routine that we don't have to call it equal opportunity, that it's just a matter of fact. I almost think we've called attention to equal opportunity long enough that we ought to be at that point. I'm hoping that one of these days we will get there. But when, I don't have any idea. I just feel that we've still got so far to go concerning equal opportunity offices and those kinds of things, but we should have been out of that range a long time ago.

I'm hoping we can do away with affirmative action. Rather than saying we ought to be two peoples who are equal, we ought to be striving to be one people. I think we ought to be one set of Americans. Okay, some are going to be dark, and some are going to be light, but that's the way it is in, say, South America, where some countries have one strong organization. I think we can have one country of people, who may be mixed in the color of their skin, but they're one people otherwise, speaking the same language and reaching for the same goals.

The Navy faces another challenge with regard to minority individuals. It is always vulnerable to talent seekers from companies in industry who are trying to get the good people. These companies seek out capable black people who have received training and experience in the Navy. This is particularly true for defense contractors that have to satisfy the Department of Defense goals for equal opportunity, or else they don't get these contracts. There's not much the Navy can do about it, because the Navy cannot automatically give Joe Blow here, who's a young black second class petty officer, more money than it is giving Joe Smith out here, who's a white second class petty officer. It can't give him more time off. In some of these cases the Navy is bound to lose in that kind of competition. What we've got to instill in its personnel—and I do not mean just the black people, but all of them—is that "We really want you. Here's what we're doing for you." And remind them every once in a while that there are lots of benefits here.

I remember an incident from my own experience. Just to expand on the event I covered earlier, in the early 1960s I was a young lieutenant commander serving on board the destroyer *Theodore E. Chandler.* Alma, our son

Robbie, and I were eating in a restaurant in San Francisco, and there were two high-level industrial types who found out I had some communications experience. They came over to talk to me, and they were tickled at how well behaved Robbie appeared to be.

Now, it's worth remembering that around 1960–61 a black family in a restaurant maybe stood out a little bit. In any event, they offered me a job that would have paid me about four times what the Navy was paying me at that time. But the one thing they couldn't guarantee me was the security the Navy offered. And they couldn't guarantee me the well-being and everything else I felt I had in the Navy. So I didn't do it. I think we've got to instill some of this thinking in our younger crowd.

What the Navy needs to do to hold on to people is convince them that this really is an area in which they can grow and prosper, and that the service has the individual's long-term interests at heart. By contrast, companies on the outside may want to use people for a short time and then get rid of them. It is interesting to me to see the number of people who get hired because a defense contractor has a contract with the government that lasts, say, for two years. At the end of two years, the company no longer has a contract, and the individual no longer has a job. And some of them stay even less time.

★★★

In thinking back on my long association with the Navy, I see quite a contrast between where I started and where I wound up. My career started with the sense of obligation I felt to serve during World War II. I really did not expect we were going to have a long war by any stretch of the imagination, but at the same time, for my part I wanted to do as well as I possibly could. Initially the motor machinist route seemed to have been the most interesting one for me. And, of course, that's where I went.

I really have always been very curious as to what would have happened to me if World War II had not come about when it did. I know now that I wasn't doing what I was capable of doing in college at that point in time. In fact, I had dropped out, and I was working as a coat-liner presser. I really got turned around when I got selected to the V-12 program at UCLA. There I began to realize I not only had to compete in a world wherein I was involved but also that a lot of other people were involved as well. I realized I had some of the same capabilities they did, and I could be fairly successful in the Navy environment.

This feeling was reinforced even further when I went to the *PC-1264*, where I was accepted for the first time, really, as a young man who was a naval officer, and I enjoyed it. I came out of the Navy, as I said earlier, for a couple of reasons. One was that, first of all, nobody asked me to stay. And, secondly, I didn't believe that there was the opportunity that did present itself after I came back. And the major reason, I guess, was that I had not completed my education, and I felt I should come out and do that. I've often wondered what would have happened if I had stayed in and tried for one of the college training programs the Navy offered at that time. I personally don't think I would have gone as far as I eventually did. Circumstances worked out in my favor. I think part of my success came about as a result of the timing—that I was called back to active duty as a recruiter and then remained because the Korean War began when it did.

Timing also helped when I transferred to the regular Navy. I lost two years of seniority, but that change gave me two more years in which to prepare myself better for promotion. I've always certainly been quite pleased with the success that I had. I attribute it not so much to me as to, certainly, the people whom I've worked with, who've worked for me and with me. This means whites as well as blacks. I enjoyed every minute of it. I don't think I would change much of it if I had to do it again, because I'm quite happy my career worked the way it did.

One by-product of my success is a role that has been thrust upon me: to serve as an inspiration for others coming along. I accept that role as graciously as I can, because there are people out there who feel I am sort of a role model. For instance, I recall a visit from a man who happened to have gone to school with my son David. He now is a schoolteacher and a football coach at one of the schools in Virginia. He's asked me to come out to speak to his kids, and I'm quite happy to do that. If there is something I can tell them, or sit down and answer a question, or something that will cause an individual to reflect and prepare himself or herself a little bit earlier, I'm just very happy to do that, really.

A lot of wonderful things have happened to me. I have a street named after me in my hometown, and in fact, I have a street sign from it in my family room: "Admiral Gravely Boulevard." I really appreciate what that group did for me. I've become an honorary citizen of so many cities from the plaques and things I've gotten from various people and organizations. I sometimes am impressed with myself, although I hope I don't show that too much.

My marriage to Alma has been one of the prime reasons for success on my part. I was very fortunate. I married a really wonderful woman. It's quite interesting to me because there was no long courtship. I met this young lady in 1940 on the campus of Virginia State College. I managed to see her for a total of five or ten minutes. I guess I went back there once after that and saw her really because she was one of the girls who lived on the same floor as my sister.

Then when I got into the service and I started looking for people to write, I found out very quickly that the best time of your day is mail call, and the only way you can get letters is if you write letters. I began to write a lot of people, and she was one of the ones who answered. We continued to correspond, and then I went to see her in January 1946, when she was teaching school in Blackstone, Virginia. Less than a month and a half later we were married.

Alma has been a tremendous lady, one whom I admire, because she's done some things for me I wouldn't do for myself. She's just a great gal. And that's been part of it, having the right kind of a partner. We didn't have any children. We adopted three children. And those guys and that gal turned out to be just tremendous people. They went around at times when things were really tough. So each of them has been a trooper, and I've been quite happy with that. I have been truly blessed in so many ways.

Afterword

Our Navy life together was still some distance in the future when I first met Sam Gravely. That was in 1940, when he was a student at Virginia Union College in Richmond and I was a student at Virginia State College in Petersburg. As he said, we met through his sister. The second time we were together was when he came up to visit one Sunday in early 1943. He was then stationed at the Navy Training School at Hampton Institute near Norfolk, Virginia, and was wearing his enlisted sailor uniform. During that visit we sat out on the front campus and talked so long that he missed his bus and had to catch the next one back to Hampton. He wound up being absent without leave—the only time he ever did that in his life.

The next time I saw Sammie was at the beginning of 1946, shortly after the end of Christmas break. By that time, I had graduated from college and was teaching in a segregated school in the small town of Blackstone, Virginia. I was also going with one of the professors at Virginia State College. He had fallen in love with me the latter part of my senior year. He was a very, very nice man, but I didn't love him.

One day, early in the New Year, I was teaching a class. The home economics department was in a full home, and I had students working in different rooms. All told, I taught 130-some children each day. I had a captain in each room. At one point I looked out through a window and saw a man approaching; all I could see was from just about the waist down. I could tell that he was coming around to the back door and had on something navy blue. But I couldn't see enough of him to be able to know who it was. I had a captain who was in the kitchen at the time. She came in and said, "Miss Clark, there's someone here to see you."

I was taking roll then and said, "Oh, who is it?"

She said, "I don't know, but he's got a uniform on."

I said, "Okay, tell him I'll be there as soon as I finish taking this roll."

So I finished, and I went into the kitchen and started looking. There was Sammie in his long blue bridge coat, the heavy one. He was supposed to have come home to Richmond at Christmastime, and he was going to come to Roanoke, where I was home for Christmas. But he hadn't come, and I never gave it another thought. I figured something had happened, that his ship had left or something. But now here he was—a big surprise.

That was my last class for the day, and the USO was right up the road from us.[1] So I talked to him a while and told him to go up to the USO, and I would meet him there after school. After we talked there for a while, he and I got together with several of my fellow teachers. We caught a bus to Richmond, which was Sammie's hometown, and went to a club. Among the group was a pair of newlyweds. The bride taught in the same school I did, and the new husband was in the Army and stationed at Fort Lee. While they were home for Christmas, they had gotten married, and now they had just come back. They were all excited, and we were all excited for them. In the midst of this mood of celebration, Sammie announced to everyone: "Well, that's okay. Alma and I are going to get married in June."

I said: "We are? I don't even know you."

That was only the third time I'd ever seen him.

I said again: "I don't know you. The man I marry, I plan to love."

He said: "That's okay. You can learn to love me."

We had a nice time that night, and he continued to say, "We're going to get married in June."

The next day the teachers and I boarded the bus, and we rode back to Blackstone. I think the new husband came back with his wife. All the others were sitting together, and I was sitting by myself. I became quite lonesome, and it just seemed like I had lost something because Sammie and I weren't together. When I got back to where I lived, I thought about Sammie more and more and more. He was still just my friend at that time, but every day,

1 The United Services Organization is a group of U.S. civilians who provide hospitality for service personnel in many parts of the world.

from that moment on, he wrote me a letter. I would write him back at times, but not every day. So the relationship developed through our letters because there wasn't really much opportunity for what would be termed a courtship. I think part of the attraction in his mind and heart was because he had lost his mother so early, when he was fifteen years old. I think he envisioned me as his mother, his friend, and maybe in his mind as his girlfriend—just to have somebody to talk with but never anything really love-wise.

After a few weeks of getting his letters and thinking about him a lot, I decided that maybe I did like him enough to marry him, but I had to love him if I was going to marry him. A little more time went on by, and I decided, "Maybe I do love him." I guess it was all those letters from him that were so persuasive because I surely didn't see him very much before I decided that he was the one for me. Once I did so, I wrote three long letters. I wrote one to my mother and father and told them that I was not going to marry the professor at Virginia State. I told them that I was going to marry Sammie the Sailor, because they knew no name for him but that. Also, I wrote a letter to the professor. I told him: "I don't love you. You are a very nice man, but I don't love you. And the man I marry I must love."

The third letter was to Sammie. I told him that if he thought he was capable of selecting my rings, then go on and do so. I said: "I want white gold. I don't want yellow gold. Everybody gets yellow gold."

One day a little package came to the house where I rented a room from the couple that lived there. I opened the package, and I found a sterling silver compact. I said to myself, "Oh, how pretty." There was a stove in the room to provide heat. I went over to it to get rid of the box and the wrapping paper that the compact came in. I opened the lid with one hand, and I had all of the paper in the other. Just as I was getting ready to throw the wrappings in there, I thought: "That's strange. He didn't have any note or a letter in there, and I didn't get a letter today. So maybe I'm not seeing something in this." So I put the lid back on the stove and sat down and went through all the paper. Inside was a beautiful engagement ring in white gold. I had come that close to throwing it in the fire.

I wrote and thanked Sammie for the ring. Soon I got a reply in which he wrote that the *PC-1264* was decommissioning in early February. He wanted to know if we could marry that month. I told him that was awfully quick. My older sister Nellie would be the one planning the wedding, and she said,

"That doesn't give me any time at all." But we got married on February 12, 1946. We picked that date because he had only so much leave, and he had to go back on duty. I didn't want to marry on the fourteenth because I didn't want to compete with Valentine's Day.

When Sammie came to marry me at my parents' home in Roanoke, it was only the fourth time I had ever seen him. I would like to have worn a silk wedding dress, but there wasn't much of that fabric available because it was being used for parachutes in the armed services. Instead, I married in a pale blue double-knit wool two-piece dress. That marriage must have been a good choice for both of us, because it lasted a long time.

★★★

As Sammie has said, the early years of marriage presented us only intermittent opportunities to be together. That was the period when he was finishing up college at Virginia Union, working on the railway mail cars, and doing Navy recruiting duty in Washington. We relished the times together and worked through the separations. During his time on the railroad, I observed his preparations. The post office provided him with a box to use at home for practice in handling the mail. The box was divided into pigeonholes for the letters going to various places. We had practice envelopes, and I would mix them up among the various slots. He would then rearrange them so they got into the correct pigeonholes. Both of us learned a good bit of geography in the process.

When he got called back to active service in 1949 and sent to recruiting duty in Washington, we had to look for opportunities to spend time together because I was still teaching school in Virginia. It became even harder when he shipped out to the West Coast to go aboard the battleship *Iowa*. I did get to see him after the ship came back from the Korean War and was home-ported in Norfolk. At least we were in the same state. I didn't make all the ship's events, because I lived in Franklin, which was forty miles from Norfolk, but I did go to wives' luncheons on board ship. I wanted to get to know the wives and be a part of them.

I remember the first time I went. When I arrived, the officers' wives were all sitting around in the wardroom, which was huge. Peg Horrall, the wife of Sammie's boss, Gene, got up when she saw me coming. We had a little social time at the beginning. She led me right into the middle of the group and gave me a big hug and a big kiss. That set the tone for the day. We became very,

very close friends. She and Gene became our son David's godparents several years later. Interestingly, even though some of the *Iowa* women may not have wanted to sit with me during the meal, the seating arrangements had nothing to do with likes and dislikes. We sat in sequence according to the ranks and seniority of our husbands, just as our husbands sat when they had their regular meals in the ship.

Probably the person whom Sammie felt the closest to outside of his own family was Clyde Hassell. He and Sammie had met in Norfolk at the end of World War II and played football together. The day I went to that first *Iowa* luncheon, Clyde and Sammie sat in a restaurant nearby, worrying about me the whole time I was gone. They said: "We're going to be right here, and you come right back here when you leave there. You come back here, because we're not going anywhere."

I told them then: "Don't worry about me. I can take anything that's dished out there to me."

When I came back, they said: "How did it go? How did it go? Were you all right?"

I said: "Sure. I'm sure some of the wives didn't want me there, probably, but they didn't show it, and that was nice enough of them." I told them about what Peg did, and they were relieved.

★★★

In Sammie's recollections he told about some of the problems we faced when traveling across country. I recall the time in the early 1960s when he had orders to command the *Falgout*, and we made a trip from California to Virginia to visit our parents before going to Hawaii. He remembered the incidents being on the eastbound trip; my memory is that we were going west. By that time my daddy had retired, and my parents lived in Christiansburg, Virginia. We drove on icy roads all the way from their backyard to Tennessee. When we got to Memphis, we needed to spend the night. We knew all along that we couldn't find anything decent in the white section. We knew that if we went across the tracks, maybe we would find something. It would probably not be desirable, but at least it would be a place to stay. We had the two boys with us at the time, and they were very little. David was really an infant. I guess he was about eighteen or twenty months old. Robbie was about three and a half. When we found this motel, the snow was almost knee deep on the ground. It was cold as could be. The office was separate from the rooms.

Sammie went in and got the key. Then we went up a set of steps to get to our room on the second deck.

When we got there, it was so cold in the room. Sammie tried to turn on the wall heater, but the handle was missing. He walked back through the snow, over to the office, and asked for the key or lever or whatever would turn it on. He came back with a pair of pliers. I'm not sure whether he ever got it on, even with the pliers. It was so cold that we tucked the children in between us and all four of us hugged together till morning came. The next morning we left and continued on to San Diego. We've thought about it since then, particularly right after Martin Luther King was assassinated. I think it was the same motel that we had stayed in that cold, cold night.

What makes me think we were on our way to the West Coast during these incidents has to do with my fair skin. I would tan when we had duty in San Diego, but when I would be leaving the East, I would be lighter in complexion—and that is a factor in the story. David and Robbie were standing up in the back seat of the car, and they begged us constantly for ice cream cones. Finally, with them standing up and looking out, they saw the Tastee-Freez ice cream trademark. They said: "There's ice cream. There's ice cream. Stop, Daddy, stop."

We looked at each other, and we said, "Well, let's try it." So Sammie pulled in, got out, and went to the window. After so long, he came back to the car and got in—with no ice cream.

I said: "What happened? They wouldn't serve you?"

He said: "No, the man at the window wouldn't serve me there. He told me that if I came to the back door, he would serve me. And I told him, 'Forget it.' Let's go."

I said, "No, pull up until you are a little out of his sight."

He said: "What are you going to do? Are you going to try?"

I said, "Yes, I'm going to try and see what happens." I got out, and I went to the window and ordered the ice cream. The man evidently assumed that I was white, which was what I wanted him to assume. He waited on me. I paid him and came back to the car. The children had their ice cream. They, of course, never knew what had happened. My husband said a few unkind words about the ice cream man, and we went on.

We didn't really have to teach our children about race. I think they just kind of grew into it. They essentially learned by experiencing life. I don't ever remember their asking questions on the subject except one time. If they had asked we would have told them that people are of different races, but as human beings we are still the same. Under our skin we are all the same.

I do remember one exception when both Robbie and David were little. This was when we were at the Naval War College in Newport in 1963–64. They were playing outside with all the neighbor children. Robbie came in one day when I was just getting over a migraine headache but was still in bed. He came running into my bedroom, and he was just tall enough to put his arms on the bed. He said, "Mama, what is a Hershey kiss?"

I said: "That's a very, very good, smooth piece of chocolate candy, Robbie. And it's wrapped in silver paper with a little tassel hanging out of it. It's really, really good and very pretty." When he asked, I was wondering how he would know about a Hershey kiss. I knew he had been playing with the children, and they were all white except him and David. I was kind of putting two and two together, so I asked him, "Why?"

He mentioned the boy or girl who had called him that. This child said, "My mom says that Robbie looks like a Hershey kiss." He didn't know what it was, of course, so he ran in to ask me. When I told him, he was so excited and happy, and then he ran back out and started playing again.

While Sammie was at the War College, the students were put in different groups. At the end of the year, each group had a party somewhere to celebrate, to let down, and whatever else. My husband's group decided to rent one of the little homes that go back hundreds of years in Newport. We all knew each other by then and had become very close in that year. (In fact, that's where I started bowling, which I still do to this day.) At the party I was sitting on the arm of a chair and talking to a fellow who was sitting in the chair. A lady came up to me; she was the wife of one of the other officers in the course. I had known her already as part of the group, but I wasn't as close to her as I was to some of the others. It was a very good party, and the whiskey was flying. She came over with a glass in her hand and feeling very good after the drinks she had evidently had previously. In a very Southern accent she said: "Alma, how did Sam get into the Navy? Did the NAACP sponsor him in?"

I said, "No, I rather think that he went in on his own merits."

She said, "Oh." The fellow sitting in the chair turned red. He was not her husband, but he was embarrassed by what she had said. I wasn't embarrassed because I grew up in Christiansburg, a small town that included white people in its population. It was the western part of Virginia. When I was little, the white girls and I used to play and cook while we were wearing my sister's high-heeled shoes. The town was segregated, so I couldn't go to the drugstore and sit at the counter to drink a Coke, ice cream soda, or anything else. I couldn't go to the library, and other black children couldn't either. But at home and in our immediate neighborhood we talked to each other. In fact, we had set up a little restaurant in a log cabin, and we ran it for three years, but we ate up the profits.

My point is that from childhood on, and in all our experiences in the Navy, I wasn't intimidated by white people. So what this lady said at the party didn't bother me. I remembered it, but it didn't bother me. Interestingly, even though the man in the chair was embarrassed, this Navy wife was not. I think at that point she was too high to feel embarrassment.

★ ★ ★

In the summer of 1968, Sammie had left command of the *Taussig*, and he had orders for duty in Washington. He flew back from overseas and came to San Diego. When he got home, I saw that he seemed uninterested in things. He just wasn't quite into what he usually did and should have been doing when we were moving. I couldn't figure out what was wrong with him; I just thought he was tired.

In making the trip across country, we planned to drive up the West Coast to Canada, cross it from west to east, and then come back into the United States at Niagara Falls. We had visited the falls when he was stationed at Com Three in New York, and now we wanted the children to see them. We left San Diego and headed north, but as we drove farther and farther on our trip, we changed our plans. It was raining so much that we had to change the blades on the windshield wipers. Perhaps because of the dismal weather, Sammie seemed even more depressed than before. So we decided to return to the States through Montana. Instead of Niagara Falls, we would show the children Yellowstone National Park in Wyoming. It was the first time our young daughter, Tracey, had seen snow. The boys got out, and they made snowballs and threw them at her. I taught her how to make them and throw them back. While all this was going on, Sammie sat in the car. It just didn't interest him. And that was not like him; in a normal situation, he would have been out there making snowballs himself.

His condition got worse and worse as we came along. When we got to Maryland, we stayed with Sammie's brother Ed and his wife, Joanie, till we could find a house. Finally, we found housing, but Sammie was worried while we were looking, and his mental outlook kept deteriorating. The stress and the medication took a toll on him. I think the major way I was able to contribute to the eventual recovery process was by forcing him to see a doctor and making him see that he was not himself—that he did need help. He went into the naval hospital at Bethesda, Maryland, for two months. Part of the treatment was changing his blood pressure medicine. While he was going through his hospitalization, I took care of the children and did all the major thinking for the family. This was a case of my doing basically the same things I did over the years when his ships were on overseas deployments. When he came out of the hospital, he was much better, which was obviously a relief after what he had been through.

★★★

Sammie's tours of duty on board ships were challenging for us as a family because of the long separations during deployments. Even though I got used to the lifestyle and enjoyed the camaraderie with other Navy people, there were wives who did not enjoy it that much and made it hard for their husbands. Some of the husbands decided to leave the Navy even though they didn't want to. But they had heard their wives' complaints and wanted to save their marriages. Yes, the deployments were long, sometimes six or seven months. Sammie talked about the time the *Jouett* was extended while it was overseas in order to go to Australia and New Zealand. We got the news about two months before the original time that the ship was due home.

That change in plans upset some of the wives, particularly the enlisted wives, and they let it be known to me. So I notified Sammie that they were dissatisfied, and he took care of it by sending those women's husbands home early. I can understand why those women were upset, because two months before the ship is due to return—in my mind and in the minds of a lot of wives that I know of—is the most critical time for the dependents at home. In the case of a six-month deployment, the crew would have been gone for four months by then, and the men's families were expecting them back in two months. So you're getting excited. You're trying to get everything together and everything done that was supposed to be done. You're trying to make yourself look nice, the children look good, and to be ready for the ship to come. It's very exciting, and it's hard to sleep. So if another month is tacked on to the deployment, then that's upsetting to you, because you're expecting them to come back. In some cases, the wives really were suffering to begin with, and the extra time just made the situation worse.

So a few of the husbands came home before the cruise was over, and the rest of the crew went on down to Australia. They got a good experience, and, of course, we would have liked to join them down there. That is one reason that Sammie took us to Australia and New Zealand to celebrate our fiftieth anniversary. He knew how much we had wanted to join them in the *Jouett* era but couldn't. So our whole family took a thirteen-day cruise down there in 1996.

In late April 1971, when the ship was almost home from the deployment, I got the news that Sammie was selected for rear admiral. That was my bowling day. In the morning I did some volunteer work at the thrift shop on the amphibious base at Coronado, across the harbor from San Diego. I had to close up the shop at noon, turn in the money, and our group went to bowl at one o'clock. I was sitting there in the bowling alley, with my head down, tying on my shoes. One of the women in the group called me from about two lanes down and said, "Hey, Alma, congratulations."

I said, "For what?"

She answered, "For your husband making admiral, you nut!"

"Oh, he made it?"

"Yes. You didn't know it?"

"No, I've been busy at the thrift shop all morning, and I haven't had the radio on."

So that's how I learned the good news. I was really pleased with it. I felt he deserved it after all he had accomplished over the years. I was very happy for him, but I couldn't congratulate him that day because it would be a few more days before the *Jouett* got back to San Diego.

In the meantime, I had a trying time, because the children and I had to take all the brunt of the blows from the news media people. The reporters even came one morning to watch me get the children off to school. David was then in elementary school, and he was getting an award. I just knew that I should be there at the school, which was at the end of my street. Also, I was scheduled to go to a meeting of commanding officers' wives.

A person with a television station in Los Angeles had called the day before to try to set up an interview, but I said that I would have no time because these other things were scheduled. The producer was persistent, despite my objections, and talked me into doing an interview following the wives' meeting, because the station wanted the interview for the five o'clock news the following afternoon. Like a nut, I agreed to do what the TV people wanted. After it was over, the station had a plane nearby to fly the tape to Los Angeles because this was still in the days before satellite transmissions became commonplace. After that I got in the car with Luddy Newcomb, the executive officer's wife, to go to David's school in Chula Vista. We went so fast that it was almost as if we were flying. When we pulled up to my house, David was just then walking home from school. I had missed the whole awards ceremony.

When five o'clock came, I watched the news; some other story got almost all of the coverage. When the interview that they did with me came on television, they flashed through it quickly and showed only a very small portion of it. It was a part that had me saying, "My husband always said that sailors belong on ships, and ships belong at sea." Just that quickly, it was over with. Because I had missed my son's award, I was so upset that I didn't know what to do.

Of course, there were positive emotions to go along with all that. The *Jouett* arrived in San Diego on May 1. I was so happy Sammie had made admiral, and I certainly congratulated him heartily, but I was also happy that he could now take care of his own business with the newspeople.

★★★

After making rear admiral, Sammie had the Navy communications job in Washington and commanded the cruiser-destroyer group in the Atlantic. His third tour of duty as a two-star admiral was in the mid-1970s, when he was commandant of the Eleventh Naval District. We lived in the commandant's quarters on Ballast Point, which is an area just north of Point Loma in San Diego Bay. One day I received in the mail an envelope that was addressed to me. I opened it, like all the other envelopes. Inside were two or three sheets of toilet tissue, and on them was human feces. There was nothing else in the envelope. I was quite shocked. When Sammie came home from work that day, I said, "I have something to show you which is quite interesting."

I showed it to him, and he said, "Well, I'll be damned." He decided to take it to the FBI, which he did. We never got any word back from the FBI on what happened about it, so we had no idea who sent it or why. All we could do was form our own conclusions about the type of person who would send such a thing to somebody. I can speculate that the event that triggered this vile piece of mail might have been the announcement of my husband's promotion to vice admiral and the upcoming transfer to Hawaii to command the Third Fleet. Another possibility was that it grew out of a newspaper article in which I was quoted. I said that some welfare recipients were misusing the payments. I said that welfare was certainly important and needed in some cases, but I also suggested that the authorities needed to check a little more closely to see whether that need was genuine. The one thing I do know is that the person who sent me that envelope was sick—very sick.

★★★

The death of our older son Robbie in 1978 came as a shock. That was truly a shock. At the time I was in Tripler Army Hospital in Hawaii for bunionectomies on both of my feet. The day after the operation the people in the hospital taught me how to walk properly on crutches. The doctor told me that I could go home, but some Japanese friends of Sammie had invited him to come over and do some fishing on Hawaii's big island on Sunday, June 4, which was his birthday. He just looked forward to that so much because it was deep-sea fishing. I decided to stay in the hospital until after he came back on Sunday night. Monday he would pick me up and take me home. I could use the additional time in the hospital to continue my recuperation.

I was asleep in my room when the lights came on around two o'clock Saturday morning. There stood Sammie. I said, "What are you doing here?"

He just stood there in the middle of the floor with his head and both hands hanging down. He said, "Robbie's dead."

I said, "What do you mean, Robbie's dead?"

He said, "He had an automobile accident, and he's dead." Then he kind of controlled himself a little, and he told me what had happened. He said Robbie had put his car in the shop earlier, and he got it out. He was test-driving it, checking it out to see how it was running. Sammie and all three children had been watching television at home that evening. When he thought it was time, Sammie got Tracey off to bed. David told me later that Robbie went to his room, then came back by and went on out the door.

David, who had graduated from high school by then, also told me he had started to say, "Wait up, Rob, I'll go with you," but then he remembered that he had to go to work early the next day. So he didn't say anything to Robbie.

Robbie went on alone, and someone told me that he or she thought that Robbie had been at the ferry that connected Ford Island with the main part of the naval base at Pearl Harbor. I found out that there was a young Navy woman who was working on the ferry. Robbie had just turned twenty in March of that year, and I think he went up there to see the girl. Apparently, though, she wasn't on the ferry that night, so then I guess he decided to test his car.

As Sammie said later, "If I were a twenty-year-old boy and I lived on a little island like this one, I would do the same thing. I would get in the car, and I would start off slowly, and I would drive a little faster the next time I go around the island. And then I'd drive a little faster and check the car." But when Robbie came around one curve, he missed it somehow and went off into the bay. The car landed upside down in the water. There was a huge rock, about the size of a refrigerator, lying about where we thought the car left the road. Robbie liked to lock himself in; I know that because he was always locking me in for safety. So I have a notion that he was locked in and just couldn't get out. Or perhaps the accident knocked him unconscious in the beginning, and he didn't get out. It was something really hard to have to take.

On that Saturday, several hours after the awful time when I got the news, the doctor came by to see how I was doing. Tripler Hospital has a screened-in veranda on the second floor, and I was out there sitting on a lounge chair. The doctor found me, and he said, "How are you today?"

I said: "Well, foot-wise I think I'm all right. Mentally, I'm a wreck."

He sat down and said, "What's wrong?" I told him what had happened. He said: "Oh, my God. What do you want me to do? I'll do anything you want me to do."

I said: "Well, if I'm able to, I want you to let me go home. There's not very much I can do. I know I have to stay in bed or lie on the couch or whatever, but Sammie says the phone is ringing off the hook. I know that I can take some of the calls. That will help. The steward is doing all he can do, but he can't do it all. Sammie has to work, and the children have to go to school. I want to go home."

He said: "You're all right. You can go. We've taught you how to walk on crutches, and when you feel like you need to get on that bed, you go straight to it or the couch or something."

So that's what I did when they let me go home, and I lay around as I continued to recover from the operation. Gradually my feet got better, but the process of grieving for Robbie and getting past his death took far longer. The loss of a child is the worst possible thing for a parent. You feel so helpless while it's going on. There's not a single thing you can do for your son at that point except arrange his funeral. Robbie died early on a Saturday morning, about one o'clock, and on the weekend you can't get hold of a soul in the offices—at least in the military. You can't start working on the funeral until Monday, and that's what Sammie had to do when Monday came.

As Sammie said, Robbie was buried in the military cemetery in San Diego. From the day I married him, I learned that Sammie loved San Diego so much. Even though I had never been there before we got married, I think I said, "Yes, I do, and yes I will retire in San Diego"—all at the same time. So all of those years we planned to retire in San Diego, and we loved it each time we went back there for duty. We made friends there, and I still stay in touch with some of them today. We had a congregation there that we had worked with. I was on the building fund; they put me on it every time we went back. They built a new church because a freeway ran through where the old one was. Now we have a pew in the new church. It has Robbie's name on the end, because the building committee was taking donations to pay for the pews. Whenever Sammie and I went back to San Diego after that, no matter for how long, we would plan to stay for Sunday and go to a service at that church.

★★★

Surprisingly, we did not wind up retiring in San Diego. Sammie's final Navy job was as director of the Defense Communications Agency. We had quarters on the grounds of the Naval Observatory, just off Massachusetts Avenue in Washington, D.C. One day he said to me that we should call a real estate agent to find a place for us to live in northern Virginia. He had come to that conclusion because most of our relatives were around Virginia or at least on the East Coast. Being in California would make it far more difficult for us to visit them and vice versa. So we found our retirement home in the community of Haymarket, which is in Prince William County, Virginia.

Sammie had originally joined the Navy in 1942, and in 1980 his active duty came to an end. I loved the Navy as much as he did. In fact, I think when he retired I missed it more than he did. If he missed it, he kept it more inside himself. We still went to various events, but it wasn't like being involved every day as we had been.

I liked the closeness of the Navy. But there was one thing we always did to keep in touch with the civilian world. We always found a church out in the city. The only time we didn't was when we lived on Ford Island in Hawaii. The Navy chapel was right there. Every other time, we always made sure we joined or became associate members of a local church.

I really liked living on the naval bases because I think you understand military life better when you do. If you're out in the city, you don't get all that is going on. I liked that part of it. I didn't like the moving, but I liked going to different places. The moving wasn't all that bad, once I think about it now. When we would be getting ready for a transfer, the children would say: "I don't want to leave. Why do we have to leave?" But when they moved somewhere else and got ready to leave there, they said the same thing. So they just went along with us. I liked the association with the Navy wives. I like people and so did Sammie. After our arrival in a new place, even when our heads were down in boxes and we hadn't found the curtains or the sheets yet, he used to say, "When are we going to have the first party?"

I would say, "Can't you just let me find the curtains?"

Another thing I liked about living on bases was that the people would stick together. While the ship is deployed, it's much easier to keep the wives together, especially when your husband is the skipper of the ship. If you're out in the city and have the initiative, you can do it, but it's a little harder.

★★★

Sammie had a tendency to use sailor language when he was away from the ship. I tried through our whole married life to change that, because he truly could curse like a sailor. They were not really, really bad words, but every now and then they would come out. He used the word "hell" and this and that a good bit—more than I ever wanted him to. So I worked on him all through the years. Finally, something happened after he had retired from the Navy. He was a trustee of the church in Haymarket, and he went to a trustee meeting one night. He came home with his head hanging down low and looking extremely sad. When I asked him what was wrong, he said, "I cursed at the minister."

I said: "Oh, no. I knew it was going to happen one day. Something was going to happen, and you were going to curse at the wrong time. What did you say?"

He said: "Something that he was talking about, and I didn't think it should go that way. I said, 'God damn it, reverend, so and so and so.'"

I said, "No, you didn't say that."

From that day on, I think he truly decided that he was going to watch what he was saying. Little by little by little he got it all straight, and his mouth was much cleaner as the years passed.

★★★

On our fifty-fourth wedding anniversary, February 12, 2000, Sammie and I were honored at a dinner held at the officers' club at the North Island Naval Air Station in Coronado, near San Diego. It was a very wonderful affair. Everybody and his brother who lived close enough to come was there for it. Also, some people came from considerable distances because they were there for a conference of the National Naval Officers Association, which sponsored the event. They went all out to make it a great celebration. It was beautiful. They were honoring my husband and me for our long involvement with the Navy. They gave us so many gifts. The cake was huge; it seems to me it was four feet by six feet. It covered an entire table. It was three layers thick, maybe four or five inches high. The decorations celebrated our anniversary and many other highlights. The cake fed all 350 people who attended the dinner, and there was some left over afterward. Sammie and I sat on tall stools while we shook hands with the long line of well-wishers; our arthritis was not going to let us stand up the whole time. It was a real pleasure as so many people came by because they wanted to say thank you. It was just lovely.

Sammie had a number of health problems during those final years of life. His kidneys were giving out. He had two operations, one in each kidney, at different times. The doctors knew that he had three cysts in each kidney, which had been the case for a number of years prior to that. So they decided they should operate on the kidneys. They were just about certain that one kidney had cancer in it and suspected the other might also. They decided to operate on the better kidney first, leaving him with ninety percent function in that kidney. That let them know what they could do when they went into the one they thought was worse. They removed that kidney completely. That happened in about 1990–91.

As the years passed, the remaining kidney was eventually working at only thirty-five percent of normal capacity. That was when they decided he should go on dialysis. He did that for a number of years—three times a week for four and a half hours each session. That was time on the machine itself, and the travel to and from took more time. He told me, "I wish I didn't have to go," or something like that. He wouldn't come right out and say that he hated it, though I know he disliked it. But, as he said, "I don't like the alternative." He never missed a time. He had dialysis in Florida, in the Outer Banks of North Carolina, in Williamsburg (where we had a time-share), and in California. We just had to plan for it when we went anywhere.

While he was going through his health problems, he lost a fair amount of weight. I remember when he was breathing a little hard one day when I picked him up from dialysis. He had also had his third replacement of the left knee. The next day, the physical therapist was at our house to help him with his recovery. I was gone for a while during the session, and the therapist was waiting for me when I got back. I had told her when she first came that he was breathing a little hard. She said: "I notice he has been breathing a little hard today too. I think you ought to take him on in." So I took him to the emergency room at the hospital, and they decided to keep him for a few days.

They called me the next day and told me that fluid had built up around his heart. The day after that they called and said: "Mrs. Gravely, I think you can come and get him. He's all right now." I went there, and I didn't recognize him. They had taken twenty-eight pounds of fluid out of him, and he never regained the weight. The dialysis people were thrilled to death. But that's how he got thin, and I think the dialysis kept the weight off.

In the autumn of 2004 he fell, and I took him to the hospital. They changed his medicine and decided to keep him in the hospital for a while to monitor him. The next day, when they took him to dialysis, he had a stroke. That happened somewhere from the time he left the bed till the time he got back to it. In addition to the stroke, he got two types of bacteria. They put him on a regular antibiotic while they were growing the specialized antibiotic that would kill that particular bacteria. Two days after they started him on the new one, the doctor met me when I got to the hospital in Bethesda and told me that the new culture was working. But then Sammie got another infection, and his body was too weak to fight off that one. So the next time I went to the hospital Sammie was in the intensive care unit. When he had gone for dialysis, the nurses found that his blood pressure was so low they called the doctor and didn't give him the dialysis. It just got lower and lower.

On the day I went to see Sammie in the ICU, David was along with me. He and his wife, Beverly, went to see Sammie often, including breaks at lunch hour. Tracey usually didn't go to the hospital, but she called and talked with him several times. Once I was there when she called, and I held the phone for him. He couldn't talk, because the stroke mostly prevented that, but he could hear and understand. I couldn't get her to go because I guess she just didn't want to see him in that condition. But she finally came when I told her he was in the ICU. David and Beverly were also there on Thursday night, October 21. The people treating him gave us a choice. They said he was living because they were giving him the medicine that would keep his pressure up. I asked the nurse, "Is that the only reason he's living?"

She said, "Yes." And then she said, "What do you want to do?"

I said: "Well, neither one of us want to be kept alive on a machine. I don't know. Let us go out into the waiting room and talk about it and see how we all feel."

Nobody else was in the waiting room at that time. It was late. When we had been there the day before, Wednesday, I asked Sammie to squeeze my hand. His eyes were closed, and I didn't know how much of a coma he was in, or whether he was in a coma. He slightly—very, very lightly—moved my hand. But on Thursday I asked again, and he didn't do it. There was no response, so I knew he was sinking even further, but he was breathing; he was alive.

As we gathered in the waiting room, I put the question to each member of the family. I asked Tracey first, and she wanted to take him off that medicine. She said: "I don't think he should be lying there suffering. Even if he's not suffering, I don't think I would want him to go on this way. I think the doctors should stop giving him the medicine."

I next asked Beverly what she thought. She said: "Well, I told you many times how my grandmother was sick to the point where the minister had come and administered the last rites to her. Everybody was preparing a funeral, but my grandmother got better and lived ten years after that, doing fine. So my answer is not to take him off."

Then I said, "David, what do you feel?"

He said: "Mom, I don't know. I have mixed emotions."

I said: "David, I do, too, so I don't know."

We just sat there, and we talked a little bit. I said: "Okay, I'm going back in, and I'm going to talk to this nurse."

They said, "What are you going to tell her?"

I said: "I'm going to tell her to leave him as he is tonight and continue to do what she's been doing all along. Tomorrow we will see how he is, and if he's still living when I come I'll make my decision tomorrow. I'm going home. There's nothing I can do tonight here. I know what is coming when he dies, and I need to go home and get my rest and get strength enough to take what will come afterward."

This was after we had gone to the hospital every day for three and a half weeks. And it's a long trip from Haymarket, Virginia, to Bethesda, Maryland—forty-four miles each way. So we were worn out. Tracey said she wanted to stay in Bethesda that night, and Beverly persuaded David to stay with his sister so she wouldn't be alone.

Early on Friday, October 22, the doctor called me from the hospital to tell me that Sammie had died at seven o'clock that morning. David and Tracey were there when he died, and Tracey called me right after the doctor did. I talked to my children and told them: "You'll know what to do. You haven't had this experience, but you know what to do. I will come to you. What you don't know to do, call me, and I will tell you. I will be there as soon as I can."

My husband's passing when he did made the decision for us. I was truly sorry to lose him but also relieved that I didn't have to make the decision, because it would have been a hard thing for me to do. I have always suffered for those people who had to decide whether or not to turn off the machines and end a life. This was a case of medicines, rather than a machine, but the dilemma was still the same.

★★★

In 2006 the Navy formally approved the idea of naming an upcoming *Arleigh Burke*–class guided missile destroyer the USS *Gravely*. My reaction was to say: "Since the Navy thought enough of my husband to build a ship for him, I am so glad you chose a destroyer. Because if you had not, be it larger or smaller, my husband would have turned over in the grave." And he would have, because he loved destroyers. That was because they were fast, and they did many jobs, not just one.

On September 12 of that year, less than two years after Sammie's passing, the chief of naval personnel, Vice Admiral John Harvey, made a speech at a conference of the National Historically Black Colleges and Universities. It was there that he announced the news. Soon afterward I received a letter from the Navy Department that invited me to be the ship's sponsor. I gladly accepted the invitation. From that time on I have been involved with the ship and its crew. The keel was laid in November 2007 in Pascagoula, Mississippi.

The first skipper of the *Gravely* is Commander Douglas Kunzman, who is really the greatest. I cannot imagine the Navy choosing anyone else to command the ship. He's just perfect, and I'm sure he's going to do a tremendous job. He and I have become so close, and he has kept me informed with every little thing that changes and everything that I had to do to be ready by the time the christening came. I think hardly anybody knows how much has to be done by the sponsor except the women who have been sponsors of other Navy ships.

After the hull and the superstructure were built, there was a ceremony called a mast stepping, and it is comparable to putting artifacts in the cornerstone of a building. A group of coins is put either under or beside the mast on a ship. Doug and I had to come up with some important dates so the shipyard could buy coins that were made in those years. We also had to write out a list that explained why those dates were important. I think I wrote down eighteen significant dates in Sammie's life. I also had to develop guest lists for the christening ceremony on May 16, 2009, and for the sponsor's dinner, which was held the night before. It took me several months to put the lists together. I wound up getting dozens of calls from people who wanted to be invited.

On the day before the christening, I went through a rehearsal. Doug Kunzman walked me to the bow of the ship, where I would be for the event itself. As I stood there with him, tears came in my eyes. I knew that it was something great, and I was very happy for Sammie, but I never thought it would affect me that way. I remembered seeing the whales that were on display at the Sea World theme park in San Diego and would come right up to the tourists. I just felt that here was a big ship that had come alongside the pier and was saying to me, "Here I am, and I'm going to do everything I can for you and the admiral." I told Doug that, and he rubbed my back and helped me in that moment. I just never thought that I would feel that way. That was the greatest surprise to me out of the whole experience.

Mike Petters, the president of Northrop Grumman Shipbuilding, was on the platform when I took my practice swing. It was amusing later to see a picture of the rehearsal in which he appeared to be backing away so he wouldn't get splashed with wine. He seemed a bit surprised that I swung with such vigor. I don't think he thought I was going to be able to break the bottle—at least on my first attempt—but I've got a lot of strength in my bowling arm. I really popped it. That picture is so cute, because everything he was feeling showed in his expression as I broke the bottle. It was a very good rehearsal.

On the day of the christening itself, several Navy officials made remarks. The principal speech was by Admiral Paul Reason, the Navy's first black four-star admiral. After that Mike Petters introduced me. I made a brief speech. When the shipyard was planning the program earlier, someone asked me if I wanted to speak. My first reaction was not to because there was so much else going on. Then I thought about all my friends, relatives, and acquaintances who were going to be there. I knew I wouldn't be able to talk to all of them amid the hectic schedule that would be involved. So I called my contact in Washington, Alicia Beck. I said: "You asked me if I wanted to say anything in the program. I don't want to say much, but I do want to say something." That was a way of reaching all those people who came great distances to be there.

After I spoke, it was time for the actual christening. I had another good swing and broke the second bottle, which I now have at home as a wonderful souvenir of that experience. I was feeling tense before I whacked the bottle against the ship because so many people had their eyes on what I was doing. Afterward I felt a real sense of relief that it all went as it was supposed to. I didn't know that I was going to be nervous, and I didn't really feel nervous. But I must have been a little bit wary as to whether or not I would break the bottle on my first swing, because I so much wanted to do it. But I knew from two pages of instructions that I got from the president of the Society of Sponsors what can happen at christenings and what has happened at christenings. I didn't want any of those problems to happen to me, so I was definitely going to break that bottle the first time, and I did—both days.

Because of all the things leading up to the christening, I was already exhausted before I set out for the trip to the shipyard in Mississippi. And I certainly didn't get much rest during the two days I was there. By the time I got home again afterward, I had added two more exhausting days to it, because I worked the whole time I was down there. I wound up being sick in bed for a while after that because I think my immune system was about gone.

That brings me to another honor for Sammie. The principal of the elementary school named for him is Michele Salzano. She is just as sweet as she can be. She lost her mother shortly before we met, and she now thinks of me as her mother. She was at the christening ceremony, and when she heard the following week that I was sick in bed, she brought me some chicken soup.

A few years earlier, a friend of mine called to ask how I would feel if she submitted Admiral Gravely's name for a school being built in Prince William County, Virginia. I gave my friend the go-ahead to submit his name at a school board meeting, but I didn't want to insert myself into the process. I said I would be happy to supply information but wouldn't help get it done. There were differing views and articles on the subject in local newspapers. Eventually, the idea was approved to name a school for him.

One morning the phone rang, and it was the county supervisor calling. He said two schools were to be named that night at a board meeting, an elementary school and a middle school. He and his people wanted to know which one I wanted to carry my husband's name. The elementary school was to be in Dominion Valley, which is only fifteen minutes from me, and it's in my community. The middle school was close to the community but not directly in it. So I opted for the grade school, and that's what the board chose that night.

Having that connection has been a real pleasure for me. I watched the building grow from the time they had the groundbreaking. I used to drive by the school during construction to keep track of the progress leading up to its opening in 2008. While this was going on, I got a call from Michele, who introduced herself. She wanted to meet me, so I suggested that she come to my home because I felt she could learn a little bit about my husband. Michele and I just enjoyed each other so much, and we hit it off from that moment. On June 4, 2009, Sammie's birthday, the new building was officially dedicated as the Samuel L. Gravely Jr. Elementary School. Our son David presented the school with an oil portrait of his father. One of the people who joined us for the ceremony was Doug Kunzman.

I go to the school quite often, and it is a spectacular new building. Just inside the front door is the motto that expresses Sammie's philosophy: "Success = Education + Motivation + Perseverance." There's also a picture of the school's mascot, Seadog. It's a cartoon figure of a cute little animal with a wagging tail, and on its head is a sailor's white hat. I'm not there every time that front door opens, and I told them from the beginning that I wasn't going to be running in all the time. But the teachers call me when they would like me to come down and do something.

Among other things, the fifth grade teacher asked me to come and judge a science fair. The second grade teacher called and asked me to come answer some questions she couldn't answer about my husband. She said she could answer the ones in which the information was available on the Internet and other sources, but they wanted to know personal things. They were making a timeline for the dedication of the school. They asked me everything. One little boy had a long list written out. They wanted to know what my husband's hobbies were and what kind of father he was, what he did when he was at home and not on board ship. The children are just as sweet as they can be. Whenever I stick my head in the door, they wave and say: "There's Mrs. Gravely. Hi, Mrs. Gravely."

One time a group of prospective crew members of the *Gravely* came up from Norfolk, where they were undergoing training prior to the ship's commissioning. On a holiday, they took time off from their training to go to the school and help with field day, which included spending time with the students. In charge of the group was the *Gravely*'s executive officer, Lieutenant Commander Mike Witherspoon. He's like my husband in that he was an enlisted man before he got his officer's commission. Also part of the group that visited the school was the ship's senior enlisted sailor, Command Master Chief Mattie Wells.

The school had expected forty crewmen and women to come and wound up with eighty-five instead. They played games with the students and talked to them about the ship. Afterward, I invited the Navy people to come to my house and get a sense of what the admiral was like. They drove over in seven Navy vans. They came and looked all around the house, including down in the basement, which has a lot of photos and other tributes to my husband.

They all lined up afterward in front of the building in which Sammie kept his pigeons. They posed for a group picture wearing their T-shirts with the ship's crest on them. I was in the middle of all of them when the picture was taken.

David and Tracey also do things on behalf of the school named for their father, although that is sometimes tough because school meets during the day, and that's when they are working. Tracey calls the principal every now and then about something. She even contributed some school supplies for the children. A while back, I ran into David's boss, and I apologized to him for all the time that David had taken off to go to events connected with the elementary school and the ship. His boss said to me: "Don't worry about it. I'm just happy that all these things are happening." And, fortunately, I knew him already because he had come to a thank-you barbecue that I held for all the people who went over and above for Sammie's funerals. He had been very helpful at the time.

David is in the computer field, and he works for contractors. I can't explain it any better than that, because he tries to explain it to me and it goes in one ear and comes out of the other. Tracey has had a variety of jobs over the years and works very hard at them. She lives in Fredericksburg, Virginia, and we see each other from time to time—but not as often as I would like.

★★★

I feel very fortunate that my husband and I could live together as long as we did because so many couples don't make it that far. We were both eighty-two years old when he died, and we had been married since we were in our early twenties. As I look back, I have so many happy memories that came about after I read those letters that persuaded me to marry Sammie the Sailor. He worked hard at his many jobs, and I have heard of so many examples of cases in which he was able to inspire young people, both in the Navy and in civilian life. His life is a demonstration of what happens when someone can take advantage of opportunities and in so doing create opportunities for others. It is truly fitting that both a warship and a school are named for him, because they embody the values that he cherished throughout his life. I was so happy to take an active part in his long journey.

Alma B. Gravely
Spring 2010

Index

A-3 Skywarrior, 145–46
Acapulco, Mexico, 158–61
Adamson, Robert E., Jr., 208
Adler, Robert, 166
adoption of children, 83–86, 105, 155, 238
AFCEA, 231–32
Air Force, U.S., 48, 131–35, 198, 221, 232
Alameda, California, 80–81
Albuquerque, New Mexico, 105
Alcohol: christening of the *Gravely*, 259; drinking on board ship, 84–85, 189–90; on liberty in World War II, 19, 27–28; on liberty in the 1950s, 49; on liberty in the 1960s, 113
Algiers, Norman A., Jr., 57
Allen, Charles Vern, 82–83, 85, 88
Aluli, Noa Emmett, 220
American Battleship Association, 223
Amphibious Group Three, 79–80
Andrews Air Force Base, 134
Antarctica, 223
antisubmarine warfare, 97–98, 144, 160, 162, 164
Arlington, Virginia, 129–30, 171, 196–97
Armed Forces Communications and Electronics Association (AFCEA), 231–32
Army, U.S., 1, 5, 7, 28, 39, 121, 131–34, 137, 171, 178, 225, 227, 230, 232, 240
Asbury Park, New Jersey, 15–16
atomic-biological-chemical (ABC) warfare defense, 67, 71
Australia, 151–54, 187–88, 222–23, 247–48
Automated Business Systems and Services, 231

Bailey, Fred, 234
Baldwin, Robert B., 211
Battleship Division Two, 52–54
Baugh, Dalton, 224
Bayonne, New Jersey, 68, 70
Beck, Alicia, 259
Bethesda, Maryland, Naval Hospital, 130, 132, 170–71, 247, 255–57
birds, 60–61, 165–67, 177, 229–30, 262
Blackstone, Virginia, 32, 239–40
Boyd, USS (DD-544), 141–142, 151–56
Brisbane, Australia, 153–54
Briscoe, Robert, 46
Brooklyn, New York, 66–67, 69–70
Brown, Bobby, 13
Brown, Galen C., 93–99
Brown, Nicholas, 179, 181

Brown, Wesley A., 63
Bureau of Naval Personnel: augmentation, 51; changed homeport of *Theodore E. Chandler*, 101; officer assignments, 45, 55, 71–72, 75, 87–88, 90–92, 99, 102–3, 107, 120, 125, 135, 169–70, 173–74, 214; rules on officer accommodations, 30

Cacapon, USS (AO-52), 146
Camp Lejeune, 208
Camp Robert Smalls, 8, 20–21
Canada, 170, 221, 223, 246
Chafee, John, 172, 202
Charleston, South Carolina, 203, 205–07
Chevalier, USS (DD-805), 164
Chicago Defender, 40
China, 178–79
Chinfo (Navy Chief of Information), 141
Christiansburg, Virginia, 70, 75, 243, 246
Christmas Island, 110–11
Clarey, Bernard A., 189
Clark, Joseph J., 46–48
Clements, William P., Jr., 217, 221
CNO's Advisory Committee on Telecommunications, 197–98
Cockell, William A., 61
Columbia University, V-12 program, 16–20, 22–23, 33
commercial ships, 178–79, 193–94
communication school, 41–44
communications: Defense Communications Agency, 131–38, 170, 226–28; Naval Telecommunications Command, 196–99; satellite communications program, 169–73; in USS *Falgout*, 114; in USS *Iowa*, 44–51; in USS *Jouett*, 189; in USS *Seminole*, 78, 83; in USS *Taussig*, 153; in USS *Toledo*, 57–61
Com Eleven. *See* Eleventh Naval District
Com Three. *See* Third Naval District
Constellation, USS (CVA-64), 140, 146
Coogan, Robert P., 219
Cooper, George C., 224
Cooper, Joshua W., 50, 52–54, 58
Coronado, California, 76–77, 81, 248, 254
Cousins, Ralph W., 172
Cruiser-Destroyer Flotilla Five, 188
Cruiser-Destroyer Force Pacific Fleet (CruDesPac), 58, 61, 91, 94, 122, 160, 162, 179–80, 187, 190
Cruiser-Destroyer Group Two, 202–09
cryptology, 47, 49–50
CTEC, 230–31
Cuba, 55–56, 113–14, 126, 191
Cuban Missile Crisis, 113–14, 126
Cummings, Edward J., Jr., 91–92
Curts, Maurice E., 61
Curtze, Charles A., 99, 103

Davis, Benjamin O., Sr., 121
Davis, Sammy, Jr., 121
Defense Communications Agency, 131–34, 136–37, 226–28
Destroyer Development Group, 205
Destroyer Division 213, 158
Destroyer Flotilla Five, 120
Destroyer Squadron Five, 91–92
Destroyer Squadron Seven, 88–89
Deutermann, Peter T., 193–94
diesel engines, 109–10
Dinneen, Gerald, 227
Distant Early Warning (DEW) Line, 107, 110
drone antisubmarine helicopter (DASH), 160, 162
Drugs, 159–62, 211
Duncan, USS (DD-874), 98

Ebony magazine, 141–44, 199
education: through AFCEA, 231–32; Gravely in college, 4, 10, 30, 32–34; in Gravely's youth, 3–4; Naval War College in 1963–64, 124–26;

Samuel L. Gravely Jr. Elementary School, 260–62; V-12 program in World War II, 12–19
Eleventh Naval District, 79–80, 209–18
Eller, James B., 117
Emancipation Proclamation, 120
enlisted personnel: at CNO's residence, 194–95; in crew of the *PC–1264,* 23–25, 27–28; Cruiser-Destroyer Group Two, 202–09; effect of Z-grams, 180–82; at Hampton Institute, 9–10, 224; opening of Navy ratings to blacks in 1942, 5–6; recruit training in World War II, 7–9, 18–21; at San Diego in 1943, 10–13; in USS *Falgout*, 112–13, 115–16, 118–19; in USS *Gravely*, 261–62; in USS *Iowa*, 49, 52–53; in USS *Jouett*, 182–83, 191–92, 247–48; in USS *Taussig*, 145, 147–48, 150, 153–54, 159–62, 165–66, 170; in USS *Theodore E. Chandler*, 98, 100; in USS *Toledo,* 57–59; in Washington, D.C., recruiting station, 38–40
Ensenada, Mexico, 213
Esch, Arthur G., 176
Ethan Allen, USS (SSBN-608), 111

Falgout, USS (DER-324): duty in nuclear weapons tests, 110–14; enlisted crew, 112–13, 115–16, 118–19; home-ported in Pearl Harbor, 102, 107–110, 114–17, 120; North Pacific barrier patrol, 118–120; ship handling, 109–110; ship's officers, 110, 112, 117–18
Falls Church, Virginia, 196, 209
Fay, Paul B., Jr., 115–17
FBI, 249–50
Fiji Islands, 154
Finneran, John G., 203–05
First Fleet, U.S., 176, 192
Fisher, Gordon, 184
Fitzpatrick, Francis J., 171–73, 196
Fleet Training Group, Little Creek, 30
Fleet Training Group, San Diego, 88
football, 3–4, 14, 27, 32–33, 243
Formosa Patrol, 97
Forster, USS (DER-334)
Fort McClellan, Alabama, 71–72
Fourteenth Naval District, 219
FRAM (fleet rehabilitation and modernization), 94, 98–101, 139
Frederick Reef, 152–53
Fremantle, Australia, 188

Gause, D. C., 59
German Navy, 26–27
GI Bill of Rights, 30, 32–33
Gibbons, Roger, 9–10, 33
Gidrofon (Soviet), 149–50
Gilkeson, Fillmore B., 210, 213
Golden Thirteen, 17, 21, 68, 224
Goodfellow, A. Scott, 156, 188
Gravely, Alma B. (wife): as college student, 4, 239; courtship and marriage in 1946, 29–30, 238–242; as a Navy wife, 52–53, 55–56, 62, 65–68, 74–75, 83–86, 88, 93, 105–7, 110, 120–21, 125–26, 128–30, 155–59, 161, 164, 170–71, 187, 190–92, 202, 209, 212–13, 224–225, 235–36, 238, 242–62; occupations, 32–34, 37, 42, 51–52, 239–42
Gravely, Betsey (sister), 1
Gravely, Beverly (daughter-in-law), 256–57
Gravely, Christie (sister), 1, 4, 29, 239
Gravely, David (son), 105–7, 110, 125–26, 129, 155, 191, 225, 237, 243–45, 248–51, 256–57, 260–62
Gravely, Ed (brother), 1, 3, 121, 247
Gravely, Mary S. (mother), 1–4, 189–90, 229, 241
Gravely, Robert (brother), 1
Gravely, Robert M. (son), 85–86, 105–7, 110, 114–15, 125–26, 129, 155, 191, 224–26, 235–36, 243–45, 250–52

Gravely, Samuel L., Sr. (father): concerns for son, 22; guidance and supervision of son Samuel, 2–6, 10, 35, 123, 190; occupations, 1–3, 33, 229–30; support of son, 30–31, 33–34
Gravely, Samuel L., Jr.: civilian occupations, 2, 5–6, 33–36; on Com Three staff, 66–75; communication school, 41–44; courtship and marriage in 1946, 29–30, 238–242; in crew of the *PC–1264,* 23–30; Cruiser-Destroyer Group Two, 202–09; at Defense Communications Agency, 131–38, 226–28; depression, 170–71, 246–47; duty at Great Lakes in 1945, 20–21; Eleventh Naval District, 210–18; enlisted service at Hampton and San Diego, 9–12, 24, 224, 239; final illness and death, 254–57; flag officer indoctrination, 194–95; Naval Telecommunications Command, 196–201; at Naval War College, 124–27; as Navy recruiter, 36–41; on-the-job training in destroyers, 87–92; recruit training in 1942, 7–8; retirement activities, 229–37; satellite communications program, 169–73; siblings, 1–4, 29, 30–31, 33, 154, 230; student at Submarine Chaser Training Center, 22–23; Third Fleet, 216–225; V-12 program in 1943–44, 12–20; at Virginia Union University, 4, 10, 32–34, 239, 242; youth in Richmond, Virginia, 1–3, 229–30, 240; in USS *Falgout*, 107–23; in USS *Iowa*, 43–55; in USS *Jouett*, 174–94, 247–48; in USS *Seminole*, 76–88; in USS *Taussig*, 139–169; in USS *Theodore E. Chandler*, 93–104, 235–36; in USS *Toledo*, 55–65
Gravely, Tracey (daughter), 155–56, 191–92, 225, 246, 250, 256–57, 262
Gravely, USS (DDG-107), 257–62
Great Lakes Naval Training Station: recruit training in World War II, 7–8, 18, 20–21
Groner, William T., 60–61
Guam, 144, 177, 221
Guantánamo Bay, Cuba, 55–56
guns: 3-inch, 108; 5-inch, 98, 146–48, 177; 16-inch, 46

Hampton Institute, 4, 9, 12, 224, 239
Hardman, Ernest, 25
Harlfinger, Frederick J., II, 196–98
Harvey, John, 258
Hassell, Clyde, 27, 243
Haymarket, Virginia, 229–30, 232, 252–53, 257, 260
Hayward, Thomas B., 219–21
Heftel, Cecil, 219–20
helicopters, 140, 160, 178, 183–84, 219–20, 230
Henderson, USS (DD-785), 98
Holloway, James L., III, 216–18, 224
Hong Kong, 61, 63, 97, 193–94
Horrall, Eugene F., 44–45, 48, 242–43
Horrall, Peg, 242–43
housing: changes by the 1970s, 196; problems in the 1950s–70s, 62, 67–68, 114–15, 128–30, 205–06
Hunters Point Naval Shipyard, 99–104

Iowa, USS (BB-61): Atlantic operations, 52–53; communications, 44–51, 59; enlisted crew, 49, 52–53; officers' wives, 242–43; size, 43, 56; West Coast operations, 43; Western Pacific deployment during Korean War, 45–50, 223
Italy, 198

Japan, 48, 50, 62–63, 66, 84–85, 97, 113, 165
Johnson, Lady Bird, 122
Johnson, Louis, 37
Johnson, Lyndon, 122, 134–35
Johnston Island, 110

Joint Chiefs of Staff, 137–38, 227
joint service, 131–38, 193, 226–28
Joint Staff, 131, 133–34, 136–38, 193
Jouett, USS (DLG-29): enlisted crew, 182–83, 191–92, 247–48; frocking ceremonies, 192, 218–19; ship handling, 175, 190–91; ship's officers, 179–84, 188–90; size, 179; on West Coast, 174–77, 179–80, 182–84; Western Pacific deployment, 177–79, 184–91, 193–94, 247–48
Judge Advocate General's Corps, Navy, 230

Kahoolawe, Hawaii, 219–21
Kaohsiung, Taiwan, 165
Keener, Bruce, III, 209
Kennedy, John F., 105, 115, 121–22, 134, 142
Kidd, Isaac C., Jr., 176, 192, 198, 217
Kimmel, Husband E., 151
Kimmel, Thomas K., Jr., 151
King, Martin Luther, Jr., 106, 122, 244
Kitty Hawk, USS (CVA-63), 200
Korean War, 39–41, 43–46, 61
Kowalzyk, Alexander M., Jr., 73
Kucharski, Leo F., 67–68, 71–74
Kunzman, Douglas, 258–59, 261

Langaleer, Bob, 171–72
Langille, Justin E., III, 158–59, 161, 188
Layman, Lawrence, 91
Lee, John W., 63, 68
Liberia, 199
Little Creek, Virginia, 30
Lofberg, USS (DD-759), 89–90
Long Beach, California: naval shipyard, 140–41, 176, 179–80, 211, 218; USS *Iowa* homeport, 43, 50, 52; USS *Toledo* homeport, 55, 60, 62, 64–65; USS *Yorktown* homeport, 162–64

Mare Island Naval Shipyard, 101
Marijuana, 159–62, 211
Marine Corps, 208
Martin, F. B. C., 57–58, 61
Mason, USS (DE-529), 23–24
Matthews, Herbert Spencer, Jr., 42
Mau, George W., Jr., 76–77, 84
McCain, John S., Jr., 189
McGuire, Gene, 83
medical problems: depression, 170–71, 246–47; eye trouble, 66–67; foot operations, 225, 250–51; high blood pressure, 130, 170–71, 247; hysterectomy, 74–75, 83; kidney dialysis, 254–57; pneumonia, 9
Melbourne, Australia, 152–53
Memphis, Tennessee, 106, 243
Mexican Navy, 213
Mexico, 158–61, 211–13
Miami, Florida, 22–23, 27–29
Middendorf, William, 215
Midway Island, 119–120, 144, 214
Miles, Milton E., 69
Missouri, USS (BB-63), 29
Monterey, California, 41–42, 44, 71–72
Moran, William J., 173
Morman, Donald G., 24–25

Nagler, Gordon R., 108
Naples, Italy, 198
Nash, David, 91–92
National Association for the Advancement of Colored People (NAACP), 6, 68, 199, 245–46
National Communications System, 226–27
National Emergency Airborne Command Post (NECAP), 133–35
National Military Command Center (NMCC), 131–34, 136–37
National Naval Officers Association (NNOA), 232–35, 254
National Security Agency (NSA), 228
NATO, 203, 217
Naval Electronic Systems Command, (NavElex), 171–72
Naval Institute, U.S., 181

Naval Investigative Service, 159–60, 192
Naval Reserve, U.S., 36, 63–64, 66, 68, 211
Naval Reserve Officers' Training Corps (NROTC), 41, 57, 110, 124, 169–70, 184, 232
Naval Ship Systems Command, 206
Naval Telecommunications Command, 196–99, 214
Naval War College: on campus course, 124–27; correspondence courses, 74; integration of, 124–25, 245–46
Navy Day, 218
Nelson, Dennis D., II, 21, 63, 68–69
New York City, 16–19, 26–27, 29, 65
New Zealand, 151, 188–89, 247, 222, 247–48
Newcomb, Luddy, 249
Newcomb, Zeanious "Zeke" L., 179, 181, 188–89
Newland, John W., Jr., 107–9, 120
Newport, Rhode Island, 124–27, 203, 205, 245–46
Newport Beach, California, 213
news media: *Chicago Defender*, 40; coverage of Gravely, 108–9, 141–44, 190–92, 199–200, 219–20, 248–50
Nisewaner, Terrell A., 91
NNOA, 232–35, 254
Norfolk, Virginia: *Iowa* homeport, 52–53, 55–56; poor housing conditions for blacks, 30; shipyard work, 27, 53
Norman, William S., 200
North American Air Defense Command, 221
North Korea, 164–65
Northrop Grumman Shipbuilding, 258–60
nuclear weapons tests, 110–14

Okinawa, 84, 97

Pago Pago, Samoa, 188
Parham, Thomas D., Jr., 63, 170, 189
Pascagoula, Mississippi, 258–59
PC–1264, USS: decommissioning, 29; enlisted crew, 23–25, 27–29; operations, 23, 25–26, 29, 33; racial makeup of the crew, 23–25; ship's officers, 23–29; size, 23, 43
Pearl Harbor, Hawaii: headquarters for Third Fleet, 216, 219–25, 250–52; homeport for USS *Falgout*, 102, 104, 107–8, 114–17, 120, 122–23; naval shipyard, 108, 110, 120, 122–23; stopover by USS *Jouett*, 188–89
Peet, Raymond E., 192
Pensacola, Florida, 233–34
Pentagon, 121, 129, 131–37, 170, 193, 196–97, 231
Perth, Australia
Petters, Mike, 259
Philippine Islands, 145, 165, 177, 187
physical fitness programs, 115–17, 142
PIRAZ, 177–78, 184, 187
Plate, Douglas, 190
Polaris missile, 111, 144
postal work, 1–2, 33–36, 123, 242
Prairie View A&M, 10, 32, 169–70, 1 84, 186
prisoners of war, 178
propulsion plants: in USS *Falgout*, 109–10, 119–120; in USS *Jouett*, 179–80; in USS *Taussig*, 149–50, 163
Prout, Russell K., 90
public affairs, Navy, 141–42, 190–91, 211, 213, 215
Pueblo, USS (AGER-2), 164–65
Purdon, Eric, 24–26, 28–29
Pyongyang, North Korea, 165

racial issues: affirmative action, 235; atmosphere in Charleston, South Carolina, 205–07; black naval officers pigeonholed as communicators, 43; difficulties in the 1950s–60s for blacks on

long trips, 56, 69, 104–6, 243–44; difficulties finding housing in the 1950s–60s, 62, 67–68, 128–30; hate mail, 249–50; imagined cross-burning, 214–215; integrated V-12 program, 12–19; integration of the Naval War College, 124–25; Navy opportunities for minorities, 233–36; Navy policy changes in the 1970s, 180–82, 200–01; opening of Navy ratings to blacks in 1942, 5–6; problems with neighbors, 114–15; segregated training at Great Lakes and Hampton in World War II, 7–9, 20–21; segregation in Richmond, Virginia, 6–7; segregation in San Diego, 10–11; shipboard incidents, 200, 202; unpleasant incidents while on liberty, 27–29, 63
radar, 110–11, 177–78
railroads, 1, 7–8, 242
Ranger, USS (CVA-61), 95–96
Reagan, John W., 17, 37, 224
Reagan, Willita "Dede," 17, 124
Reason, J. Paul, 259
recruiting stations, Navy: Richmond, Virginia, 7; Washington, D.C., 36–41
religion/church, 3, 6, 86, 117–18, 225, 252–54
Rhodes, Stanley, 25–26
Richards, John K., 16–17
Richmond, Virginia: home for Gravely in his youth, 1–6; Navy recruiting station, 7; segregated conditions, 6; Virginia Union University, 4, 10, 14, 32–34, 239, 242
Ritter, Walter, 220–21
Roanoke, Virginia, 34, 240, 242
Robinson, John G., 183–84
Robinson, Rembrandt C., 183, 193–94
Rock, Herman K., 48–49
Rowan, Carl, 23
Rowan, USS (DD-782), 141–142
Royal Navy (Britain), 151–52
Rumsfeld, Donald H., 217

Saigon River, 147
Salzano, Michele, 260–62
Samoa, 188
Samuel L. Gravely Jr. Elementary School, 260–62
San Diego, California: Eleventh Naval District headquarters, 209–18; homeport of USS *Jouett*, 175, 183–84, 188–92; homeport of USS *Seminole*, 75–76, 83, 86; homeport of USS *Taussig*, 139, 155–57, 162–63; homeport of USS *Theodore E. Chandler*, 93–94, 104; naval base in World War II, 10–13; Robert Gravely's burial site, 225, 252; site of Gravely's on-the-job training, 87–92; site of schools for crew members, 101; training site for USS *Iowa*, 43–44
San Francisco, California, 56, 62, 80, 86, 99, 101–4, 218, 220
Sasebo, Japan, 49, 62–63, 165
satellite communications program, 169–73
Scarborough Shoals, 145
Scotia, New York, 70–71, 74
Seal Beach, California, 140–41, 176
Seattle, Washington, 61
Second Fleet, U.S., 203, 208–09
Seminole, USS (AKA-104): communications, 78, 83; deployment to Seventh Fleet, 84–85; intelligence publications, 78–80; ship handling, 81–82, 95; time on the West Coast, 75–83, 85–86
Seventh Fleet, U.S., 46–47, 60–63, 97, 152, 217, 221–22
Seventh Naval District, 28–29
Shanker, Benjamin, 24
Shepherd, Tazewell T., Jr., 121–22
ship handling: in USS *Falgout*, 108–110; in USS *Jouett*, 175, 190–91; in USS *Seminole*, 81–82, 95; in USS

Taussig, 140–41, 144, 149–50; in USS *Theodore E. Chandler,* 95–96, 108
Sickles, Albert, 180
signaling, visual, 22–23, 45–46, 59, 111
Singapore, 187
Skubinna, Myron A., 100, 102
Smalls, Robert, 8, 108
Smedberg, William R., III, 44, 48–49, 114
Society of Sponsors, 259
Somers, USS (DD-947), 91–92
Son Tay, North Vietnam, 178
sonar, 140–41, 144
South Atlantic Force, U.S., 208
South Korea, 230
Soviet Navy, 149–50
Soviet Union, 71, 107, 111, 119, 126
Sperandio, Joseph L., 103–4
St. George, William R., 218–19
Standing Naval Force Atlantic, 203
Staten Island, New York, 74–75
Stephan, Edward, 44, 223
Subic Bay, Philippines, 145, 165, 177, 187
Submarine Chaser Training Center (SCTC), 22–23, 27
Surface Force Atlantic Fleet, 207–08
Surface Force Pacific Fleet, 218–19, 222
Suva, Fiji Islands, 154

Tachen Islands, 62
Tahiti, 222–23
Taiwan, 165
Task Force 77, 46, 178
Task Group 70.8, 147, 154, 156
Taussig, USS (DD-746): enlisted crew, 145, 147–48, 150, 153–54, 159–62, 165–66, 170; 1966 deployment to Western Pacific, 141–54; 1967–68 deployment to Western Pacific, 164–68; ship handling, 140–41, 149–50, 144; ship's officers, 142, 147, 150; Vietnam War service, 146–57; on West Coast, 139–41, 156–64; 156–57
Taylor, Sam, 33
Tecumseh, USS (SSBN-628), 144
Terrier missile, 174, 176
Theodore E. Chandler, USS (DD-717): deployment to Seventh Fleet, 97–98; enlisted crew, 98, 100; ship handling, 95–96; 108; shipyard FRAM overhaul, 99–104; on the West Coast, 93–97, 140–41
Third Fleet, U.S., 209, 216–25
Third Naval District, 64, 66–75
Thomas, Gerald E., 169–70
Thompson, George I., 124–25
Thompson, William, 126–27
Thomson, James W., 76–77, 80–82, 85
Tidd, Emmett H., 211
Tijuana, Mexico, 158–61, 211–13
Tiru, USS (SS-416), 152–53
Toledo, USS (CA-133): communications, 57–61; deployments to Seventh Fleet, 60–63; enlisted crew, 57–59; ship's officers, 57–58, 60–61; size, 56–57; on the West Coast, 55–60, 64
Train, Harry D., II, 206
Training Command Pacific Fleet, 89, 92
Tripler Army Hospital, 225, 250–52
Truman, Harry S., 29, 36–37
Tubman, William V. S., 199
Turner, Stansfield, 127, 205, 208–09, 216

UCLA: V-12 program, 13–15, 18, 33; NROTC, 124–25, 236
Underway replenishment, 149, 151–52, 177
Urban League, 68
USC, V-12 program, 13
USO, 240

V-12 program, 12–20, 22–23, 109, 236
Vallejo, California, 101
Vendetta (Australia), 153

Vietnam War, 146–49, 177–78
Virden, Frank, 122–23
Virginia State College, 4, 29, 238–39, 241
Virginia Union University, 4, 10, 14, 32–34, 224, 242
visual signaling, 22–23, 45–46, 59, 111

Wainwright, USS (DLG-28), 204
Warner, John, 202
Washington, D.C.: CNO's residence, 194–95; housing situation, 129–30; Navy recruiting station, 37–41; White House, 120–22, 134, 193–94
Washington Post, 220
Watkins, James D., 214
weather, 111–12, 118–120, 145, 165
Wells, Mattie, 261
Wentworth, Ralph, 203
Weymouth, Ralph, 163, 165–67, 169
White House, 120–22, 134, 193–94
Whittle, Alfred J., Jr., 217
William H. Standley, USS (DLG-32)
Wilson, Pete, 211, 215
Wilson, Ralph E., 63
Wilson, Robert, 211
Witherspoon, Michael, 261
Wonsan, North Korea, 46

Yarbrough, Herbert A., 44, 57
Yokosuka, Japan, 49–50, 62–63, 84–85, 97–98
Yom Kippur War, 204
Yorktown, USS (CVS-10), 162–67

Z-grams, 180–82, 187–88
Zumwalt, Elmo R., Jr., 126–27, 180–82, 194–95, 200–02, 216

About the Authors

Vice Adm. Samuel L. Gravely Jr. was a Navy pioneer. After growing up in Richmond, VA, he enlisted in the Naval Reserve in 1942 and was among the very earliest black officers to be commissioned through the V-12 training program. Following a brief post–World War II return to civilian life, he was recalled to active duty in 1949 and served until his retirement in 1980. He had many tours of duty at sea and ashore. Ship commands included the radar picket destroyer escort *Falgout*, the destroyer *Taussig*, and the guided-missile frigate *Jouett*. In 1971 he was selected as the Navy's first black rear admiral; in 1976 he became the first black vice admiral. Admiral Gravely died in 2004.

Paul Stillwell served on the staff of the U.S. Naval Institute from 1974 to 2004. At various times he was an editor with *Proceedings*, editor in chief of *The Naval Review*, first editor in chief of *Naval History*, and director of the organization's oral history program. He served in the Naval Reserve from 1962 until his retirement in 1992. Among his notable active-duty tours were the tank landing ship *Washoe County* during the Vietnam War, the battleship *New Jersey*, the Second Fleet staff, and as a historian in the Persian Gulf during the Iran-Iraq War. He is the author or editor of numerous books, including *The Golden Thirteen: Recollections of the First Black Naval Officers* (Naval Institute Press, 1993). He and his wife Karen live in Arnold, Maryland.

The Naval Institute Press is the book-publishing arm of the U.S. Naval Institute, a private, nonprofit, membership society for sea service professionals and others who share an interest in naval and maritime affairs. Established in 1873 at the U.S. Naval Academy in Annapolis, Maryland, where its offices remain today, the Naval Institute has members worldwide.

Members of the Naval Institute support the education programs of the society and receive the influential monthly magazine *Proceedings* or the colorful bimonthly magazine *Naval History* and discounts on fine nautical prints and on ship and aircraft photos. They also have access to the transcripts of the Institute's Oral History Program and get discounted admission to any of the Institute-sponsored seminars offered around the country.

The Naval Institute's book-publishing program, begun in 1898 with basic guides to naval practices, has broadened its scope to include books of more general interest. Now the Naval Institute Press publishes about seventy titles each year, ranging from how-to books on boating and navigation to battle histories, biographies, ship and aircraft guides, and novels. Institute members receive significant discounts on the more than eight hundred Press books in print.

Full-time students are eligible for special half-price membership rates. Life memberships are also available.

For a free catalog describing Naval Institute Press books currently available, and for further information about joining the U.S. Naval Institute, please write to:

Member Services
U.S. NAVAL INSTITUTE
291 Wood Road
Annapolis, MD 21402-5034
Telephone: (800) 233-8764
Fax: (410) 571-1703
Web address: www.usni.org